Tribal Dancing

Tribal Dancing
and Social Development

W. D. Hambly

Noverre Press

First published in 1926 by H. F. & G. Witherby

This facsimile reprint published in 2009 by
The Noverre Press
Southwold House
Isington Road
Binsted
Hampshire
GU34 4PH

© 2009 The Noverre Press

ISBN 978-1-906830-01-4

A CIP catalogue record for this book is available from the British
Library

TRIBAL DANCING
AND SOCIAL DEVELOPMENT

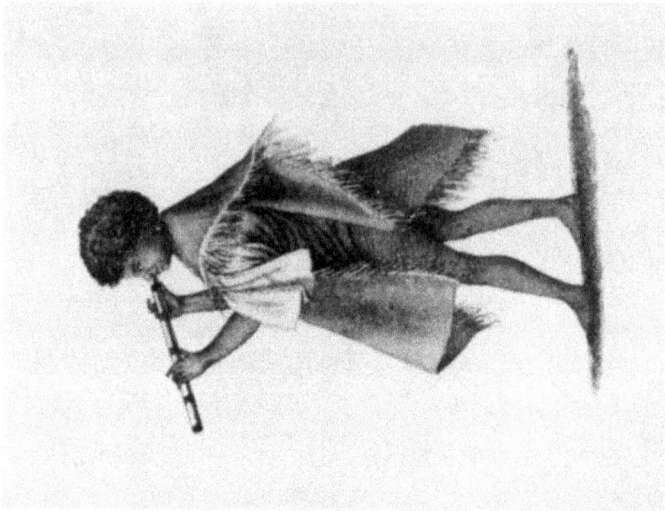

PLAYING THE NOSE FLUTE, TAHITI (CH. V).
(By permission Whitcombe & Tombs, Ltd)

THE PERUPERU WAR DANCE (CH. I).

Frontispiece.

TRIBAL DANCING
AND SOCIAL DEVELOPMENT

BY

W. D. HAMBLY, B.Sc. (Oxon)

Anthropologist to the Wellcome Expedition, Sudan.
Assistant Curator, African Ethnology, Field Museum,
Chicago. Author of " The History of Tattooing,"
" Origins of Education Among Primitive People "

WITH A PREFACE BY
CHARLES HOSE, Hon. Sc.D. (Cantab.)

PHOTOGRAPHS, SKETCHES AND A MAP

LONDON
H. F. & G. WITHERBY
326 HIGH HOLBORN, W.C.
1926

Printed in Great Britain

PREFACE

I have much pleasure in writing a foreword for Mr. W. D. Hambly's book on the Music and Dancing of savage races. The subject is one of great interest, and of wider scope and significance than might at first sight appear. It really is part of that large field of investigation which has been receiving more attention and recognition of recent years—an enquiry into the habits and customs of primitive peoples with a view to a better understanding of the development of human institutions and the growth of mental conceptions regarding natural phenomena and spiritual beliefs. It is remarkable how much there is in common between remote and disconnected races in this respect, whether they have lived their lives like the Indians in the North American Continent, the Bushmen in the arid wastes of the Kalahari, the Polynesians in their numberless islands, or the extinct savages in Tasmania. The human mind in its most primitive forms showed similar modes of development whether in the interpretation of the puzzling world around them or in the expression of their own physical activities and emotions. The great problem forces itself on one's mind—and it is too large to be more than referred to here—whether primitive man appeared in one isolated area like the Southern part of Africa and spread thence over the world, or evolved himself more or less simultaneously in widely separated parts of the globe. In any case it is of importance to note that all over the world the natural energy of youth

and the expression of emotions displayed themselves
in the form of dances varying according to the climatic
conditions or the habits of the peoples, and were
accompanied by rhythmic sounds or songs that
harmonised more or less with their saltatory movements. The primitive simple step of the Bantu, the
weird gyrations of the Medicine man, the slow snake-
like motion of the Oriental women dancers, the folk-
dances of old England, and the highly developed
Russian ballet have their roots deep in the same
primitive soil.

As one interested in anthropology and the psychology of primitive races, I have of course given
much attention to the researches that have recently
been made in this wide field, but my own personal
experience has been confined mainly to Borneo, and
especially to that part of it known as Sarawak. It
was probably the highway through which passed the
stream of early migration from the shores of Asia to
the isles of the Pacific and New Zealand and perhaps
to Australia. Its present native inhabitants include
some of the earliest types like the Kayans, Punans,
and Kenyahs as well as descendants of other Mongo-
loid and Caucasian stocks. Since the dawn of history
they have engaged in internecine strife. Dancing,
accompanied by vocal efforts as well as by instrumental music, ranging from the tom-tom to reed-pipes and
drums, is greatly in vogue on all festive occasions.
Harvest festivals, victorious raids, and general
entertainments are celebrated with dancing and
music. These performances take place in the spacious
verandahs, or in the galleries of the long houses dimly
lit by resin torches or wooden fires. Some tribes, like
the Punans, dance on a single narrow board with
wonderful balancing feats, twisting and turning in
perfect harmony with the accompanying music.
These exhibitions of skill are not restricted entirely

to occasions of joy and merrymaking. When, in serious illness, unconsciousness is fast seizing upon its victim, the medicine man chants a dirge, and contorts himself in a frenzied dance, gyrating and mimicking frantic efforts to overcome the powers that are endeavouring to withdraw the patient's soul. Sword in hand, he strikes in all directions in harmony with the music, glancing from time to time at the sheen on his sword, in which his soul may perchance see reflected that of the patient in its wandering to the confines of the nether world. Frequently the patient is so stimulated by the energetic example of the medicine man as actually to arise and join in the dance, usually with the result that he collapses in a state of exhaustion. If the medicine man is successful in securing the soul, he passes it over the head of the patient in the form of a grain of millet, rice, or something similar; thus apparently making it re-enter the body. In order that it may be secured there he binds the patient's wrist with a strip of palm-leaf or tattoos a bracelet, and afterwards sacrifices a cock in gratitude to the unseen powers.

His frenzy then subsides, the music ceases, and he becomes normal once more. After he has warned the patient against certain kinds of food, he suddenly ends the ceremony. The patient believes that his soul has been recovered, and his faith in this belief doubtless often helps in his cure.

The method of dancing of the women differs greatly from that of the men. Their movements are sinuous and slow, with their arms moving in greater measure than their feet. The men, on the other hand, are full of action, and while they keep time to the music, their steps and motions are vigorous, consisting of jumps and jerks and twistings of the body, as if they were engaged with shield and sword in deadly combat. Then retiring, crouching, and squatting with an almost sitting posture, the dancer with a shout springs suddenly upwards with arms extended and defiant air as if challenging his enemy to come on. He circles about, all the time in tuneful motion, as if he were prepared for hostile attacks from all sides, his long raven locks whisking round his gruesome visage. In all these dances, the movements, however exhilarating or fantastic, are rhythmical and in tune with any improvised side-steps or attitudes that he may effect. The audience and the musicians may get warmed to their work and quicken the music, but the dancer keeps to time often up to a pitch of frenzied excitement. Burns' description of the witches dance in Alloway's auld haunted kirk is quite appropriate to the scene :

> And, wow ! Tam saw an unco sight !
> Warlocks and witches in a dance !
> Nae cotillion brent new frae France,
> But hornpipes, jigs, strathspeys and reels
> Put life and mettle in their heels.
> At Winnock bunker in the east
> There sat auld Nick, in shape o' beast ;
> A towzie tyke, black, grim and large
> To gie them music was his charge :
> He screwed the pipes and gart them skirl,
> Toll roof and rafters a' did dirl !

.   .   .   .   .

> As Tammie glowred, amazed and curious
> The mirth and fun grew fast and furious :
> The piper loud and louder blew ;
> The dancers quick and quicker flew ;
> They reeled, they set, they crossed, they cleekit,
> Till ilka carlin swat and reekit,
> And coost her duddies to the wark,
> And linket at it in hersark !

" Even Satan glowred and fidged a fain, and hotched and blew with might and main "—which shows us that in the calisthenic art there is some affinity between the wild tribes of Borneo, and the invisible inhabitants of Ayr !

Mimicry frequently plays a part in these dances. The peculiar motions of birds and animals like the hornbill and the monkey are represented by a regular two-step in the case of the former, and of appropriate scratches and other actions in the latter.

Just as the belated youth of Surrey whistles as he passes through the dark woods to keep up his courage, so does the lonely boatman of Sarawak sing loudly in a falsetto voice as he paddles his tiny craft on the crocodile-infested waters of the river, feeling some courage and comfort at the sound of his own voice in the deadly stillness of the night. The same feelings and desires for active expression belong to human beings, whether primitive or civilized, and the advance in culture in many areas obliterates characteristics which might well have been retained. The survey of this phase of primitive social life which Mr. Hambly has prepared will repay the reader who is fortunate enough to peruse it.

C. H.

CONTENTS

CHAPTER I

INTRODUCTION

CHAPTER II

HISTORICAL EVIDENCE

CHAPTER III

HEAD HUNTING AND THE WAR DANCE

ILLUSTRATIONS

13

Facing Page

MAP

Facing Page

CHAPTER I

INTRODUCTION

THE SCOPE OF THE SUBJECT

The reticence of primitive man and his inability to express in words a philosophy which is the well-spring of actions, renders the study of conduct of great importance for a right understanding of primitive society. A recent investigator in the Andaman Islands states that " The Psychology of Dancing offers a wide field for study, that has, so far as I know, been barely touched. The dance produces a condition in which the unity, harmony and concord of the community are at a maximum."[1]

On the side of technique, no less than as an expression of emotions both lofty and debased, music and dancing are worthy of detailed study. As a harmoniser the savage is undeveloped, but his knowledge of, and ability to utilise, complex rhythms is far beyond the power of civilized musicians.[2]

The evidence collated in the following pages, though illustrative rather than exhaustive, will serve to show the variety of emotion and sentiment which may find adequate expression in song and dance. There would appear to be no fibre of human passion, hope, or despair left untouched by the ingenuity of the primitive musician. In the words of Claridge,[3] Congo music may make the nerves tingle with unearthly sensations. " At another time it is sentimental and carries one away to mental scenes which

leave one sad when they have faded away. Now it
is melancholy; it puts a weight on the soul. Then
it is wanton, when it makes men see fire and feel it
in their bones. Happiness, misery, sadness, wicked-
ness, hope, contentment, all are found in Congo
Music.''

An investigator of primitive music and dancing is
at once impressed by the contrast between the importance of these aesthetics in primitive and
civilized communities. The modern social dance of
pairs of men and women is peculiar to civilization,
and in so-called backward societies every branch of
musical expression is a communal concern, an essential of juvenile training, though there are, of course,
composers and specialists who give exhibitions.

Dancing in particular has functions in primitive
social life which have fallen into disuse in modern
society, as the following table will show:—

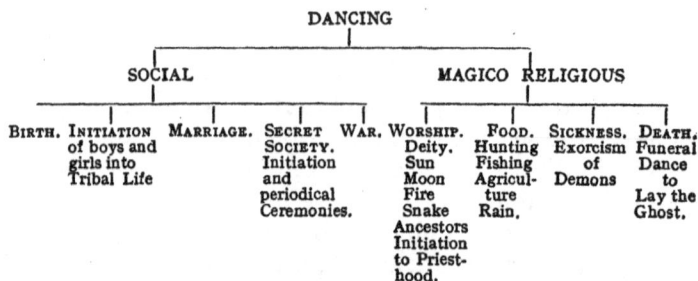

DANCING

SOCIAL — MAGICO RELIGIOUS

BIRTH.	INITIATION of boys and girls into Tribal Life	MARRIAGE.	SECRET SOCIETY. Initiation and periodical Ceremonies.	WAR.	WORSHIP. Deity. Sun Moon Fire Snake Ancestors Initiation to Priest-hood.	FOOD. Hunting Fishing Agricul-ture Rain.	SICKNESS. Exorcism of Demons	DEATH. Funeral Dance to Lay the Ghost.

SYMPATHY OF THE READER

The student of primitive music and dancing will
have to cultivate a habit of broad-minded consideration for the actions of backward races. In other
words he must have imagination and sympathy

combined with the power of temporarily detaching himself from his own mental training and view-point. Music and dancing performed wildly by firelight in a tropical forest have not seldom provoked the censure and disgust of European visitors, who have seen only what is grotesque and sensual. The observer who is shocked by the sight of swishing petticoats showing tattooed thighs, or is merely horrified without being interested in the devil dance and war dance, will find little gratification in these pages, for we are regarding crude survivals of the social life of prehistoric man.

Early travellers are amusing in their contempt for the customs of those they visited, though one cannot do other than admire the courage of these pioneers. An early explorer in Kamchatka and the Kurile Islands says that the manners, customs, and religion of this barbarous nation were loaded with absurd practices, idle ceremonies, and unaccountable superstitions, which show the precise state of an unpolished, credulous, and ignorant people. "Their manners are quite rude, for they never use any civil expression or salutation. They do not take off their caps nor bow to one another and their discourse is stupid, for it betrays the most consummate ignorance. Their chief happiness consists in idleness and satisfying their natural lusts and appetites, which incline them to singing, dancing and relation of love stories."[4] Turner says that dancing in Samoa was a common entertainment on festive occasions, and is practised still, but only by people who make no serious profession of Christianity. "At these night dances all kinds of obscenity in looks, languages, and gesture prevail, and often the people dance and revel until daylight."[5] Jesters follow in the train of chiefs, and by oddity of dress, gait, gesture and lascivious jokes, they excite their audience to laughter.

B

The dancing in Otahite does not appear to have
met with the approval of Captain James Cook,[6] who
says that among other diversions they have their
heivas, very nearly corresponding to the ancient wakes
of England. The young people meet together to
dance and make merry, and at these meetings their
minstrels and players constantly attend as formerly
persons of the same character were wont to do all
over England. At these *heivas* however the girls in
their dances have no regard for decency and though
the same end was no doubt in view in the institution
of the wake and the *heiva*, yet what in England was
concerted with the greatest secrecy is in Otahite
publicly avowed and practised.

There are however broader views even in an early
Victorian Age of prudery, for E. Dieffenbach[7] says
that Maori dances had by 1843 become classed as
vices, so they were not exchanged for others, but were
given up altogether. The observer thinks that
missionaries, while abolishing these dances, might
with safety have introduced those of England. The
suggestion is intelligent and well meant, but it is
doubtful whether an exotic dance would find favour,
for dancing like a language is part of the society with
which it has grown up. There is however an important principle at stake, namely the undesirability
of unduly interfering with native institutions unless
they are positively cruel and pernicious.

Aborigines of Tasmania, who became extinct in
1872, showed in their wild dances a good-humour
which was remarkable considering the excitement
that prevailed. It is stated that though exhibition
in a state of nudity must necessarily shock the eyes
of Europeans there was no conduct which would offend
the most scrupulous observer.[8]

HUMOURS OF THE DANCE

Mrs. Grundy will have to concede to primitive dancing and festival a peculiar humour of the unconscious type, though there is a touch of pathos in the mingling of what is genuinely primitive with incidents of European intrusion. Mr. R. W. Williamson⁕ says that when watching a dance of the Roro people in New Guinea he was " much exercised by the extraordinary white, shining, disc-shaped ornament hanging on the back of one of the members of the party from a village where there is a station of the London Missionary Society, and his interest was aroused in the new form of native decoration. The object proved to be a card on which was printed ' Prepare to meet thy God'. The ludicrous incongruity was due to the fact that the man was wearing it as an ornament and not as an exhortation to his friends."

The Maoris, like many other people, passed through a stage in which articles of European clothing were highly prized and worn in combination with native ornaments at public festivals such as the welcoming *haka*. The faces of the dancers were daubed with a red solution to which stains of blue earth were added round the right eye and temple. Feather head-dresses were worn by all performers in addition to fragments of European clothing. The sole attire of one performer was a tattered brown waistcoat that reached some eighteen inches below his throat, the nether man being entirely exposed *in puris naturalibus*. A companion wore a shirt fastened round his loins by the sleeves, so forming an apron. One youth had inserted himself into the body of a woman's gown, his extremities being encased in an old red baize shirt, the sleeves of which answered the purpose of trousers.

"A pair of duck trousers were tied round the throat of one young chief, whose extreme delicacy was attested by an old worn-out red night-cap being placed in the identical spot for a sporran. One of the equipage wore a single low shoe and an old top boot."[10]

Crude the savage may be, but he takes first-class honours for persistence. An Andamanese will always compose his own song, singing it over softly to himself as he cuts his canoe, and not resting satisfied until the refrain suits him, and the chorus has been taught to a group of his womenfolk on whom he will rely for hearty applause and vocal assistance at the public ceremony in view. At this function he is expected to sing several songs, each of which is repeated without interval several times, and the duration and noise of the applause help him to judge which compositions may be added to his permanent repertoire.

Of the Abipiones of Paraguay it has been said that when they begin singing they will never leave off. The chanter is admonished to conclude his song by women who stand round separated from the men. After repetition lasting a quarter of an hour or more these vigilantes signify that it is time to desist by repeatedly pressing their lips together and pronouncing the words "Kla-leya," meaning "It is enough," an admonition with which the singer immediately complies.[11]

Marco Polo,[12] staid and precise chronicler as he was, did not fail to see the humour of a musical festival in Shansi province about the middle of the thirteenth century. Describing a convivial gathering round the Grand Khan, he says there were two officers with great staves to prevent guests touching the threshold on entry, and obliging them to step over it as a mark of respect. If by chance anyone is guilty of this offence these janitors take from him his garment, which he must redeem for money, or when they do

not take the garment they inflict on him such number
of blows as they have authority for doing. " In
departing from the hall, as some of the company may
be affected by the liquor, it is impossible to guard
against the accident of touching the threshold and
the order is not strictly enforced." It would indeed
be an exacting test of sobriety after a merry evening
to walk backward, bowing reverentially, and at the
same time carefully judging one's paces.

" At the moment his majesty drinks, all the
musical instruments, of which there is a numerous
band, begin to play, and continue to do so until he
has ceased drinking." A mark of respect, no doubt,
but a seemingly unnecessary comment on the imbibing capacity of his highness.

Music, dancing, and liberal potions marked the
royal festivals of a court in mediaeval India in 1040
A.D. Ghazni-Amir said : " ' Let us begin without ceremony.' Accordingly much wine was brought and fifty
goblets and flagons were stored in a small tent. The
Amir said : ' Let us keep fair measure and fill the
cups evenly in order that there may be no unfair-
ness ' ; each goblet contained nearly a pint. They
began to get jolly and the minstrels sang. Bul-
Hasan drank five goblets and his head was affected
at the sixth ; he lost his senses at the seventh, and
began to be ill at the eighth, when the servants
carried him off. Bi-l-Ala the physician dropped his
head at the fifth cup, and he also was carried off (one
might reasonably have expected more discretion from
a physician). Singers and buffoons all rolled off tipsy
and the Sultan alone remained. When the Khwaja
had drunk eighteen cups he made obeisance and
prepared to go, saying to the Amir : ' If you give
your slave any more he will lose respect for your
Majesty as well as his own wits.' The Amir laughed
and gave him leave to go, when he got up and departed

in a most respectful manner. After this the Amir kept on drinking and enjoying himself. He drank twenty-seven full goblets of half a maund each; he then arose, called for a basin of water and his praying carpet, washed and read mid-day prayers as well as the afternoon ones, and so acquitted himself that you would have said he had not drunk a single cup. He then got on an elephant and returned to his palace. I witnessed this scene with mine own eyes, I, Abi-l-Fazl."[14]

DANCING FROM CRADLE TO GRAVE

Birth

The Kayans of Sarawak, more especially those of the Upper Rejang, sometimes perform a dance which is supposed to facilitate delivery. The actor is usually a female friend or relative of the labouring woman, and her dance includes the dressing of a bundle of cloth in the form of an infant. With this she dances before placing the dummy in the type of cradle which a Kayan woman usually carries on her back. An old story relates the origin of this ceremony as follows: A widow died in childbirth and the infant was given to a woman who happened to be dancing at the time of the birth. The fact that the child afterwards became influential and prosperous set a precedent for the custom of dancing with an effigy of the newly born child.[15]

Primitive races generally regard twins with superstition, even repulsion, and it is no uncommon thing for one or both children to be put to death. The Bagesu of Uganda, however, regard a double birth as auspicious and special ceremonial dances are held. The medicine man is called, and after he has sacrificed a goat some of the blood is sprinkled on each member of the family, also on friends assembled to take part in the ceremonies. During four days, dancing continues while drums are beaten day and night, a practice which calls to mind the Hindu birth custom of drum beating to drive away hostile demons. The Bagesu husband has to see that all guests are well supplied with food and beer, which he has taken some pains to collect from his relatives. It is said that there must be no temper or quarrelling, as these would be harmful to the twins.[16]

The Lango, a Nilotic tribe of Uganda, regard twin birth as auspicious, bringing good luck not only on the family and clan, but on the whole village, for which reason special birth ceremonies are required. From the day of birth two small drums are beaten each evening while the village girls dance and sing. There is a long ceremony of offering food and presents to the mother followed by a sacrifice of chickens. The entertainment is prolonged far into the night with dances and indelicate songs, and again at the next full moon the girls of the village dance by themselves for four days.[17]

Performances of dancing boys and musical accompaniments are Persian methods of giving welcome to a baby boy. But should a girl arrive, the beautiful hammock and cradle are replaced by something inferior. The baby is not weighed, no distribution of sweets takes place, and musical honours are cancelled. A rumour is circulated that the child is a boy, a ruse which is said to " save the face of the parents," for when the truth is broadcast the public will take no notice of the disappointment.[18]

Initiation

Exhausting dances play an important part in many systems of physical training leading to tribal initiation, and no doubt the boys feel some incentive to effort on account of the fact that it is at these dances that a girl falls in love and decides which boy she will select as her husband.[19]

Akikuyu boys dance the whole night long before the morning of circumcision, so that they have to face the ordeal when thoroughly tired.[20]

Yao boys during preparatory isolation undergo exhausting dances which are a severe test of physical stamina.[21]

Boys who are about to be incorporated with the tribe have a special masked dancing performance to carry out in front of a large audience. The boys make their own disguises, which must completely hide the head and prevent identification. A fall during this dance is regarded as the worst possible augury for the future of the youth concerned, and he must try to avoid the evil consequences by remaining on the ground as if dead. Grass is sprinkled over him, and when all spectators have departed the lad creeps away from the spot, which is liberally splashed with the blood of a fowl. No doubt this ceremonial is intended to deceive the evil spirit, who would be led to believe that the faulty dancer had died, and no vindictive measures would be taken by the demon, who had been offended on account of imperfect dancing on such an important occasion.

Social and Anti-Social Dances

Blackmailing dances of New Guinea recorded by Hardy and Elkington[22] appear to be related to the Secret Society dances of New Britain, for performers, hideously painted and grotesquely attired, visit by night the hut of the person from whom payment is

(*Upper*) WELCOMING DANCE, ARUNTA TRIBE.
(*Lower*) FIRE CEREMONY, WARRAMUNGA TRIBE.
  (*Photos, Sir Baldwin Spencer and Messrs. McMillan*)

to be extorted. On arrival the blackmailers commence a wild fantastic whirl accompanied by song in which threats are shrieked until the unfortunate victim consents to make a payment.

Certain forms of corroborree are in Australia a purely social form of entertainment, though in all probability there is a deeper significance which has been lost. A form of welcome dance, though certain incidents suggest a war dance, is performed when a wandering Australian tribe enters the preserve of another. The fact that the approaching party is accompanied by women and children shows the absence of hostile intention, but the men wear in their hair curious flaked sticks which are a sign that they mean to kill someone if they can. These are the sticks which Australian aborigines wear when forming an avenging party, and after the victim has been killed the sticks are broken and thrown on the dead body. The hosts, who are armed, take no notice of the visitors for half an hour, then one of the old men invites them to come up, in response to which the visitors form in a square and advance at a run, with high knee-action and spears held aloft. A preliminary welcome is given by old women of the entertaining group, who go through grotesque dancing antics, meanwhile yelling at the top of their voices. Three of the local groups on a hill near by dance wildly with spear, shield, and boomerang, to show the visitors they are quite prepared for hostilities if necessary. The visiting men run round and round with prancing steps and the whole performance is a make belief, in which the savage is trying to persuade himself that he is much more valiant than is the case. A leading man of the visiting tribe collects all the sticks worn in the hair, and after being presented to the local headman these are burnt as a sign that the visit is of a quite friendly character."

Sex Attraction and Marriage

The gaiety of sex dancing is seen at its best in certain South Sea Islands, for example the Marquesas, where the dancing movements are a combination of glide, swim and whirl, in which every part of the body is in motion at the same time. The young girls very often dance by moonlight in front of their dwellings. There are a great variety of these dances of a romping, mischievous kind, bringing every muscle into play. Not only do their feet dance, but their arms, hands, fingers and even eyes seem to dance. The damsels wear nothing but flowers and their gala tunics, which make them look like gay insects on the wing.[24]

In Hawaii and other Polynesian islands the daughters of chiefs used to give an exhibition dance, for which their finest dresses were reserved. The performance was designed to bring to notice the daughters of chiefs in order to introduce them to eligible young men of rank and station, who, it was hoped, might be so charmed by their dancing as to become their future husbands. There were many dances, says an early missionary, " all too indelicate or obscene to be noticed." The ceremony took place in a spacious roofed dancing hall without any walls. Dancing mats covered the floor and images of gods were introduced to " sanction and patronise the debasing immoralities connected with them."[25] The reader will do well to accept with caution the phrases in quotation, for they express a view all too common before the missionary had acquired ethnological interests and broader views.

Although the surroundings of a coral island give an ideal setting for the dance of sexual joy and selection, people of the snowy tundra and mountain waste are by no means slow to discard their fur clothing

in order to trip a measure, so we find that among
Siberian tribes there are very normal uses of music,
song, and dance, in addition to the mystic performances of the Shaman. At a Yakut wedding there is
great feasting followed by dancing and singing, in
which young people of both sexes participate. " Ho,
boys, ho ! Let us enjoy ourselves while we are young,"
shout the young men, to which a girl responds, " Sing
aloud my throat." Then follows a musical dialogue.
" Boys, let us dance and laugh while we are still
unwed," and the maiden's answer : " Girls, let us play
while we are still unwed, while we are yet uncaught
by the hands of men."[26] Old women flock to the
scene, and in improvised verses lament the departure
of youth and the approach of infirmities—

" How welcome is the warmth of the sun to my aged bones,
How joyful to dance with you my children.
This may be the last time I shall sing.
Soon will the earth cover my sightless eyes.
Next year again you will come here to play,
But on my grave the young grass will be green.
Cold I shall be there, nor can the hearth fire warm my old
body.
Dance and sing then, oh youth.
When in the grave my happy bones will dance to your merry
songs."

Mimicry of Animals

It is not improbable that mimetic dances which
are of world-wide distribution have survived from a
most ancient means of increasing supplies of game
by symbolic magic.
Young girls of the Chukchee tribe of N.E. Siberia[27]
are fond of performing dances in imitation of the

movements of animals, and the motions are accompanied by peculiar guttural noises which are described by a Chukchee word meaning "to call with the throat." The performers arrange themselves in a circle or perhaps in opposite rows, and produce a series of notes, guturally at first, later in a much higher key, meanwhile swaying their bodies to and fro in time to the music. Young boys who sometimes take part in these mimetic dances hold up their hands, snap the fingers, and produce clicking noises with the tongue. The "Raven" song is very popular, so also is a humorous mimetic performance relating to a dialogue supposed to have taken place between the fox and the bear. The former is described as a cunning doctor who attempted to heal the bear's wounds by applying hot stones, a process which resulted in the death of the latter. Performers taking the part of the fox sing in shrill treble voices, while those representing the bear, reply in gruff accents, which grow gradually more feeble as the narrative relates the dying of the bear. The dance and song of the fighting sandpiper is an imitation of the movements and notes of that bird during the pairing season. There are also songs of the long-tailed duck, the swan, the seal, wolves, and the reindeer, all of which are accompanied by mimetic dances representing the movements of these animals. It is not improbable that widespread dances relating to animal life had their inception in remote prehistoric times in connection with cults for increasing animal fecundity. Such totemic ceremonies with their appropriate " emu," " kangaroo," "frog," or " opossum " dances are a regular feature of Australian aborigines' procedure at the present day.

In mimetic dances the performers have no scruples about imitating the sex display and movements of animals in the breeding season. That such realism

(*Upper*) A NYAM-NYAM HUNTING DANCE, BAHR-EL-GHAZAL
PROVINCE, SUDAN.
(*Lower*) NYAM-NYAM DRUMS.

(*Photos, Major R. Whitbread*)

arouses the disgust of some observers is due to the fact that our higher culture has forgotten the natural, unfettered attitude of the savage toward matters of sex.

Among Indian tribes, as is the case with most primitive people, the bodies of animals are credited with having a spirit counterpart which may be invoked by song and dance, hence before commencing a bear hunt the Sioux Indians dance in honour of bear spirits, which are regarded as having a separate and invisible existence.

The chief medicine man is, of course, the principal performer in these grotesque and amusing scenes, in which he impersonates a bear by clothing himself in the skin of that animal and dancing in imitation of its movements. The spectators and supplementary performers, too, are clad in bearskin, and very amusing are their imitations of the animal's ambling walk and queer way of sitting with drooping paws. Catlin,[18] who travelled extensively among the North American Indians in the years 1830-4, gives a detailed description of one of these mimetic dances conducted with a view to attracting a herd of buffalo to the vicinity. Such a dance was at times kept up by relays of dancers, who performed continuously for three weeks.

Approaching the Spirit World

The savage differs from modern man in feeling that he can bring pressure to bear on spiritual powers by use of suitable dances, musical instruments and incantations. So in every part of the world there are intermediaries who learn the will of the spirits when in ecstatic condition resulting from wild dancing, drumming, and use of narcotics.

Among primitive tribes inhabiting the frozen

wastes of Siberia the magician, medicine man, or
" Shaman," is a most important person, and of greater
significance than his robes and amulets is the musical
drum, whose notes produce in the Shaman a hypnotic
trance, during which he communicates with the
spirit world.

A boy of neurotic temperament, who is subject to
fits of hysteria, is selected for training, which consists
of fastings, ceremonials, and seclusion in the loneliest
mountain ravines. Such a course naturally emphasises
physical weakness and mental abnormality, until at
last the youth is in such a highly sensitive state that
hysteria, followed by trance, can be self induced by
violent dancing, singing and drum beating.

The Shaman's drum is everywhere regarded with
the utmost awe, and many superstitions centre
round its manufacture and use as an instrument for
assisting communion with the world of spirits.

India, from Ceylon to Tibet, is a region where
the devil dancers, who claim to exorcise disease, wear
hideous masks with staring eyes. In Tibet there are
said to be man-eating devils, fiends of pre-Buddhistic
mythology, who are driven out by suitable dances
and texts from Buddhistic scriptures.

The Veddas, a shy and primitive people of Ceylon,
have a Shaman or medicine man who undertakes
special dancing ceremonial to cure sickness, to give
thanks for success in hunting, or to celebrate a funeral.

An altar and pole are erected, then a pot of milk
is placed on a rough stand. From this supply the
sick man and the dancers are fed until only a small
quantity remains to be thrown into the jungle as a
libation to Kapalpei, a powerful foreigner who reached
Ceylon in a ship. Kapalpei sees the food and is so
appeased as to withdraw the sickness. As the dance
proceeds, the rippling motions of the muscles become
more violent until, as the performers move round and

effect a "Dance of the Departure of the Spirit," a ceremony in which three persons represent the death of one of them and his restoration by the waters of life. This liquid is supposed to be brought from the country which is traversed on the journey to the land of shades.[32]

IMPORTANCE OF DANCING

A brief summary of the musical performances of primitive people in Africa, North America and Oceania emphasises the importance of music, not merely as a recreative faculty serving to express emotions and complex sentiments, but as an integral part of a well-organised social system, whose stability it serves to maintain throughout long periods. True it is, that rigid customs have exerted a repressive influence on the development of music and dancing among primitive people. A creative genuis would find his powers curbed by tribal precedent, and one cannot fail to be impressed by the manner in which backward races have selected certain stereotyped forms of musical expression, to which the community resorts on occasions of tribal importance.

With savage races, as among ourselves, the individual, and the unit to which he belongs, is continually striving to select some form of outward expression capable of reflecting the emotions arising in response to social intercourse, and crises of all kinds, nor are the powers and beauties of nature negligible.

The beauties of a full moon, the force of a hurricane, the playful eccentricities of a breeze, and the havoc wrought by lightning, are regarded with a full measure of awe which expresses itself in song and dance. Hunting peoples are daily brought into con-

tact with various forms of animal life which never
fail to arouse interested observation, resulting not
infrequently in the invention of mimetic dances that
form a faithful portrayal of animal movement. Perchance the grip of disease is felt by the community,
fear is rampant, and all unite in a grotesque devil
dance calculated to drive away the hostile demons
of disease. Bellicose neighbours are advancing,
war is imminent; fear, pugnacity, rivalry, self-
assertion and jealousy compel the community to a
violent expression of feeling, which most probably
vents itself in some wild, fantastic war dance, accompanied by the thumping of tom-toms and the blast
of trumpets. Enemies are routed, the victors, intoxicated with the excitement of battle, and filled with
feelings of pride and self-assertion, organise an
orgy of feasting, music, and dancing, all of which
provide a safety valve for turbulent passions capable
of doing incalculable mischief. Peace reigns within
the tribal domain, and the earth has brought forth
her fruits abundantly. What function more appropriate than a communal dance could be devised in
order to express joy and give thanks to the God of
agriculture ? Praises of this kind must not, however,
be rendered in a trivial manner, without due regard
for the importance of ritual and tribal precedent. For
generation after generation, the same honorific dances
are performed to the accompaniment of songs, and
the playing of musical instruments, which have been
sanctified by centuries of use on these special occasions.
Every detail of ritual is punctiliously followed, even
to refreshing the exhausted soil with human blood,
or plucking the heart from a victim and holding it
up to the sun, and no method is so likely to offend a
deity, as one which departs from the orders laid
down by tribal elders. Perhaps the time has come to
celebrate a marriage or the initiation of boys into

tribal fellowship ; or it may be that youths are being admitted to the sacred membership of a secret society. On all such occasions social emotions quicken, and once more music and dancing, adapted to the circumstances, are the means employed to express adequately all the alternating feelings of joy, reverence, and excitement which such important events stimulate. Mysteries of birth, growth, sickness and death never fail to impress primitive man with a sense of awe for powers lying outside his normal life and experience, hence there naturally arises the problem of directing these unseen spiritual forces into channels useful to the community. Medicine men, specially trained from youth, are exercised in various rites deemed necessary to bring the natural into touch with the supernatural. Tradition has sanctified particular songs, dances and musical instruments, which are employed according to precedent, in order to enable a mortal man to approach a spiritual world, where he learns the will of the gods and makes himself acquainted with precepts that are to be followed by the community for which he is acting as mediator.

CHAPTER II

ANTIQUITY OF DANCING AND VOCAL MUSIC

So far as dancing in prehistoric times is concerned, the oldest evidence which the archaeologist has to offer is that of ancient stone age paintings on the walls of caves in Spain. In the gloom of caverns, and in parts so difficult of access that it is unlikely that the artist went there for mere pastime, are figures of dancing women, contemporary with the well-known realistic pictures of such animals as the reindeer and bison.[33] Such works of art are approached with a reverence for the past, for they have survived from a remote period in the childhood of men, since which time has to be measured in geological periods rather than years.

Can it be that Bushman works of art representing dancing human figures, mythical beings, and animal life, are due to the efforts of a migrant branch of the Aurignacian people of the late stone age in Europe ? The imagination is kindled as one is left to speculate on the possibility of dancing and magical ceremonies being part of a rite, performed in gloomy caverns, by prehistoric man, in order to increase the supply of animal life on which he depended.

Among primitive people, all the world over, at the present time there are mimetic dances which may or may not be associated with totemism, a kind of

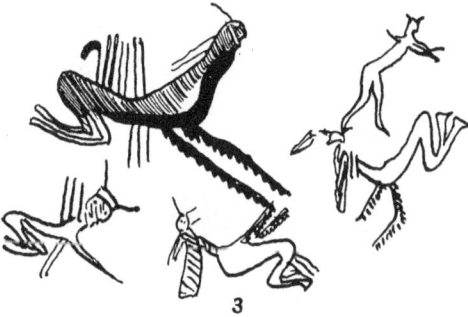

(1) HUNTERS FROM FRIEZE, ALPERA, S. SPAIN.

(2) BUSHMEN PAINTINGS.

(3) MYTHICAL BUSHMAN PAINTINGS, BIGGARDSBURG, S. AFRICA.

(4) DANCE ATTITUDES, ON WALL OF ROCK SHELTER, LERIDA, SPAIN.

(5) ANIMAL-HEADED MEN IN DANCING POSTURES.

magico-religious cult of animals and ancestors, thought to have a most important bearing on social organisation and food-supply.

Bushman paintings representing events which may or may not be entirely legendary are found in caves and rock shelters of the Biggardsberg mountains. The human figures are painted in brown, red, yellow, and the insects in blue with graduated tints. The originals of these are to be found near Konigsberg on a range running out from the Drakensberg mountains. Four strange-looking monsters with toothed arms appear to be part men, part insects, possibly they are men disguised as insects for some form of mimetic dance. Certain figures suggest the praying mantis regarded by Bushmen as a living symbol of the great Kaang, who is the central interest in a long series of folklore stories which show that he was appealed to for success in hunting.

The figures include animal-headed men in dancing postures,[34] and I should not hesitate to describe these pictures as the earliest evidence of animal cults of which the present day mimetic dances, often performed to increase animal fecundity, are a fragmentary survival.

Among dances of Bushmen of the Kalahari Desert there was one, represented in cave paintings, which was of special importance because ordained by the great Kaang himself. Apparently this and similar historical paintings have not retained a sanctity which may at one time have been theirs, for the works of art are not now concealed from women and the uninitiated. One has to read the ethnology of Australian aborigines fully to realise how carefully sacred objects are concealed from women and young children.

The Mo'Koma, or " Dance of Blood," so called because its delirious performers often fell to the ground with blood falling from their noses, is represented in

Bushman paintings of incalculable antiquity. Women
revived the prostrate man by placing two sticks in
the form of a cross on his back, while an initiated man
conjured from the patient a foreign body alleged to be
the cause of the faint. By excessive indulgence in
this dance the performer's health was ruined, so that
Kaang became angry, carried off the victim, trans-
formed him into a beast, and chastised him with a
digging stick.[35]

At Orange Springs the Mantis dance is depicted in
mural paintings showing the rite in progress, as witnessed by some Bushman artist with a gift for realism.
The five central performers symbolise the praying
mantis, while two or three others appear to be musicians providing an accompaniment. The onlookers
are men and women whose attitudes suggest supplication or applause.[36]

Vocal music, in the earliest stages of its development, might have originated in an imitation of the
whistling of birds and the cries of animals. Many
dances of the Tasmanians were imitative of the movements of animals, and amongst pagan tribes of Borneo
aborigines of Australia and North American Indians
such mimetic dances are extremely common. These
dances are not merely recreative, or aesthetic ; they
are conducted in the hope of placing primitive man
in closer touch and sympathy with the animal life on
which his livelihood depends. The Baganda people
of East Africa seek to propitiate the spirit of a
slaughtered leopard by dancing round the suspended
skin in imitation of the movements of leopards.
North American Indians do homage to their totem
animals by mimetic dances, and in the succeeding
pages many examples of primitive dances, imitative
of animal movements, will be discussed. It must be
clearly recognised, however, that all theories respecting the origin of vocal and instrumental music, or

of dancing, whether supported by archaeological evidence, psychological inquiry, or present day observation among savage races, are extremely speculative, and no dogmatism may justly be attempted on the evidence available.

RHYTHM IN CHILDREN AND ANIMALS

Psychologists have noted a general resemblance between the mental development of children and that of primitive man. In more technical language there is a theory of culture epochs, which suggests that the history of juvenile development recapitulates the phases of mental progress through which the human race has toiled. The emotional life and want of foresight in children have a parallel in the career of primitive man, whose emotions, easily roused, are often productive of immediate vigorous action, while at all times he has a tendency towards improvidence ; the tribe will eat, drink, and be merry without a thought of the famine ahead. With respect to the development of musical faculty in children, it may be said that there appears to be some inherent emotion which is gratified by rhythm however crude, and a very young infant will attempt rhythmic movements and show signs of gratification when someone plays the piano. In most musical performances of primitive people rhythm is the dominating factor which may take the form of a simple monotonous beating on a dried skin, or a more complex expression by means of synchronising various rhythms beaten on drums of lizard skin, no two of which produce the same pitch. The child resembles the savage inasmuch as his musical sense is not shocked by sudden and violent changes in intensity, and an energetic individual effort productive of much noise is as gratifying as elaborate orchestration. The psychologist Bernard Perez[37] goes so far as to say "Sounds of all sorts, sharp or flat, intense or feeble, impressive or not, give him pleasure, provided they are accompanied by rhythm," and one is inclined to believe that a very striking parallel might be established between the development of the musical sense in children and primitive man. Psychological study of animals might assist the inquiry into origins of musical expression, with special reference to rhythmic movements, for it is a matter of common observation that many animals, especially the horse, whose nervous system is sensitive, are susceptible to the influence of music. The cobra is dormant in its basket until roused by the pipes of the snake charmer, whose musical effort causes the creature to raise its head and body which are swayed in time to the music. A well-trained horse, performing a rhythmical dance on hind legs, delights the children at a circus, while irrespective of training, the same animal shows keen appreciation of martial music which causes a quick natural response in the form of stepping and general alertness. Dogs and bears are easily trained to perform muscular movements adaptable to varied musical sounds, and birds, such as the jackass and parrot, readily exercise an imitative faculty in copying the notes of various songsters. This general susceptibility of animals towards musical sounds was picturesquely expressed in the legend of Orpheus, whose sweet pipes rallied animals both timid and ferocious. Many Indian legends dealing with origins of music refer to this well-known power of musical sounds over animals.

To the student of music this imitative faculty is of great interest, for primitive man, like modern musicians, is ever ready to incorporate new songs and dances. Corroborees travel over vast areas of Australia, and not only are the movements correctly taught, but there is a readiness to learn the words which accompany the dances, in spite of the fact that such words are not understood by the pupils. Bishop Codrington has noted the check placed by primitive musicians on this imitative tendency, and something akin to copyright prevails in Melanesian villages, where songs and dances may not be reproduced by the musicians of one village without permission of the villagers who invented them. The tutors may consent to teach their neighbours, and for this purpose they reside with their pupils, who reward them with lavish hospitality and payment in kind.

MUSICAL INSTRUMENTS

There has been a great expenditure of effort to solve problems connected with the origin, not only of musical faculty, but of the instruments, sometimes of great ingenuity, by means of which primitive man has sought to express his feelings and emotions. A convenient classification of musical instruments might be made under the headings "wind," "stringed," and "percussion," but musicians interested in origins are reluctant to make a definite statement respecting the priority of any one of these, with regard to time of appearance in the course of human history. Those who give favour to the theory that percussive instruments preceded all others, point to the simplicity of origin. In the dances of present day primitive people there is considerable hand clapping, combined with slapping of the legs and thighs, so at a very remote date our earliest progenitors had in their own contours an ever-ready percussive instrument.

Amongst present day Australian aborigines, a simple orchestra is provided by a group of women who maintain a rhythmical clapping, and here, too, one may observe the use of a most simple percussive instrument, the drum, which might easily have been improvised by the earliest representatives of the human race. The instrument is made by stretching a skin tightly between the knees of a squatting operator, usually a woman, who uses the palms of her hands as drumsticks. In considering the archaeological evidence respecting antiquity of musical instruments, the investigator must bear in mind the perishable nature of the material of which drums are made. Skin and wood undergo rapid decay, while on the other hand bone, earthenware, and ivory preserve their form for long periods ; hence examples of wind instruments, chiefly whistles made in prehistoric times, are to be found in most archaeological museums.[38] From the stalactite deposit on the floor of Kent's Cavern, near Torquay, perforated bones of the hare have been obtained, and their previous function is suggested by the fact that they do still admit a shrill note when the operator blows into a perforation which prehistoric man probably drilled with a sharp flint instrument. During 1863 the researches of M. Lartet in the cave of Laugerie Basse, Dordogne, brought to light a number of bone whistles made from the small bones in the foot of the reindeer. These very early instruments are ascribed to the Magdalenian and Solutrean periods which closed the old stone age.[39] What was the function of these early wind instruments ? Did they summon stone age man to combat ? Were they the hunter's shrill call ? or for use by the principal operators in magical ceremonies ? as is the case among present day " Blackfeet " Indians of North America.

During the stone age period in North America the slender bones of birds were often made into whistles, an exact replica of which is still in use among primitive medicine men concerned with exorcising demons of disease. Clay whistles are characteristic of the "neolithic" or new stone age, a period marked by the polishing of flint implements, and examples are numerous from such widely separated areas as Southern Europe, Colombia, Peru, and Mexico.

The bronze age of course yields a number of ancient musical instruments, amongst which trumpets[40] and harp-keys are numerous, but the inference, based only on archaeological evidence, that wind instruments preceded percussive in the evolutionary series would be unwarranted, in view of the perishable nature of skin and wood from which the latter are made. Plaintive whining of the wind amongst thin bamboo, and the twanging of early bow-strings might have originated ideas concerning stringed instruments. The acolian harp employed by Indians of Guiana is an example of the ingenuity of primitive man, exerted in the cause of musical development. Palm-leaf fibres separated from the matrix are raised by a little bridge, and this simple contrivance erected on the tops of high trees produces musical sounds when the wind blows. Mr. Henry Balfour has clearly demonstrated the evolution of the musical bow from an occasional adaptation of the hunter's bow, and has collected a series of illustrations explaining stages of development.[41]

Psychologists are concerned with the distribution of primitive musical instruments, for the study of this subject confronts the investigator with the rival questions of multiple or single origins. Nose flutes are common in large areas of Brazil, Northern and Central India, the Southern Malay States, Borneo, and many islands of the Pacific, and the question naturally arises, have these instruments had an independent origin in widely separated areas ? Or may we assume a single origin and subsequent distribution ? The conch shell trumpet found in Central America, Northern India, and Melanesia suggests similar queries, so also does the almost universal distribution of the syrinx Pan pipes, and the widespread use of the musical bow. Ethnographers concern themselves with the collection of a great variety of examples of these musical instruments which are, or should be arranged, not merely geographically, but according to musical principles involved in their construction and use.

Ecstatic dancing as an adjunct to religious cere-monial has been a feature of all civilisations, but it is perhaps not so well recognised that this form of excitation has its prototype in magical dances of primitive medicine men and their followers who are concerned with rain making, avoiding supposed dangers of an eclipse, causing animals to multiply, or driving off demons of disease. Many musical instru-ments, including drums, whistles, and flutes, appear to have a sanctity which has been acquired from long contact with magico-religious ceremonial.

In many rustic villages of the British Isles there is a simple toy known as the " bull roarer," " buzzer," or " hummer," which is easily constructed by attach-ing a string to a hole bored through a thin slat of wood. Such a toy, when rapidly whirled at the end of a taut string, produced a shrill note, which in some parts of Scotland is thought to be a charm against thunder, while in many districts the noise is found to be of use in herding cattle.

This simple contrivance for producing a shrill musical note has an almost universal distribution. In many parts of Central Australia, notably among the Arunta tribe, the bull roarers are decorated and classed with sacred objects known as " churinga," all of which are carefully preserved from the gaze of women and children, who would, in all probability, suffer the penalty of death, or loss of eyesight, should they gaze, even accidentally, on objects of such potent magic.

When a boy arrives at the age of puberty and has undergone a part of his initiation into the tribe, he becomes acquainted with the mode of producing this weird music, which forms an important part of all ceremonies designed to cause rainfall or an abundance of animal life. Very reverently the old men of the tribe lead the way to some rocky defile, and from a cleft in the rocks take forth the sacred bull roarers, which for untold ages have been the most highly venerated tribal assets.

Among the Yuin of South East Australia, novices about to be incorporated in the tribe are carried into a clearing, where they are laid round a large fire. Elders of the tribe, blackened with charcoal, and grotesquely clad in bark fibre, dance into the circle, and test the physical endurance of the youths whose central incisor teeth are knocked out with a stone implement. During this terrifying performance, men stationed in the adjacent bush whirl the magic bull roarers, whose shrill notes are declared to be the voice of the god Daramulun ; and on this impressive occasion moral precepts respecting the iniquity of adultery, lying, and stealing are taught. Magical properties of the bull roarer may be employed to alleviate pain, and in the Arunta tribe an affected part is rubbed with this sacred musical instrument.

In Central Europe, North America, Brazil, the Malay States, Sumatra, West and South Africa, New Guinea, and Melanesia the bull roarer is in wide circulation, though with the advance of civilisation there is always the tendency for the instrument to degenerate into a mere plaything.

To many primitive people of West and South Africa the shrill musical note of the buzzer is the voice of Oro, a god of terror and vengeance. Bushmen of the Kalahari Desert use the noise as a means of driving game, and Kaffirs believe in the instrument as a means of producing a wind. Amongst the Indians of Arizona magicians twirled the bull roarer rapidly, and with a uniform motion, swinging it around the head from front to rear; a performance which resulted in the production of a musical note, said to be infallible in compelling a rain-laden wind to visit the crops.

A religious procession among the Zuni Indians is headed by a priest gaily decorated with embroideries and war-paint, carrying in his arms a ferocious-looking wooden idol heavily ornamented with shells. Slowly the procession winds along to the accompaniment of shrill, weird music, produced by a priest, whose function is to whirl the sounding slat. Amazonian Indians of the Xingu area have a fish-shaped bull roarer decorated with red and black, also with a snake design at one end. At funeral feasts, when the property of a dead man is burned, the bull roarer is whirled in order that its musical note may assure the spirit of the departed that no property has been withheld. The notes of the instrument are thought to have power over the spirit of the deceased, and when the corpse is conveyed out of the village, the shrill notes induce the ghost to follow the bones instead of remaining behind to annoy the residents. Women may not look with impunity on this sacred instrument, and, as is the case in Australia, there are among the Xingu Indians severe penalties; usually a woman who sees the sacred bull roarer has to take the poison cup.

There is in wind instruments a variety of form; adaptation of construction to the nature of the

"BULL ROARERS" OF WOOD.
(1) "GOPEGOPE," FLY RIVER DELTA, NEW GUINEA; (2) "PERI-
PERIO" OF MULGRAVE BLACKS, QUEENSLAND, AUSTRALIA;
(3) NEW ZEALAND; (4) W. KIMBERLEY, AUSTRALIA; (5) BALUBA,
BELGIAN CONGO; (6) IBADEN, S. NIGERIA; (7) HOPI BULL
ROARER, ARIZONA.

(By permission of Trustees, British Museum)

material; alternative arrangements of stop-holes, in order to produce different notes and intervals; great ingenuity in selection of resonators; and recognition of the law that pitch depends, among other factors, on the length and thickness of a vibrating string. A psychologist would quickly note these manifestations of a developing intellect, and its application to the production of a more efficient musical instrument. Thus the ethnographer and the psychologist should, in collaboration, produce an arrangement of musical instruments, based on psychological principles.

No phase of primitive life is complete without musical accompaniments, which the social anthropologist studies with a view to estimating how far the religious, magical, and purely social life of primitive people have found expression through musical channels. Social emotions called into play by birth, puberty rites, marriage, warfare, religious and magical ceremonies, and funerals, have all found expression in songs and dances, which are carefully recorded by modern methods which have received a somewhat detailed description in the following pages.

MYTHICAL ORIGINS OF SONG AND DANCE

In dealing with problems of origin and migration, great attention should be paid to the existence of myths which account for the introduction of tribal songs and dances which are accurately performed, and bequeathed from one generation to another.[41]

A legend of the Haida Indians of Queen Charlotte Island states that at some remote period four of their tribesmen, when sitting fog-bound in their canoe, were startled by the sudden appearance of a man who emerged from the depths of the sea, and holding on to the gunwale said, " The chief invites you." The summons was irresistible, and after a journey to the ocean depths the four wanderers found themselves in a large house, the walls of which were adorned with rattles and dancing aprons. In this abode the four hunters learned mystic dances and songs which they faithfully communicated to their tribe when safely returned to their native village. Rattles, dancing aprons and blankets are all manufactured according to patterns seen by the four hunters who visited the house of mystery at the depths of the sea.

The importance of myth and tradition in connection with the origin of music and specific dances may be illustrated by reference to the foundation of the " Brave Dog Society," by " Generous Woman," and her husband " Red Blanket." When weary and despondent after a long and unsuccessful search for his dog, " Red Blanket " heard the words : " Lone Chief invites you to prepare for a dance." A drum sounded, but as no one was in sight " Red Blanket " lay down and composed himself to sleep. Again the notes of the invisible drum reverberated, and once more the same voice called : " Lone Chief invites you to come and eat, for he is ready to give a dance." Half awake, but convinced of the reality of what he saw, " Red Blanket " gazed around, and to his amazement was confronted by a large female dog to which he gave a piece of meat. According to the chief's story the dog addressed him saying : " I am giving a dance to-night on behalf of a mother dog and her six little baby dogs, who were left behind when the camp moved, and I am trying to help them. We will show you our dance, and when you return to camp you can make use of it to found a dog society." ' Red Blanket ' went through a long course of dancing

under the tuition of these mythical dogs, and on returning to camp proceeded to teach the movements to his
tribesmen. The primary motives in these dances of
" The Brave Dog Society " appear to be cultivation of
cunning and adoption of the fighting qualities of
brave dogs. No man of the " Brave Dog Society "
who has undergone the ceremonial dances may retire
from a foe or turn his back on danger, while to teach
cunning, members of the Brave Dog Society have to
live for periods of several days by no other means
than hunting without weapons, or stealing portions of
food after the manner of dogs.

THE MOST PRIMITIVE MUSIC AMONG BACKWARD RACES

The present day musician, who has made a comparative study of mediaeval and modern schools of
music, might complete the cycle of thought by turning
to a consideration of the music of primitive tribes.
Such music is not a mere drumming without variation
or import, as one might suppose after a cursory consideration of some few examples of primitive instruments and dancing. There is for the sympathetic
musician and anthropologist a recognition of the
common striving of humanity toward the expression
of simple emotions, which, in course of time, tend to
become stable in the form of well-defined social and
religious sentiments. The gulf separating modern
music from primitive rhythmical expression may be
realised by a consideration of the corroborree of now
extinct Tasmanians.[43]
The moon is full ; and the hills which had glared
in the noontide heat now sleep in the soft and sooth-
ing light. The laughing jackass has carolled his
farewell note, while from the valley there rises a

strange mysterious sound. We go nearer; there amidst that dusky mass we distinguish the plaintive chant, the tapping of time-sticks, and the muffled murmurs of opossum rug-drums. Various companies are sitting round small fires, which are occasionally bursting into blaze as dried boughs or a few leaves are laid upon the embers. Women have folded their rugs and placed them between their thighs, and now beat them with the open palms of their hands. Some are seated cross-legged, singing a mournful dirge, with their eyes downward, and with a melancholy aspect which seems to check conversation.

A livelier air succeeds, the old men beat their sticks quicker, the tum-tum is louder, eyes brighten, a laugh is heard, the prattling begins, and this soon develops into a tumult of noisy merriment.

But the corroborree is to begin. Certain important elders are gliding about, consulting and giving direction about the fête. The performers see that the pipeclay lines of beauty upon their bodies are in proper order, redaubing where necessary. After an amount of coquetting, fidgeting, and confusion, resembling that of a more civilised reunion, there is a fall to places. The women squat near the fires, clear their throats for a song, and give extra tightening to their drums, while the old men sit or stand in groups. The young men spring blithely into the centre accompanied by an involuntary ha ! ha ! of admiration from the throng of ebon beauties. Some little bantering passages between the sexes are silenced by the seniors ; in growls from their white-haired lords, and spiteful snappings from the shrivelled hags of mammas, silence is called, and the ranks are formed. The moon's beams rest upon the naked performers. With bunches of gum-leaves in their hands, and others round their ankles, like flying Mercuries, the dancing men are ready, and the band strikes up. Slowly

moving their bodies from side to side, the young
men gracefully and tremulously move their hands to
the measure. At a signal the legs commence a
similar motion, having a most grotesque unnatural
appearance. The flesh of the thigh and calf is seen
quivering in an extraordinary manner, which excites
deep interest in the spectators. Exclamations of
delight issue from the eager witnesses of the performance, at some peculiarly charming and difficult
wriggling of a limb. After sundry side-stepping, the
men break their line, rush together in a mass without
disorder or confusion, leap upward in the air, wave
their boughs over their heads, utter a loud " waugh,"
and bursting into laughter join in a *mêlée* of chattering,
during which they receive the hearty congratulations
of their friends.

Such then is the primitive orchestra which boasts
a rhythm marked by the beating of a single instrument, the drum, hastily improvised by stretching the
skin of an opossum between the knees, and beating
it with open hands. Such rudimentary accompaniment is sufficient to stimulate the dancers to perform
simple muscular movements in which, once again,
rhythm is emphasised by an attachment of leaves,
whose crisp rustling adds a not unmusical accompaniment. Elementary human emotions, complex sentiments, and social feelings are finding, what is to
ourselves, a crude and non-aesthetic mode of expression, though for the Tasmanian, the simple muscular
movements, guttural exclamations, rhythmic tappings,
and social surroundings, provided a most delectable
evening.

A number of early voyagers were interested in
Tasmanian musical ability, as expressed by vocal
performances and the reception of European music.
Peron,[44] quoted by Ling Roth, states that when the
Marseillaise was played the savages at first appeared

more troubled than surprised, but after some moments
of uncertainty they listened attentively. Signs of
satisfaction were soon given by strange contortions
and gestures which made the sailors shake with
laughter. One young man raised to ecstasy pulled
his hair, scratched his head with both hands, shook
himself, and repeatedly raised loud shouts. La
Billardière[45] says: "Our musician had brought his
violin ashore, but his self-love was truly mortified by
the indifference shown to his performance. The
tune was a lively one, but the savages seemed in
doubt as to the reception they should give. The
musician redoubled his exertions, but the bow dropped
from his fingers when he beheld the assembly stopping
their ears with their fingers so that they might hear
no more." The natives themselves sang duets, one
performer always keeping one third above the other,
so forming a concord with great correctness. James
Backhouse,[46] a keen observer who spent four years
in Tasmania, says that a native woman to whom a
musical box was shown, listened intently, while her
ears moved like those of a dog or horse to catch the
sound.

If the information gleaned from a study of Tasmanian music is a guide to the performances of
prehistoric man of an early stone age, we must believe
that vocal music and dancing can be well developed
without any musical instruments whatever, for the
aborigines of Tasmania had no accompaniments save
the marking of time by clapping hands, or beating a
skin stretched across their knees.

Australian dances are complex, and there are no
musical instruments, but the tones employed in singing give more variety than those of other isolated
people who have gained little from contact with
civilisation. The Andamanese, who have been shut
off in their island home for a long period, have songs

of a simple recitative kind. Each man composes his own ditty, which describes every-day occupations, for example : " Knots are very hard to cut with an adze, they blunt the edge of the adze ; how hard I am working cutting these knots." The only musical instrument of the Andamanese is a sounding-board on which a man marks time with his foot for singing and dancing. The dances are not highly specialised, thus the ceremonial dance marking the conclusion of mourning, or the intention to attack enemies, is the same as the evening dance of amusement. An area of open ground in the centre of the village is swept clean and lit up with little piles of burning resin round the edge, near which sit the men who intend to take part. The man who has volunteered the first song takes his stand on the sounding-board and reels off his own composition at least twice. Women take up and repeat the chorus while beating time with their hands on the hollows of their thighs.[47]

The Veddas of Ceylon are a shy remnant of a pre-Dradivian people hiding themselves in the forests, where they live by hunting and gathering honey. We may therefore reasonably turn to them when in search of information which will assist us to picture the musical abilities of human beings before the dawn of history.

Knowledge of Vedda music is based on tunes recorded by Dr. C. G. Seligman[48] and analysed by Dr. C. S. Myers.[49] Thirty-four different phonographic records were examined, and of these, nine tunes were composed of two notes only. In three tunes there were two notes with the addition of one or more unimportant grace notes. Nine of the songs contain four notes each, and one song has as many as five different notes. Not only is Vedda music primitive because the notes of the song are few and the range small, but also because the natives are ignorant of any other than vocal music. Dr. Seligman says that uncontaminated Veddas, for example those of Sitala Wanniya, have no musical instruments whatever. Other Veddas have borrowed the drum from their Singhalese neighbours.

In Vedda music we have an object-lesson in the beginnings of melody-building shown by employment of two notes, the song descending from the higher to the lower. In a second group of songs a third note higher than the two others is added. Lastly, in the third group a fourth note is introduced, generally a tone below the tonic, and throughout most songs the influence of this fourth note is very clearly felt.

Australian music is more advanced in complexity than Vedda music, for though the intervals between successive tones are small, the range of tones throughout any one song is considerable. Among American Indians it is also rare to find a song consisting of only two notes. The music of the natives of New Guinea, Borneo, and Africa is decidedly more complex than that of the Veddas. To these quiet glades of Ceylon we may still turn for a survival of the primitive' dances and tunes which are used to lay the ghost at funeral ceremonies, to approach the spirit world, and as incantations. And as we watch, the imagination goes back to the gloomy recesses of caves in palaeolithic Europe, where man, still in his social childhood, performed his simple rites, leaving only a few polychrome paintings of animals and human attitudes to suggest that he, like the present day Veddas, knew how the forces of nature might be approached by spell and rhythm.

MUSIC OF ANCIENT CIVILISATIONS
Egypt

The musician who interests himself in the origin and evolutionary aspect of his art would do well to turn to the great "Dark Continent" where, six thousand years ago, the pre-dynastic Egyptians were giving artistic expression to their emotions, by means of religious exercises, building, decorative art, pictorial writing, music and dancing. Students may consult the earliest historical records, consisting chiefly of scenes depicting court musicians, male and female, and from such a study, combined with perusal of papyri, may build up an accurate knowledge of the musical abilities of a civilisation, which, year by year, is made to yield its secrets to excavators in the desert sands.

The sands of Egypt, unlike the soil of the Euphrates Valley, are favourable for the preservation of musical instruments, and in the British Museum (5th Egyptian Room, Table Case E) there are stringed instruments of wood covered with parchment. Harps have four or five keys, and flutes of bamboo have four, five, or six stopholes. There is no drum among these instruments, but a figure of the god Bes holds some such instrument.

In Ancient Egypt music and religion were interdependent, though in all probability the latter had a modifying and controlling function to which the former had to conform. Bands of female singers, dedicated to serve the god in whose honour the temple was erected, were constantly employed in performing honorific dances, accompanied by hymns sung in eulogy of a particular deity, of whom the women were the peculiar property. Similar practices prevail in India at the present day, where "Basavis" or dancing

girls are fully dedicated to service in the temples,
to the physical requirements of whose gods they have
to minister.

Among Egyptian women the dance most frequently
consisted of slow posturising with studied and graceful
movements made to the accompaniment of male
voices. One foot was slowly raised and placed in
advance of the other, while the arms were lifted above
the head to their full extent with the palms turned
inward. A third movement placed the right arm
obliquely upward and the left downward behind the
body. At various periods, drums, lutes, harps,
tambourines, castanets, and hand clapping, were
employed to supply tune with emphasis of time and
rhythm. Every royal household possessed a retinue
of musicians and dancers, most frequently under the
control of a superintendent of music who organised
the performances for state occasions, at which groups
of blind singers and musicians were much appreciated.

Symbolic dances, embodying a kind of primitive
drama, were very popular, and at times one performer
representing a conquering monarch would seize a
kneeling dancer by the hair and swing a sword above
him as a suggestion of the triumph of Egypt over her
enemies the Syrians. It is of interest to note from the
pages of Adolf Erman[50] that female dancers of Egypt
sometimes represented the wind by bending backward,
in imitation of pliant reeds, until their hands touched
the ground, a movement not uncommon among
modern gymnastic dancers of our own day. The
dress of female dancers was light and of the finest
transparent texture, so as to show the form and
movement of the limbs, which were covered by a
loose flowing robe reaching to the ankles. Occasionally this was fastened tightly at the waist, and round
the hips was a small narrow girdle adorned with
beads or ornaments of various colours.

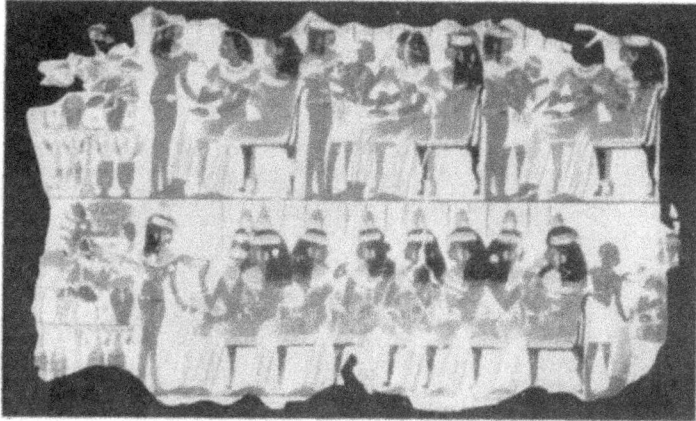

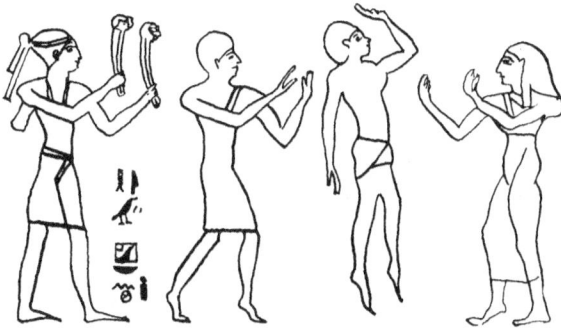

(*Upper*) FESTIVAL SCENE, TOMB OF AMENEMHEB, THEBES, ABOUT B.C. 1500.
(*Middle*) PIROUETTE AND OTHER EGYPTIAN STEPS, B.C. 2000.
(*Lower*) MALE ATTENDANTS OF HATHOR DANCING.

Sometimes the figures appear to be quite naked, but there is difficulty in saying whether this is intentional or whether the outline of the flowing robe has been effaced. One can scarcely suppose that a highly civilised people were so depraved as to admit artists to record the dances of naked women in the presence of men, or that the priesthood would permit such exhibitions. Slaves were taught dancing as well as music so that they might entertain guests in the homes of their wealthy masters. Free Egyptians who gained a livelihood from dancing appeared at parties. Guests travelled to the feast in chariots with runners alongside and were met by servants who invited them to partake of fruit and drink laid out in the house ; then they entered the banquet hall. The grass mats were spread, cakes lay in rows with pans of drink ; and hands were washed in anti-splash finger-bowls of silver. When the guests were seated damsels went round placing garlands on their necks and pouring ointment on the conical piles of hair on the top of the head, which held it as a sponge ; a lotus flower was given into the hand of each guest. Wine was then handed and was plentifully renewed during the feast. Dancers and musicians afterwards added gaiety to the gathering while a mummy was carried round to exhort all people to make the best of present joys. Herodotus was responsible for this statement, but possibly the " mummy " was a small figure of Osiris.

> " Put song and music before thee,
> Behind thee all evil things,
> And remember thou only joy
> Till comes that day of mooring
> At the land that loveth silence."[51]

From Egyptian cities of all periods there is graphic and plastic art indicating that some four or five thousand years ago the tambourine, drum, sistrum, bells, cymbals, straight metal trumpets and cross flutes blown through a lateral hole were all known and used.[52] Stringed instruments of the plucked variety were numerous, so also were those of the lute type with a vaulted resonating sound-box.[53] Unfortunately there is no Egyptian text which gives descriptions of dances, but there is conclusive evidence that dances were in remote times regarded as acts of worship.[54] So far back as the Ist Dynasty 4,000 B.C. a wooden plaque of King Semti shows dancing as a devotional exercise. The posture of the King suggests that he is stepping rhythmically to the accompaniment of simple instrumental music or perhaps to the clapping of hands. A high official who lived in the reign of King Assa in the IVth Dynasty brought from Punt a " tenk " or pygmy who knew how to dance the dance of the god, and was said to come from the land of the spirits. A text of the pyramid of Pepi I mentions a " Pygmy of the dances of the god who rejoiceth the heart of the god before his great throne." The occurrence of these amusing gymnastic dances of Pygmies in Central Africa to-day provides an impressive example of the persistence of conventional forms of expression over astonishingly long periods, in this case some six thousand years. Schweinfurth[55] says that the agility of a pygmy, Adimokoos, was marvellous. The steps included leaps and attitudes accompanied by such lively and grotesque varieties of expression that spectators shook and held their sides with laughter, as no doubt did the Egyptian courtiers of six thousand years ago.

Egyptian bas-reliefs of all periods contain many illustrations of kings dancing before Osiris and other gods. It was King Pepi's earnest desire to dance before the god in order to comfort and strengthen the deity. Budge says: "We may be sure that the naturally conservative spirit of the people faithfully preserved all essential characteristics of the dance which tradition had handed down to them."[56] Such comment, in conjunction with what is known of the preservation of Pygmies' dances, agricultural dances in connection with fertility cults, sun dances, moon dances, and many others, introduces a speculative inquiry into the problem of origins and dispersal. But the detail involved in mapping out geographically and discussing the differences and resemblances of all these ceremonies would make the work tedious for a general reader.

Babylon

Musicians formed a class to themselves, though whether as a trade or profession it is difficult to say. Babylonians distinguished between composer and performer; the latter was frequently a slave or captive and occupied but a humble place in society. He is frequently represented in the Assyrian bas-reliefs, and in one instance is wearing a cap of great height shaped like a fish. Musical instruments were numerous and various. They included drums, tambourines, trumpets, horns, lyres, guitars, harps, zithers, pipes and cymbals.

Besides single musicians there were bands of performers, and at times the music was accompanied by dancing or by clapping the hands. The bands were under the conduction of leaders who kept time with a double rod.

There is a sculpture of three captives playing lyres, an incident which calls to mind the complaint of Jewish exiles that their Babylonian conquerors required from them a song.[57]

Our knowledge of Babylonian and Assyrian musical instruments is derived from a study of sculptures, for the actual objects have not been recovered.[58] The interested specialist will find the following references useful.[59]

Aztecs of Mexico

It is impossible to think of the civilisation of Ancient Mexico without visualising the sanguinary rites of sun worship for which a victim was prepared. The youth whose heart was eventually held up as an offering to the Sun was considered to be a god, and as such he enjoyed every privilege, including the companionship of six beautiful maidens for a period of six weeks.

But all too soon was heard the drum throbbing, that "devilish music" that Cortez heard after his first repulse before Mexico. The sounds lasted the whole night and curdled his blood with horror as he thought of his captured companions being sacrificed to Huitzlipochtli, the Aztec War God.

Drums of the type illustrated were in use for religious and public festivals, and the noise made by these was supplemented by the beating by hand of gongs formed from the carapaces of tortoises. Rattles and rattle staves were also used; wind instruments included several forms of conch shell trumpets, likewise bone or reed flutes and whistles. Small bells or rattles of "hawk bill" pattern were worn as ornaments.

Music was not highly developed, and there was but little variety in musical instruments. Rattles of gourd or pottery were common, but the principal instrument of percussion was the gong formed of a hollow cylinder of wood with two tongues, of different notes, which were struck with beaters sometimes

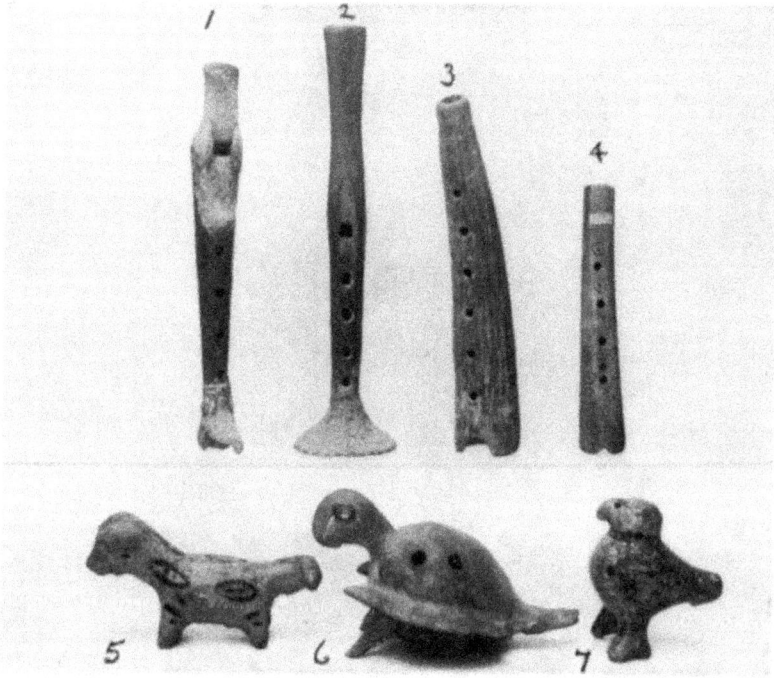

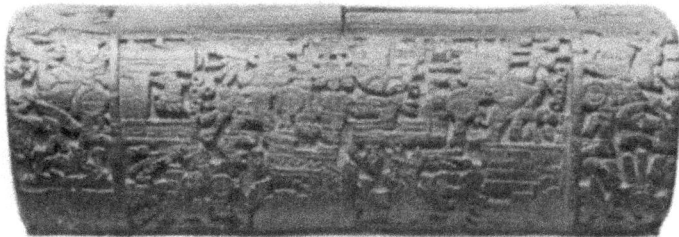

(*Upper*) (1 & 2) ANCIENT POTTERY FLUTES, MEXICO; (3) POTTERY
FLUTE, AREQUIPA, PERU; (4) BONE FLUTE, TRUXILLO,
PERU; (5 & 7) POTTERY OCARINA, TALAMANCAN, PANAMA;
(6) POTTERY OCARINA, MEXICO.

(*Lower*) "TEPONAZTEI" OR WOODEN GONG, USED BY ANTECS OF
MEXICO.

(*By permission of Trustees, British Museum*)

headed with rubber. Drums with skin membranes were also in common use, while instruments of rather a special nature consisted of tortoise carapaces, or their facsimiles in gold, which were struck either with a stick, or serrated bones, or were rubbed with short rods. Wind instruments were few in variety; conches, provided apparently with a wooden mouthpiece like those of New Zealand, were sounded in most religious ceremonies, and quantities of whistles and ocarinas have been discovered. The finger-holes do not exceed four in number, and are frequently less in case of instruments of flageolet type. Whether the Mexicans, like tribes of the North-West Coast of America, were acquainted with reed instruments is uncertain, at any rate none *are* known to exist. Singing was important in religious ceremonies involving human sacrifice, when the temple choir sang as the sacred fire, produced by friction, was lit on the chest of the wretched victim.

Many of the hymns have been preserved and illustrate well the poetical cast of Mexican thought. A species of primitive drama was said to exist; and this was recited on a terrace in the market-place or temple court. Dancing was highly developed, for every feast had its ceremonial dance, which was carried out with great solemnity and decorum. In some performances the dancers formed large circles, the members of each belonging to one sex and rank. In others the sexes mingled, while some dancers performed in pairs with their arms round each other's waists or necks. This appears to have been a privilege of the upper classes. In combined figures a long garlanded rope was held by the dancers, who moved their bodies and limbs in unison as in Peru, while occasionally they danced in threes, two women and one man, or two men and one woman.[60]

The Maya civilisation of the Peninsula of Yucatan

has left behind sculptures which show the priests using musical instruments.[61] The principal form of amusement appears to have been a dance, of which there were many varieties. Maya nobles were addicted to dancing and debauchery, and amid the sounds of revelry could be heard the throbbing of hollow gongs of wood which were sounded with rubber-headed beaters, so as to give a noise that could be heard for a distance of two leagues.[62]

Incas of Peru

South American rites, especially those of the Incas of Peru, centred largely around sun-worship and human sacrifice. In Colombia a chief was invested with the insignia of his rank amid shouts of the multitude and shrill sounds from bone and clay whistles. He then proceeded to a lake, where he washed off in its waters the offering of gold ornaments. At the same time gold-dust and emeralds were thrown in, a proceeding which makes somewhat painful reading in these strenuous modern times. Some of the whistles used were made of beaten gold formed into the fashion of a human face.[63]

During September an important harvest festival ceremony was held at Bogota, where all the people decked in finery, and led by priests wearing golden tiaras, assembled in a broad street leading to the chief's house. Many were dressed in skins of wild beasts, a custom also found in Peru. Prayers were chanted to the sun, and appeal to his pity was made by wearing masks with tears painted on them. Priests made their way along the streets followed by a troupe of worshippers manifesting every sign of joy and announcing that the sun had heard their supplication. Then came a number of men wearing gold masks ; and these mummers spread beautiful textiles before a

richly adorned band of musicians who escorted the
highest chief and his attendant rulers. Offerings were
made to idols, then the proceedings ended in a drinking
bout and merry-making, during which two men sat
at the gate of the dancing enclosure. These janitors
played mournful airs on flutes ; they represented
death and funeral dirges, the proceeding being a
reminder to the revellers that life is short, hence
pleasures must be seized while at hand.[64] This brings
to mind the Egyptian custom of carrying round the
mummy at the feast.[65]

ORIENTAL MUSIC AND DANCING

Our survey of primitive dances, which are the
social life of all backward races, expressing their
joys, sorrows, and spiritual aspirations, would be
incomplete without a brief consideration of Oriental
music, for in this one might hope to find and actually
does discover, a transition from the truly primitive
to the modern. Modern dancing as a social function
and educated form of sex expression falls outside the
scope of present inquiry, but there is interest in
gauging the extent to which the dances and musical
ceremonies of the Arabs, Hindus, Chinese, Japanese,
and Javanese have been developed from aboriginal
practices.

Arabia

The Arab war dance has already been described,
and there is no doubt that this " Rhaza Dance " as
originally performed with naked swords at Manga in
Muscat is the truly primitive expression of turbulent
emotions, which by concerted muscular action impart
the collective consciousness necessary for successful

warfare. In the "Shebwari," or wedding dance, men only, and these without weapons, dance in two facing lines some ten paces apart. The performers bend their knees and bow their bodies slightly forward in unison in time to the beating of drums. They also sing a song together, marking the rhythm by hand clapping, the most primitive form of metronome, and the only one known to Tasmanians and Australians, except that of beating on a tightly stretched opossum skin placed across the knees. The Arab "Zamil" dance is performed by day or night in front of the house of an exalted person to whom it is complimentary. The leader of the dance starts singing a solo, usually a song of praise, after which the others take up the chorus, and without musical instruments preserve time by hand clapping and rhythmical swaying of the body." This performance is primitive in conception and execution; there are no musical accessories, and the underlying idea is reminiscent of the primitive dances in which a warrior steps forward to sing his own praises or those of his ancestors

India

From Oriental music, as expressed by both educated and semi-civilised people of India, it is well to exclude that of the wild jungle tribes whose primitive agricultural dances—originally connected with human sacrifice which prevailed as late as 1860—are as old in concept and execution as any in the world.

In the oldest Indian literature of the Veda, "Dawn" robes herself in the attire of a dancing girl, and in the "Mahabharata" there is a curious account of Ragput lords and ladies going on a picnic where they are entertained with dancing. On

Buddhist monuments dancing is often represented, but a revival of Brahmanism shows Manu decreeing that dancing is an impure amusement to be eschewed by the " twice born."[67] The better class Hindu of our own day never dreams of dancing or of permitting his women to dance, and it is only among the people of the hills that public dancing of girls and youths is to be seen. These performances are usually celebrated at great agricultural festivals to promote the fertility of the soil and the ripening of crops. Among the people of the plains dancing is confined to the troupes of professional Nautch girls, and no respectable villager, Hindu or Mohammedan, would allow his women to perform in public.[68]

Some of the village dancers of India serve well to illustrate the way in which custom degenerates.

In our chapter on " Music and Magic " we shall have to investigate the pristine form of agricultural dance at which human blood refreshed the depleted earth. At present we have to note dances of the Kols of Chota Nagpur, and those of the Santals. These exhibitions have for many years been robbed of their essential features and grosser aspects by government supervision and contact with various advanced religious beliefs. The Kols still retain an aboriginal dance, which is being Hinduised, called Kartarama, because it is danced at the cutting of the branch of this sacred tree. The women stand in a line, each with her arms around a neighbour's shoulders. They bend their heads modestly, then advance and retreat slowly in front of a band of men, who beat their drums violently and encourage the women to greater exertions. Occasionally the latter bend down and pat the ground with their hands, invoking Mother Earth. These observances are rapidly passing, and in a few years' time the ancient fertility cult will be nothing but a series of invocations addressed to Hindu gods.

E

When liquor is plentiful the dance is still capable of becoming the orgy which it certainly was a century ago.[69]

The Santals erect a lofty stage from which radiate numerous strings held by women. These performers, twenty or thirty in number, have hold of each other by the waist-band. With right shoulder and breast bare, and hair decked with flowers, they dance the wildest and maddest of music drawn from pipes, flutes, and drums covered with monkey skin. The postures of the women are absurd, and the grotesque display is controlled by male musicians who dance in front of and facing the women.[70]

Performances of the Santals are of exceptional interest in giving a present day display of the ceremonies described in the chronicles of the Vishnu Puran.[71] Such a fortunate combination of ancient description and modern practice must not be ignored.

The Santals are distinguished by great proficiency with a flute made of bamboo not less than one inch in diameter and about two feet in length, which gives deep rich tones. At an early age children are taught the use of this instrument along with singing, dancing, and the mysteries of concocting the home brew which gives life to the musical ceremony. A large open space is reserved as a dancing ground, and to this the young men repair after the evening meal. To this spot the young women, with hair smoothed and decorated with flowers, are attracted by the sound of flute and drum. The ancient text would serve for a correct description of the maidens decked with flowers and ornamented with tinkling bracelets, while the young men add to these decorations peacocks' feathers. The dancers are closely compressed, so that the breast of the girl touches the back of the man next to her as they go round in a circle, one man between two girls. All limbs move as if they belonged to one dancer, the feet following in perfect rhythm the music supplied by players grouped in the centre of the ring. In this way sported Krishna with his favourite companions, "making sweet melody with voices and flutes, but more frequently they took their places in the ring, each feeling the soft pressure of two maidens in the great circling dance."[72]

To Western ears modern Indian music has little or no meaning because of inability to detect and appreciate tone shading, which is said by admirers to be as varied and fleeting as a summer rainbow. On ancient Indian instruments of the classical kind fine gradations of pitch are developed from the extreme thinness and length of the strings. On such instruments are produced elusive delicate sounds, to Western critics, much too thin, but to the Eastern mind expressive of deep thoughts and subtle imagery. Indian music of this classical, mystical type is at least three thousand years old and is accorded a divine origin which gave a mysticism based on religious faiths, observances, legends, and traditions of the country.

When the modern musician reads that there are six " Raags " or male tunes in Indian music he is puzzled, but his wonder grows as he reads of the " Raagnis " or female tunes, also the child tunes, and the " Muts " or laws which govern their classification and combination. Each tune has a season of the year and an hour of the day for rendering, and any departure from these seemingly useless harmonics is said to invalidate the beauty of the composition.

If, however, one turns to the imagery of productive thought behind the music there is a dawn of understanding of these apparently meaningless laws of melody. The tune "Lord of Rain" has to be played in July and August ; it is a spell to bring forth torrents, so in conception if not in practice the idea is of a type fundamental in primitive society. Megh, the " Lord of Rain," is represented as a dark handsome man of formidable appearance. He holds in his hand a naked sword which he flourishes in mid-air as if to rend the skies. Scowling and snarling with rage he breaks the clouds with streaks of lightning so that the rain pours forth.[73]

Another tune is a musical picture of a female Jogi seated beneath a tree to which animals are attracted by her sweet music. Serpents and peacocks lose their natural timidity and advance toward her, fascinated, entranced, her humble worshippers.[74]

The tune " Todi " is expressive of sunrise personified by a young maiden of ravishing fairness, dressed in white and gold with the sacred mark of camphor and saffron on her brow. She stands on a hilltop in the jungle concentrated on the music she is making. Her dark eyes reflect the gleams of rising sun, the only time at which the tune is to be played, while timid deer, their fears allayed, advance in meek adoration.[75]

An instrument the " Been " has a legendary origin, for it is said to have been invented by Mahedo, god of music, who was inspired by a glimpse of the beautiful woman Parbati in graceful repose, her perfumed breath making dulcent music. Her arms and wrists were adorned with bangles of gold, and her delicate breasts rose and fell with the rhythm of her song. Mahadeo watched entranced, and carried away with him a memory which gave no peace until he had invented a musical instrument which was a facsimile of his vision. The long neck of the instrument represents the long slim figure of Parbati, the two gourds are her ivory breasts, and the metal frets her bracelets ; the exquisite tone of the " Been " is her musical breathing.

(*Upper*) CHINESE FUNERAL PROCESSION, PROBABLY DEVELOPED FROM THE ANCIENT DEATH DANCES.

(*Lower*) CHINESE MUSICAL SCORE OF " HYMN OF A THOUSAND YEARS."

Burma

Burmese music is truly oriental in the fact that it is not played without a purpose, or as an aesthetic exercise only, on the contrary it is an adjunct of some important religious or social function. There is no dancing in couples, for this is a Western invention, and the Burman who wishes to see dancing hires people to do it for him. This is characteristic of Asiatic dances of Turkestan, China, and Japan. It is true that a Burman, perhaps greatly excited at a boatrace, a buffalo fight, or a religious ceremony, may tuck up his robe and prance about until his legs are tired. Young people dance in procession at the initiation of a youth into a monastery, or at a great religious festival or funeral. This processional dancing is a definite stage in the development of the terpsichorean art for religious purposes. It is a very ancient form of dancing known in early dynastic times of Egypt, and still interesting to Europeans, who perpetuate it in their religious processions on Saints' days. In Burma there are no teachers of music and no written scores. A musician begins his career by listening carefully to the performance of a good band, presently he enters a village band as a clapper player and so learns the rhythms of well-known tunes. Drums of different notes are supported on a frame which is mounted on a cart, and the instruments are beaten either with the hands or a knobbed stick. Tuning is carried out by tightening the drum heads and smearing the membrane with a paste made from husks of burnt rice. Other Burmese instruments are the gong, harmonicon, trumpets, clarionets, flutes, cymbals, and a long drum like the Indian tom-tom.[76]

China

No vestige of ancient Chinese music has come down to us, and what passes for music at the present day has been built up from the fragments which have survived the Burning of the Books in 212 B.C. The first emperor of the Chin Dynasty issued instructions that all records of previous dynasties and all copies of existing books, with the exception of those dealing with medicine, divination, and husbandry, should be burnt. This wicked iconoclasm was to flatter the emperor by making all literature date from his reign, and not only were the books burnt, but with them several hundred scholars who had attempted concealment. In this way there perished many valuable works, and it was only by accident that certain portions of the Chinese classics, hidden away by devoted enthusiasts, were subsequently discovered and preserved for future ages. There is a Chinese legend which says that Confucius was so impressed with good music that " for three months he could not tell one kind of meat from another." Perhaps the modern caterer has something of this kind in view when providing musical accompaniments for meals.

Present day Chinese music is divided into ritual, which is written in a minor mode, and popular or theatrical. Notation is exceedingly cumbrous, for though a note indicates a certain sound by pitch there is no indication of time value, hence the impossibility of learning a tune from the notes. Rests are marked, but their duration is a matter of taste."

It is clear, therefore, that such a method of writing music is very imperfect because the written notes are chiefly useful for refreshing a musician's memory. He has to hear a tune before he can render it and it may become unrecognisable when rendered according to the taste of new performers. There is a sign to denote a higher octave ; a cross × signifies a rest of undetermined value, while the beginning of the bar is marked by a small circle. There are no signs for sharps, flats or naturals, as such changes are unknown. The mark \ on the right side of a note tells the musicians to strike on one side of the drum, and a circle, except at the beginning of a bar, indicates that the drummer has to reverse his stroke and tap the other side of the drum. Two strokes thus ‖ indicate that the drummer and player of the castanets must strike together, but this sign is most frequently used to mark the end of a passage.[78] Although present day Chinese music is said to have been a new creation since the "Burning of the Books," the scale is the same as that laid in 2679 B.C., when twelve notes were selected, six masculine to imitate the notes of a male bird, and six feminine to imitate those of the hen bird. This arrangement of male and female tones brings to mind the Indian sex arrangement of notes, but one looks in vain for evidence of a common origin or definite reference to the origin of such a strange musical basis. Non-Christian Chinese may sing or play, but no congregational singing is permitted even in their temples. They have string bands, but their instruments give us no idea of music. The only element of music is that of time, they usually keep time. This is remarkable in view of the fact that the rest sign has no fixed value. Chinese are reported to have capacity, but no inspiration; this is said to be given by Christianity, the adoption of which shows that the Chinese can develop into good musicians.[79]

Chinese musical instruments are of wood, stone, metal, bamboo, skin, gourds, and earthenware. Bell metal is skilfully made with a mixture of six parts of copper to one of tin. The great bell at Peking, cast at the beginning of the fifteenth century, is a

triumph of the bell-makers' art. It has a height of
fourteen feet, a diameter of ten feet at the mouth,
a thickness of eight inches, and a weight of fifty-three
tons.   It is covered inside and out with Chinese
inscriptions.   The Kaang is an upright framework
from the bars of which a number of slabs of metal,
wood, or ivory, are suspended, and these the operator
strikes with a hammer.   Buddhist influence from
India has been considerable in influencing the development of Chinese musical instruments, and drums
were introduced from Central Asia, a very interesting
kind being those of earthenware filled with bran and
covered with skin.   The Chinese pigeon whistle is
a clever contrivance of musical tubes played by the
wind when the instrument is fastened to a pigeon.[80]

The gipsy population, who are, perhaps, akin to the
Mias-tsz often mentioned in the ancient books, live on
river-boats at Canton.   These people have shrill
weird songs which are not without melody, but from
their very nature they are destitute of harmony yet
quite free from the discord of Chinese music.   With
regard to the serenade music of the southern hill
tribes it has been said :   " To this day the wild music
rings in my ears suggesting mysterious passions in
unseen worlds and carrying the thoughts beyond the
sordidness of this."[81]   No special significance, religious
or erotic, is attached to the dancing of the Lolos, who
are extremely fond of both music and dancing on fine
moonlight evenings.

" I knew the Headman of the particular village
where these photographs were taken (S.W. of Szemao)
quite intimately, and he kindly arranged that some
of his people should give one of their dances for my
benefit.   I may add that the practice of serenading
is also quite common amongst some of the hill tribes
of S.W. Yunnan.   The young men may be heard any
fine evening playing on the flute or the gourd-pipes."[82]

DANCING LOLOS OF S.W. YUNNAN, CHINA.

(*Photos by F. W. Carey*)

Considerable knowledge of local ritual is required to distinguish between a Chinese funeral and a Chinese wedding, but the difficulty is not so great as in Korea, where the coffin bearers have to counterfeit jollity by singing and making drunken movements so that the coffin sways from side to side. Wailing concubines follow in sedan chairs cracking pea-nuts and smoking pipes at intervals between the wailing.

Leaders of the funeral procession carry streamers of soul cloth, and are followed by two men bearing banners on which are inscribed sentences expressing a hope that the deceased may be enjoying himself in company with the blessed. One man holds a white cock, which is supposed to summon the soul to accompany the body. Behind him follow two sedan chairs, in the first of which are varied ancestral tablets of the dead and in the second a portrait of the deceased. Supporting themselves on the shafts of the sedan chair two of the principal mourners drag themselves along. The eldest son affects complete inability to walk and has to be supported on either side ; he leans on a wooden staff if mourning a father, and on a bamboo staff for the death of his mother. Paper money is scattered to appease the hunger of the wandering ghost.

In the Chinese theatre there is no scenery except a few coarsely painted views at the back where the actors make their exits and entrances. The performance may go on the whole day without change of scenery, and in this arrangement there is the advantage of simplicity with the consequent inconvenience that the performer has to explain his supposed surroundings before attempting any acting. No wonder the performance may last all day, nothing but Oriental placidity could survive such an exhibition.

Musicians are seated on the stage, and these keep up so continuous an accompaniment as to make

inaudible a great many of the actor's remarks. Not
only are the songs accompanied, but on the expression
of any lofty sentiment or moral injunction they come
in with a crash of their instruments to add emphasis
to the utterance.[83]

Chinese musical attainment is undoubtedly at a
low ebb ; there is no question of a hidden mysticism
which cannot be appreciated by the Western mind.
In addition to the musical efforts mentioned, there are
blind women singers who are sometimes engaged to
sing to workmen, while puppet shows are popular.[84]

Java

The puppet show as a musical entertainment is
better developed in Java than in any other part of
the world, and along with street dancing and the
staging of historical plays it constitutes the chief
source of amusement. From the evolutionist's point
of view the most interesting fact is that Javanese plays
and puppet shows are rendered in an obsolete language.
This is not an isolated instance of the survival of
language for a particular purpose after it has ceased
to be used in everyday intercourse.[85]

Japan

Japanese music has from our Western point of
view everything against it and nothing for it. Japanese instruments give forth thin tinkling sounds
entirely lacking the volume associated with Western
ideas of what is pleasing. Written music is the
exclusive possession of the best professional players,
and a pupil can learn in no way other than listening,
watching, and committing to memory. A Japanese
lady is unable to find refuge in the excuse that she

has forgotten her music, for it is well known that everyone has a well-memorised repertoire of pieces for playing on the Koto.

Of all musical instruments flutes are the most sacred. Many of these are said to be over a thousand years old and there are descriptive lists of them in the temples ; each instrument has a distinctive name such as " Snake Charmer," or " Green Leaves." The Samisen, sometimes erroneously described as a banjo, is at the present day the resultant of many intermediate forms which saw their early development in China. The Samisen appears everywhere and on all occasions, being used to accompany dancing, acting, singing, begging, eating and drinking. The music is a thrumming tinkling sound produced by use of a plectrum.

Three instruments, frequently played in unison, are described by a Japanese word meaning " The Chamber Trio " ; these are the Samisen, Kokyu and Koto. The Kokyu is the Japanese fiddle which was originally imported from Hindustan to China, thence to Japan. The instrument has an interesting legendary history, for it is said to have been used by the barbarians of Southern China to ward off venomous reptiles by its mournful tone. The bow used for playing the Kokyu was originally an ordinary archery bow with one stout string which has now been replaced by a bundle of horsehair, two and a half feet long. The Koto, the chief modern instrument of Japan, is the last of a long series whose members vary in the number of strings. Several forms are known to have developed in China, and from there they passed to Japan, where further evolution took place. The instrument consists of several strings stretched over a long narrow sounding-board, and the sounds are produced by plucking the strings with " tsume," or playing nails.[86]

Japanese singing has been described as " mere
horrid sound disfigured by excruciating quarter tones,
nor have I ever found a Japanese express any admiration for it. It is accepted and tolerated."[87] Another
observer says that singing girls enliven social gather-
ings by their vivacity and pleasing abandon in which
singing is interspersed with conversation. The education of these Geishas is begun when they are seven
years of age and the instruction includes lessons in
dancing; so begins a career almost impossible to
quit except by becoming married to a wealthy patron,
a not infrequent outcome of the bright entertainments
given. Both classical and modern dances consist of
posturing, in which the arms are used more than the
legs. One of the oldest Japanese dances is the Kagura,
still to be seen in temple gardens, performed by
people disguised in masks and gowns. This is described in folklore as the dance which shortly after the
origin of the world lured from her cave the goddess
of light whose retirement had plunged the world into
darkness. Dancing and drama are combined, for as
some performers play and dance others describe the
legendary history which the music expresses.

The accounts of English residents should be
supplemented by opinion from Japanese sources[88],
and turning to these we find that the Geisha's praises
have been sung abroad because her equal is not to
be found, and unlike other demi-mondaines, her
lapses from virtue leave her still in possession of grace
and modesty. The organisation of Geishas has not
had a long history, perhaps not more than a hundred
and fifty years, but sufficiently long to secure the
affection of Japanese and Europeans alike, though a
government with an eye to economics rather than
aesthetics imposes a tax of two yen per month on
dancing girls.

In the Japanese Fan Dance the dancer is a girl

of thirteen years elaborately dressed as a page in a closely folded robe. The feet and legs are not much used, the feet indeed never leave the ground. Time is marked by undulations of the body, waving the arms, and deft manipulation of a fan. One movement succeeds another by transitions singularly graceful. The arms describe innumerable curves, while the fan is so skilfully handled as to seem instinct with a life and liberty of its own. The Jon-Nuké is a famous but immodest forfeit dance performed by Japanese girls, who pay forfeit for any failure to imitate each other's gestures when challenged by a loud " Hoi ! " by throwing off one article of clothing each time, until nothing remains, when they disappear behind a curtain at the back. Part of the performance consists of singing a song beginning with the words " Jon-Kino, Jon-Kino."[89]

Summary

The antiquity and origins of musical ability in the form of vocal effort, dancing, and the invention of instruments is from the very nature of the subject bound to lead into a realm of conjecture and hypothesis. Archaeological evidence is suggestive on the point of prehistoric dancing as indicated by cave paintings, but whether the perforated bones were used as whistles is a matter of speculation. In favour of the suggestion that they were so used it may be said that similar bones have been and are still used among North American and Eskimo tribes, as whistles. Sense of rhythm is something fundamental, and in all forms of natural muscular action such as walking, running, or the flight of birds, there is preservation of a regular sequence of actions which minimise fatigue. Animals of many kinds respond to musical notes, so also do very young children. To raise the question what is an instinct ? would be to enter upon an abstruse psychological problem, but rhythm of muscular movement is something basic, an economy of nature which has been artificially developed into dancing for specific purposes of great variety. With regard to vocal music, which leaves behind no tangible evidence, the investigator will have to be content with an analysis of the tunes of primitive people such as Veddas or Australians in order to form a concept of the probable early efforts of prehistoric man, unaided by musical instruments. Consideration of the most backward races of to-day, and the Tasmanians of half a century ago, suggests forcibly that vocal effort and dancing are the precursors of artificial aid from musical accompaniments. Of these the percussive variety, first tested experimentally by slapping the limbs, then by tapping a skin or piece of wood, would appear to be the most ancient, for the method will mark rhythm, which is more elementary in a biological and psychological sense than is a discrimination of pitch and the power to produce it.

Mythical origins of songs and dances might help, if carefully studied, in tracing out the beginnings of what are probably the most ancient of all dances, namely " mimetic," to increase animal fecundity, and agricultural dances performed to renew the fertility of the soil. These undoubtedly take us far back to the hunting and early agricultural stages of social development.

The music of Ancient Civilisations, likewise Oriental music of the present day, assist historical inquiry in showing that by historical times, say 6,000 years ago, instruments and purposive dances, with vocal music, were advanced so far as to indicate a very long pre-historical evolution. Oriental music makes clear the loss of free expression and definite purpose attendant on the progress of civilisation. Dancing in Asia has degenerated from the most important form of social expression to mere exhibition work, or it may in some areas have become a tolerated adjunct of public ceremony instead of the vital essence which it used to be.

When dealing with the antiquity of music and dancing we may be sure that our historical survey rests on safe foundations if attention is primarily paid to festivals connected with the main aspects of human endeavour. These are the quest for food by hunting and agriculture, display of sex charms either in the form of beauty or endurance, and a cautious approach to powers and forces outside the ordinary experience of everyday life.

With this important truth in view an endeavour will be made in the following chapters to give special prominence to agricultural dances and those connected with animal fecundity. In addition, our survey will emphasise the importance of display dancing among young unmarried people, and, what is perhaps more important still, an investigation will be made into the ritual dances by which medicine men and others approach the spiritual world.

CHAPTER III

MORALITY OF THE WAR DANCE

The number of observers who have deprecated this form of dancing is small compared with the many investigators who have criticised the immorality of festivals at which a display of sexual feeling is in evidence. Yet the war dance is immoral, and disgustingly so, in its faithful portrayal of every incident of combat, pursuit, mutilation, rape, and cannibalism. On the artistic side, the best that one can say is that war dancing represents a perfected form of primitive dramatic art and tragedy. With regard to the social importance of the war dance it may be justly said that no other is so essential for strengthening communal bonds and arousing the right mental attitude for aggression and defence.

In this form of display is seen a maximum of ferocity and concord which are to be used for self preservation. Probably the war dance has a secondary function of aiding sexual selection, for when women are spectators, their choice of lovers is influenced by exhibitions of skill, pugnacity, and endurance.

Dancing in connection with head hunting is a practice extremely common among the Nagas in Assam, in Formosa and Borneo, also in the Philippines, and right through New Guinea, The Solomons, the New Hebrides, and Fiji. The Maoris exposed to derision the mokoed heads of their foes. The Australian

KAYAN HOUSE, BORNEO, WITH HEAD HUNTING TROPHIES.
(Photo, Dr. C. Hose and W. McDougall, " Pagan Tribes of Borneo.")

aborigines are not head hunters, but nevertheless they have their dance of the avenging party about to track down a victim, though they appear chiefly to value his fat for magical purposes, and there is no evidence of taking the head. Along the Amazon and its tributaries head hunting is rife, and the specimens of dried diminutive heads with long black hair, taken by the Jivaro Indians, are familiar in ethnological museums.

In North America there does not appear to have been any collecting of heads, though it is probable that taking of scalps was a convenient modification of the head-hunting practice.

ORIGINS OF HEAD HUNTING

Like all widespread customs these head-hunting proclivities may be attributable to some basic idea which has been locally modified in many ways. Perhaps the generic concept was one relating to human sacrifice, possibly the immolation of slaves at the death of a king, so that their souls might be liberated for service in a ghostly world. Or the original object may have been to acquire a head for sacrifice to the gods, the custom having now degenerated into a collectors' hobby.[90] However this may have been, it is undeniable that a successful head hunt was the preliminary of proposals of marriage ; no girl would accept a man who had not shown his prowess in this gruesome enterprise. Again, head hunting is to this day thought to be closely connected with successful agriculture, therefore there is great difficulty in suppressing the custom among the Nagas of Assam, and various tribes of Sarawak. Tattooing of honorific marks for success in head hunting is found in Formosa, Borneo, and New Guinea.

F

THE WAR DANCE AND HEAD HUNTING

Eastern Archipelago and India

The Ibans of Borneo have up till recent times been inveterate head hunters, and there is the probability that they adopted the practice from the Kayans a few generations ago. Dr. Hose[91] suggests that the head hunting custom arose from extension of the practice of decorating shields and sword hilts with human hair. On shields a terrifying human face is made more realistic by the addition of hair.

Perhaps the converse is true, and the Kayan and Iban, finding a head somewhat cumbersome as an ornamental display, substituted the hair only in their warlike equipment.

A successful Bornean war party returning home makes no secret of its success, and the villagers come out to gaze. At their own village the war party is received with loud acclamations, people coming down to the riverside to receive them. Before ascening to the house the heads are safely lodged in a small hut specially built for their reception, and the young boys are brought down to go through their first initiation in the arts of war. Each child is made to hold a sword, and with the assistance of some aged warrior to strike a blow at the newly captured heads. Some of the older boys engage in mimic warfare with one another, using wooden swords and spears. Each head which is brought by a newly arrived war party is decorated and carried by an elderly man or woman into the home, followed by all the people of the house, men, women, and children, in long procession. The procession marches up and down the gallery many times, the people shouting, singing, stamping, and pounding on the floor with padi pestles or playing the Keluri.

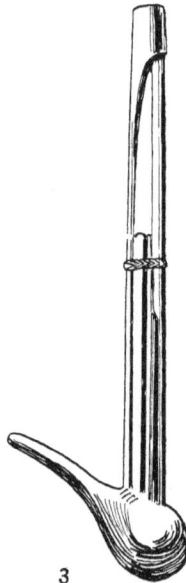

(1) SINHALESE MASK USED IN DEVIL DANCES.
(2) PUPPET OF STAMPED LEATHER USED IN SHADOW-PLAYS, JAVA.
(By permission of Trustees, Brit. Museum)
(3) A KELURI, MUSICAL INSTRUMENT WIDELY USED IN BORNEO.
(Drawing by Dr. Hose. By permission of Messrs. Macmillan & Co.)

In the course of the feasting the women usually
take temporary possession of heads and perform with
these a wild uncouth dance, waving the heads to and
fro and chanting in imitation of the men's war song.
The procession may be resumed at intervals until
the heads are finally suspended by the old ones over
the principal hearth of the gallery.[92]   The " Toh " or
spirits associated with these heads are thought to be
the ghosts of persons other than those from whose
shoulders the heads were taken.   It is said that the
spirits are resident in or about the heads, though not
inseparable from them.   At all times the heads are
respectfully treated and greatly feared.   When it
is necessary to handle them some old woman undertakes the task.   Children especially are forbidden to
touch the heads, for incautious contact is thought to
result in a curse of madness from the offended Toh.

A party of young men in full war dress forms up
in single line, the leader and two or three others play
the battle march on the Keluri.   This is a rude form
of bagpipes made from a dried gourd which has the
shape of an oval flask with a long neck.   The closed
ends of a bundle of six narrow bamboo pipes are
inserted in the body of the gourd through a hole cut
in its wall, and are fixed hermetically with wax.
Their free ends are open, and each pipe has a small
lateral hole or stop at a carefully determined distance
from the open end.   The artist blows through the neck
of the gourd and the air enters the base of each pipe
by an oblong aperture which is filled by a vibrating
tongue or reed.   The holes are stopped by the fingers,
each pipe emitting its note only when its hole is
stopped.   Varieties of this instrument are made by
all the tribes of Borneo as well as by many other
peoples of the far East.[93]

The bigger boys are taught to take part in the
dance in which the return from the war path is

dramatically represented. Perhaps the movement would be most accurately described as a musical march. A party of young men in full war dress form up in single line, the leader and perhaps two or three others play the battle march on the Keluri. The line advances slowly up the gallery, each man turning half about at every third step, the even numbers turning to the one hand, the odd to the other hand alternately, and all stamping together as they complete the turn at every third step. The turning to the right and left symbolises the alert guarding of the heads, which are supposed to be carried by the victorious warriors.

A more violent display of warlike feeling is given in the war dance, which is executed by one or two warriors only. The youth in full panoply of war and brandishing a parang and shield goes through the movements of a single combat with some fanciful exaggeration. He crouches beneath his shield, and springs violently hither and thither, emitting piercing yells of defiance and rage, cutting or striking at his imaginary foe. Beside watching these martial displays, the boy is instructed in the arts of parrying, striking, and shielding by the older men, who lunge at him with a stick, but stay their blow before it is completed. This care probably results from a reluctance to shed blood, which would involve payment of a fine.[94]

It was evidently this dance that Dr. A. C. Haddon saw in Borneo some thirty years ago. He describes a solo dance by a man dressed in a war coat decorated with hornbill's feathers and wearing a long plumed war cap. First he danced without his weapons, then he picked up his shield and later his parang. There were indescribable crouchings, jumpings and squirming, movements in which the approved positions of actual warfare were blended with gyratory motions and posturing of more ordinary dancing. Crouching on the ground, the war coat trailing behind him, and brandishing his shield in front, the warrior turned, or rather hopped like an amorous cock sparrow first to one side then to the other, as if warding off blows from an unseen adversary. Then as if perceiving his advantage he would leap to his feet and take the initiative "The numerous and rapid graceful movements, the finely harmonising colours of the buff skin, the shield, the black and tawny clouded tiger's-skin coat and red loin cloth, also the bold contrast of black and white feathers of hornbill, lit up by a blazing fire and yellow flickering lamps against a dim background of eager semi-nude natives and spaces of outer darkness, made a fascinating picture of savagery, in which beauty of dexterous movements with harmony and contrast of colour, were combined with deeply-seated human passion for bloodshed."[95]

In Formosa a boy celebrates puberty by taking part in his first head-hunting expedition at which several youths of the same age are initiated into the same group or sub-tribe by older and more experienced men who consult an omen, for example the flight of birds, before starting. The Taiyals favour an odd number of men, so that when a single boy is to be initiated he will make up an even number.

During the absence of this party women are forbidden to weave or even handle the material. Fires are not allowed to go out, and should they do so accidentally the omen is a bad one. Loud cries intimate the return of a victorious or defeated party, and in the former case preparations are hastily made for a great dance, feast and wine-drinking, in which the women take part. The heads are placed on a skull shelf of the village so that wine and food may be offered to them, the ceremony usually being carried out by a priestess or chieftainess. A toast

is given which runs : " O warrior, you are welcome to
our village and to our feast ; eat and drink, and ask
your brothers to come and join you in eating and
drinking with us."[96] This procedure is supposed to
have a magical effect in giving further victories. The
Paiwan believe that ancestral spirits dwell in knives
used for severing heads, consequently these instruments are handed down as valuable family heirlooms.

The Nagas, who are still incorrigible head hunters,
have in connection with this ceremony a review or
sham fight in which there is a large number of participants. These warriors are armed with spears which
are used as javelins, and to these are added battle-
axes and shields of buffalo hide or bamboo work
covered with tiger skin, the protection being large
enough to shield the entire body. An advance is
made in extended order, nothing being seen but a
line of shields making rapid progress. When
sufficiently near to an imaginary enemy the actors
spring up and fling the spear. This is supposed to
slay the enemy who is represented by a large tuft
of grass, which is seized with the hand and cut out
with the battle-axe. The warriors retreat, each carrying over his shoulder the tuft of grass symbolising a
head, and the ceremony is ended by a triumphant
song and dance in which the women join.[97] This
ceremony is definitely descriptive of the head hunt,
but there is a more general warlike display in the
form of a dancing game suggestive of combat. A
young man armed with a spear and shield spins the
former and utters shouts in the traditional manner
of challenging braves of the opposing force. One step
in particular which is much practised and admired,
consists of a high leap during which there is crossing
of the legs three times before the feet again touch the
ground.[98]

Women, so often excluded from ceremonial dancing,

apparently play an important rôle in connection with many war dances and head hunting festivities. While the Kafirs of the Hindu Kush region are on the war path their women have to perform a ceremonial war dance which is intended to give the raiding party strength and courage while keeping them alert and wakeful.[99]

The Pak-Don sword and shield dance was formerly executed on the eve of battle, or on the triumphant return of a war party of Santals who inhabit a strip of country in Central Bengal, they also occupy a rugged range of hills bordering on Chota Nagpore. The dancers gyrate round and round in an uneven circle, flourishing their shields and brandishing sticks that have taken the place of swords.

Each dancer wears only a loin-cloth, anklets, and a necklace, so that his fine supple limbs have free play as they spring and leap in the wild measures of the dance. The dancers form a complete circle round the drummers, and with wild ear-piercing shouts the exhibition begins. Onlookers act as waiters, passing round from time to time with jars of rice beer, which they pour from a rolled leaf down the parched throats of the performers. The scene is a wild one, and when witnessed by torchlight at its climax, one can imagine something of the madness and unbridled passion with which the tribe danced in the old days, on the eve of battle, or perhaps on a victorious occasion when returning with the spoils of war.[100]

War Dance of Australian Aborigines

There is in Australia no practice strictly comparable with head hunting, but warlike displays are frequent—in fact, much more so than actual hostilities.

Near Alice Springs, if the death of a tribesman is thought to be due to magic, for example use of the pointing bone, a decision is made to send an avenging party against the suspected person. The brother of the dead man wears a girdle made from hair of the deceased, for with this ornament the spirit of the murdered man is said to be closely associated. Each tribesman in camp rubs his thighs with this girdle to make him strong in fighting, also as a solemn pledge that he will join the expedition, whose members wear in their hair " Ilkunta," or flaked sticks that signify intention to kill.

Fully armed with spears, boomerangs, spear throwers and shields, the members of the avenging party form a close square, meanwhile dancing and yelling loudly. The brother of the dead man, who acts as leader, rushes in advance, then wildly circles round the whole party, assuming a look of intense fury, crouching and pretending to launch his spear at an imaginary foe. Other men join the party, yelling " Wah !   Wah ! " while dancing furiously with high prancing.

This blood feud is finally ratified either by drinking blood drawn from the veins of the war party, or rubbing blood over one another to make all lithe and active, also as a sign of unison and a preventive against treachery. All spears are bunched together to form a central point of the dancing circle, the most prominent performers being the men who intend to spear the victim. These men simulate the death of their intended victim by falling to the ground and remaining as if dead for several minutes.

On the morning of the tenth day after departure, the party observed returned decorated with black paint and wearing little leafy twigs in their noses and arm bands. They pranced along in a square, each man holding aloft his spear in one hand and his shield in the other. Presently, the men stood in perfect silence while an old woman whitened from head to foot with pipe-clay performed a grotesque dance to the accompaniment of her own yelling. By-and-by she tested each shield by rapping it sharply, then paused suddenly in front of a man whose shield gave forth a hollow sound. This signified that the owner was haunted by the spirit of the murdered man, which was supposed to have followed up the avenging party in the form of a small bird. The man so haunted has to sleep for several nights wearing tail tips of the rabbit bandicoot, a nocturnal alert creature. Such a precaution prevents surprise attacks by a hostile ghost. The avenging party had slain, not the intended victim, but his aged father, who according to primitive ethics was equally culpable, for he had known of his son's homicidal intention without preventing the deed.[101]

The early days of Australian exploration were concerned with geographical survey rather than ethnological research, and it is quite probable that many native ceremonies, whose meaning was then ascertainable, have since lost their significance from contact with Europeans, and loss of tribal authority which was vested in the old men.

The explorer E. J. Eyre[102] witnessed among Murray River natives a day-time dance, performed by both men and women, who appear to have given a dramatic pantomine of combat, though their rendering is not in any way comparable with the vigorous action of Maoris or Fijians. The performers advanced carrying boughs, while in the centre of the group was borne a crude representation of a human figure made of grass and reeds, bound together and enveloped in a kangaroo skin with its flesh side outwards, the whole effigy being painted with small white circles. The limbs were represented by projecting sticks.

Presently this human figure was abandoned so that each dancer might take up a pole decorated at the top with feathers of hawk and emu. The dance took place at Moorunde on the Murray, and the visitors kept advancing and retiring toward and away from the Moorunde natives, who were seated. When the third great advance was made, spears only were carried by the visitors, who discarded their feather-topped poles. The Moorunde natives sprang to their feet and speared two or three visitors in the shoulder and all was over. The final act of spearing may sanction the inclusion of this ceremony among war dances though, to be frank, the classification, and still more the interpretation of Australian dances, is obscure. Totemic dances to increase animal fecundity are well known, and there are what appear to be purely social functions. There are in addition, however, many so-called dramatic performances whose symbolism remains unexplained.

War Dancing in Melanesia and Polynesia

Fortunately, New Guinea has been studied before contact with civilisation has obscured the meaning of dances, and the acts are either self-explanatory, or capable of interpretation by the older members of the society.

Mekeo people used to have a big war feast after a victorious raid on an enemy or a successful defence against an enemy's incursion, and this feast was the occasion for donning the *Kefe* or the *Iofo* by such fighters as had succeeded in killing an enemy. *Kefe* is a large disc of white shell, in front of which is fixed a piece of turtle shell fretted in an ornamental design which is worn on or over the forehead. *Iofo* is an ornament made of a tuft of white feathers, also quills of cassowary feathers and red feathers, which are worn on the top of the head. Formerly only a man who had killed an enemy was allowed to wear these, and they were insignia of which the wearer was very proud. Mekeo is now under Government control, but pride creates a wish to transmit these ornaments to descendants at special ceremonies, similar to those of the old fighting days.

At the *Paangi* ceremony a man who has killed his enemy and is therefore entitled to wear " *Kefe* " and " *Iofo*," brandishes a spear at the height of his head, and in a loud voice sings a song peculiar to his family, and then in softer tones recounts his act of daring or an act of his ancestor. Sometimes a man who has not done the deed begins this solo ceremony as a deliberate act of aggression, and challenge to provoke combat in which he may earn the coveted distinction. *Aipa* is a warlike parade at which men in rows of three run rapidly through the village brandishing spears, with intervals of slow measured movement. Sometimes the warriors are attended by large numbers of boys who beat their drums when the men are running, and during intervals stamp their feet upon the ground in a rhythmic tread corresponding to that of the men.[108]

A realistic picture of the head hunter's dance as it was rehearsed in Prince of Wales Island (Muralug), Torres Strait, in 1888, is given by Dr. A. C. Haddon.[104] The dance was performed after dark on a sandy shore fringed with gloomy mangrove swamps, from which there stretched away to right and left a bay edged with a beach of white coral sand washed by gently lapping waves. Above was a blue-black sky studded with stars, while a crescent moon shed a silvery light over all. Near the fire sat the primitive orchestra beating their drums in rhythmic monotone and accompanying the sound with a wailing chant.

Gradually, from the distance, swarthy forms appeared, advancing in sinuous line as if on the war-path, every movement being timed to the throb of the drums. As a mass of dried herbage was flung on the fire, the flames shot up to reveal a picture of primitive savagery. Each dancer had painted the lower part of his body black, and the upper part red, while the ankles were adorned with yellow leaves. White shell ornaments showed effectively on red chest ; black plumes of cassowary feathers waved from the gauntlet worn on the left arm, and in their black frizzly hair danced plumes of pure white. No incident of the war-path was omitted. There was skipping quickly from cover to cover, stealthy stealing, and a sudden encounter of the foe with a loud " Wahu ! " All the dancers raised their right legs, and with exultant cries went through the movement of decapitating a foe with their bamboo knives. In actual practice the victorious warriors threaded the heads on rattan strings, then in the triumphant dance these ghastly trophies were swung to and fro with jubilant cries.

Mass meetings of warriors provide a remarkable example of the power of suggestion, imitation, and contagious excitement, leading to powerful dramatic effect. Milder manners and methods have made rapid progress in the past twenty years, but in Fiji, as Sir Basil Thomson[105] saw the island in 1887, the war dance was a realistic affair. A great council of chiefs assembled at Nandronga, bringing with them from the mountain regions a large number of expert warriors and dancers. These marched into a square in twenty ranks of ten, and squatted with their spears poised to listen to a quickening chant, after which there was a sinister silence. One man began to flutter a fan, the singing was taken up again on a shrill note to the rhythm of a tattoo on the war drums. There was a mighty deep-toned shout which acted as a signal for a third of the party to leap up with spears poised, and so to march the length of the arena before retiring to allow the other section to follow. All the warriors kneel with bodies bent and spears poised ready for stabbing or hurling, while their legs are like steel springs which, suddenly relaxed, cause the men to leap into open order. In mad realism they pursue, stab at a fallen foe, dodge blows by a sideward jerk of the head, or run in rhythm with a tramp that shakes the hard earth. Their eyes blaze, teeth grin with fury, and sweat rolls in channels through the soot and paint which decorate their bodies. The plains folk, who at the outset had given ironical applause, retreat in headlong flight, so realistic is the show; it is the vivid drama of attack, pursuit, capture, slaughter, mutilation, and devouring.

Intrepid camera-men bring from the New Hebrides stories which show that the interior districts have been little affected, if any, by the march of civilisation. It is no wonder that Captain Bligh, forcibly cast adrift from his ship the " Bounty," ordered his distressed crew to pull with all their feeble strength in order to out-distance canoes sighted near these islands.

A personal observer[106] says : " I have never seen a more eerie spectacle. In the centre of the clearing, before a devil-devil, an old man was dancing very precisely. He lifted one foot and very slowly put it down, then he lifted the other foot and put it down, chanting all the while in a hoarse whisper. At the farther side of the clearing a group of old savages were squatting near a smouldering fire, intently watching one of their number, the oldest and most wizened of them all, as he held in the smoke a human head impaled on a stick. Near by, on stakes set in the ground, were other heads. The head curer said that the head was first soaked in a chemical mixture that hardened the skin, and to a certain extent made it fire-proof. The curer then held it over the fire till the fat was rendered out and the skin dried. It was next smeared with clay to prevent burning, then baked several hours. After this treatment it was hung in the owner's hut or in a ceremonial house, but for a year it had to be smoked at intervals."

So greatly have the surviving Maoris, now some 45,000 in number, profited by education which has developed a natural intelligence, that it is difficult to realise the former ferocity of their dances, and one has to refer to the accounts of early observers in order fully to realise the dramatic power of the war dance.

This was performed by entertainers who placed themselves in extended line in ranks four deep. The dance, to a stranger witnessing it for the first time, was calculated to excite the most alarming fears ; the entire body of performers male and female, free and bond, were mixed together without reference to rank held in the community. All male performers were quite naked except for a cartridge belt filled with ball ammunition. All were armed with muskets or bayonets put on the ends of spears or sticks. Women, including wives of chiefs, joined in the dance of rejoicing and welcome. The females had left exposed their budding charms to the waist from which were appended two stout handsome garments of silken flax. In the chant that accompanied the dance proper time was kept, as was equally well displayed in the various performances of agility exhibited in these *hakas*, especially in the perpendicular jump from the ground, which was often repeated in a simultaneous manner, as if the whole body of performers were actuated by one impulse. Implements were brandished, and the distortion of the countenance surrounded by long tresses of hair that often adorn

(*Upper*) WAR DANCE OF MAORIS, 1827.
(*Middle*) MAORI CHIEF ADDRESSING HIS TROOPS.
(*Lower*) MAORI WAR CANOE.

(*From old prints, British Museum*)

each sex gave them the appearance of an army of Gorgons with snake-like locks.   The ladies performed their utmost in adding to the singularity of the scene, wielding spears and paddles made from the Kaikatoa-tree.   Countenances were distorted into every possible shape permitted by the muscles of the human face, and every new grimace was instantly adopted by all performers in unison, even so that only the whites of the eyes were visible.   "Altogether their faces, aided by the colours with which they had bedaubed themselves, presented so horrible a spectacle that I was fain glad to relieve myself by withdrawing my gaze.   The tongue was thrust out of the mouth with an extension impossible for Europeans to copy, early and long practice only could accomplish it."[107]   There was a resounding noise when the performers struck themselves with flattened hands on their left breasts. The exhibition gave a lively picture of the effect these dances must produce in time of war, in raising the bravery and heightening the antipathy that is felt by the contending parties against each other.[108]

"As the party approached a sham fight began. It was conducted with so much fury on both sides that at length I became quite horrified, and for some time could not divest myself of the feeling that our visitors were playing false, so closely did this mock combat resemble a real one.   The dreadful noises, the hideous faces, the screeching of the women and the menacing gestures of each party, were so calculated to inspire terror that stouter hearts than mine might have felt fear."[109]

Major Robley[110], whose active service in New Zealand during the Maori wars has enabled him to give vivid word-pictures and life-like sketches, speaks of the constant thrusting out of the tongue in defiance during the war dance.   This frequently-repeated action involved so much distortion of the features that the blue tattooing formed a quivering network. The time or cadence of the dance was marked by striking the palm of the left hand against the thigh.

In addition to pictures of the Maori when worked into this state of fury, there are in many museum collections staves, the upper ends of which resemble a distorted human face with a protruding tongue of surprising length. Some flutes in the British Museum collection show the same kind of ornament.

The dances are performed with astonishing agility that habitual practice can alone bring to perfection. Every member of the body is actually employed— fingers, toes, eyes, tongue, being as much engaged in it as the arms and feet. All bound simultaneously from the earth, then with loud exclamations clapping the left breast with the right hand flatted give a sound that is unequalled, save when the yell or war screech is added to the astonishing din. These performances are taught to children from earliest infancy, and raise the passion of masters and pupils to such a degree that a legion of the diablerie in a melodramic incantation scene, gives but a subdued representation of the demoniacal horrors that chill the European with abhorence and disgust. Obscenities of a most revolting description are imitated in some dances to represent the contempt with which they regard the enemy, and the intentions they would practically perform if the foe fell within their power.[111]

The war dance of Gela in the Solomons,[112] where the head hunters still have an evil reputation, is a realistic piece of acting in which each man stoops low so that his body may be entirely covered by his shield, though the eyes are kept just above the top of the guard. This formation results in a fierce grotesque array of swaying bodies, wagging heads, rolling eyes and quivering spears.

The War Dance in Africa

There still survive old settlers and ex-soldiers who well remember, and with some uneasiness, the steady throbbing of signal drums which night after night passed the command to assemble Zulu hordes, in order to exterminate the white man. African warriors, like those of most primitive peoples, have to rouse themselves, not only by listening to the speeches of their chiefs and witch doctors, but by a prolonged and frenzied dance.

The Matabele war dance began with a march past the King, who soon retired into his kraal with the witch doctors to make medicine. Women and girls danced in front of the warriors, and when the King later joined the party, everyone was expected to join in, and the witch doctors and their attendants ran about with thorn-sticks, beating all who through weariness or boredom were reluctant to do so. The stick was also applied to those who did not dance with the necessary vigour. There was a ceremonial slaughtering of cattle, which had to be struck in the left side with an assegai, and following this incident the king threw a spear in the direction in which the next raid was to take place. When the dance was over, the warriors, before returning to the village, burnt the huts which they had temporarily erected for the ceremony.[113]

A glance at the pictures of Shilluks, who are usually six feet four inches in height, will give a good idea of the impressive nature of the war dance among these tall Nilotic negroes to whom the Lango are akin.

On approaching their village after a victorious battle, these warriors beat the drum and each slayer blows his call on the war whistle. At a short distance from the village they break into the victory dance,

G

running forward in line, shields at the ready, and spears poised shouting their particular war cries. Thus they run advancing and retiring, until the women come out to meet them, raising the shrill undulating screech of victory, and running with knife in hand to stab the shields of the victors in a riotous mêlée, until finally the women receive all weapons from their elated menfolk.[114]

Among the Angoni there is a very popular war dance, in which hundreds of warriors leap simultaneously into the air, at the same time clashing their spears loudly on the shields,[115] and it is improbable that any African tribe is totally devoid of some dance performed in order to stimulate warlike passions.

The Baloki war dance is reminiscent of the Roman practice followed by warriors, who stepped forth and showed their wounds to the admiring crowd. At a given drum-signal a Baloki advances, and in a solo tells of his recent fighting exploits in a manner which does not in any way minimise his own prowess and the discomfiture of the enemy.[116] Many North American Indian tribes follow a similar custom.

War dancing in Sierra Leone is a weird fantastic performance requiring great skill and powers of endurance. Warriors are summoned to the arena by a lively beating of tom-toms, and the ceremony does not commence until a line of naked warriors, each with a shining sword held at arm's length from the body, is drawn up in front of a vast audience. When drums are beating their loudest, each warrior describes circles with the point of his weapon, slashing at an imaginary foe with lightning swiftness, and working himself into a fearful frenzy while loudly applauded by the audience. From the line a warrior steps forth to perform a solo dance, which is a marvellous exhibition of prancing and sword-whirling, all in perfect time to the steady thumping of the tom-

(*Upper*) ZULU WARRIOR IN FULL WAR DRESS.
(*Lower*) ZULUS MASSING FOR THE WAR DANCE.
(*Photos, S. African Railways.*)

toms. When at last the point of exhaustion is approaching, the frenzied dancer rushes forward, and kneeling before his chief drives the sword blade deeply into the earth.[117]

The American War Dance

Many South American warriors of the Amazon Basin and Peruvian highlands are inveterate head hunters who, on account of their truculence and elusive habits in the dense jungle, have defied a close ethnological study. No one has, for instance, explained the significance of the tattooed marks right across the men's faces ; it is not unlikely that these indicate prowess in war, as is the case in Formosa, Borneo and elsewhere. The explanation usually given is that South American tattooing of men is chiefly tribal and ornamental.

The solemnity of night in an Amazonian forest is broken by the throb of signal drums carrying their call to the war dance over fifteen miles of swamp and jungle. Presently the performers prance into the arena in pairs, advancing, turning and stamping with their feet while playing bamboo flutes. Then the instruments are laid aside, and the dance becomes a mimic battle,each side advancing in line for a distance, then suddenly kneeling or lying prone to go through the movements of using the blowpipe or discharging arrows.[118]

Such is the dance of the Parintintins, who at times perform their war dance by moonlight in deference to good and bad spirits of light and darkness. Beginning with loud cries of " Yataipehe ", meaning " We are the Parintintins ", they make the forest resound with weird war-cries which are accompanied by wailings from women who hide in the shadow of the trees.

The dancers, gaily decorated with feathers, then begin their wild display of stabbing with long tufted spears at dark shadows cast by the trees, or at clouds drifting across the moon. Without apparent signal the confused mass of naked savages suddenly forms into a line of archers, who have left behind their spears stuck point upwards in a clearing. The line of warriors alternately advances and retreats or runs in circles from time to time pausing to go through the actions of discharging arrows to the sounds of yelling and stamping feet. Such a barbaric display appears to be a realistic use of the war dance in some form of moon worship.[119]

The Itogapuks begin their war dance with a slow shuffling of feet and a swaying of their naked bodies, as they alternately advance and retreat, meanwhile sounding their shrill cries to an accompaniment of flutes and hollow gourds. The final act illustrates the abduction of women by the conquerors, a piece of symbolism taking us back to early days of marriage by capture. In the dance each warrior chooses a girl, and throwing her over his shoulder runs away with the screaming captive.[120]

Indians of Jivaran stock, whose gruesome head-hunting trophies we have mentioned, celebrate the end of a successful raid by giving special dances in pairs, each man carrying his lance. In turn each warrior makes a short address glorifying himself, after which he gives an exhibition dance with lance ready to strike and movements simulating advance and retreat.[121]

Such dances enable the observer to realise with a shudder what the actual post-war celebration must have been. The gloomy rolling of signal drums provided a fitting prelude to the cannibal orgy at which warriors broke from the dancing party to stir huge troughs of liquor with the limbs of their enemies. After drinking from large calabashes they stagger back to the further intoxication of the dance. Songs degenerate into demoniacal shrieks, while captives young enough to be worth saving from the earthern pots cower in the darkness, there to suffer the gibes of women. For eight nights the mad celebration continues until all are surfeited with their excesses.[122]

The successful war party of North American Indians has returned, and without delay preparations are made for " dancing the scalps of their enemies "[123] for fifteen successive nights, while the performers give most lurid and exaggerated accounts in song and verse of the discomfiture of their foes, and their own prowess in war. A number of young women enter the ring holding up the scalps as a signal for the commencement of a dance in which the performers, simulating single combat, brandish their weapons while feigning attack and conquest of an enemy in the most realistic manner. Very frightful are these scenes enacted in the dead and darkness of night when the torches' uncertain flare cast grotesque shadows, and the horrors of the scene are enhanced by fearful yelling, barking, prancing and facial contortion. Usually the ceremonies conclude by public and respectful burial of the scalps which have previously been subject to indignities, and in this concluding ceremony the emotion of fear shows itself in sharp contrast from the feelings of boldness and strong self-assertion which have been manifest throughout the performance. Under all conditions primitive man has a fear of ghosts, and among savage races there seems to be a common consciousness of a non-material existence of the dead who may do incalculable harm. Hence, prior to the burial of these scalp trophies, a propitiatory song is rendered, in which the ghosts of deceased enemies are addressed in flattering and conciliatory terms.

The contrast between the beggars' and scalp dances is very noticeable, not only in the outward forms of expression by song, music, and dance, but in illustration of the varied emotions which may find expression by means of bodily movement, with vocal and instrumental accompaniment. Young Indians of noble birth dancing for charitable purposes, for example to beg alms for widows, are exercising complete self-abnegation, and the music is representative of sympathy combined with all the higher altruistic feelings ; while on the other hand the same people, when executing a scalp dance, are employing music to assist in the interpretation of every form of the crudest pride, pugnacity and self-assertion. In connection with scalp dancing it may be said that adult tribesmen take great pains to train young boys in the correct and most intense forms of emotional expression. Among the Mandan Indians[124] sham fights are organised among youths, who use bows and blunt arrows with which they carry on a very realistic combat, which is invariably followed by a scalp dance organised for the purpose of vaunting and reciting deeds of valour, so that there may be serious preparation for the more earnest expression of adult life. The more recent researches of W. McClintock[125] among primitive tribes of North America tend to show that with the Blackfeet, at any rate, civilisation has left untouched the ancient desires for crude forms of emotional expression by means of singing, dancing, and performing on elementary musical instruments.

A travelling railway engineer who was deeply interested in Indian tribes, who did what they could to arrest the progress of the great trans-continental railway lines in the sixties, has left reliable records of the Siouan war dance performed by painted, feathered warriors, some of whom danced round their fires clad in the hides of animals. Each of the trium-

phant party returned with his face painted black and
a scalp transfixed at the end of his lance. In single
file they marched up and down firing their fusees
and receiving warm congratulations and smiles from
the older men and squaws. Boys also, who were too
young to go on the warpath, were loud in their acclamations while eagerly assisting in preparations for
singing and " dancing the scalps all night." The
leader was " Long Hair," so called from the length
of his natural hair, which trailed to the ground as he
walked into the camp at the head of a band of young
women. Long Hair acted as master of the ceremonies, beating his large drum-like tambourine and
directing the movements of the women, who circled
round with shuffling steps. Louder and louder he
shouted " Hi ! Hi ! Hi !—yah," to which the squaws
answered " He ! He ! He ! Hee-ee ! " The writer
of this incident says that in spite of the cruelty of
Indians they have many excellent qualities : " If
in all my dealings with white men I had found the
same sense of honour that characterised my savage
friends my appreciation of my own countrymen would
have been much higher."[126]

Martin Dobrizhoffer[127] was a courageous missionary anthropologist who lived with the Abipoines, now
almost extinct, in Central South America in the
latter part of the eighteenth century.

He says that the anniversary of victory was marked
by festivities including singing, dancing and extrava-
gancies. Preparations for the great day included
the collection of large quantitites of honey and the
brewing of beer. The people never sang all at once,
but only two at a time, and these greatly varied their
voices from high to low, one either taking up or
following, or interrupting the other and sometimes
accompanying him. Now one then another was
silent for a short interval, and the tones were well

varied according to the subject of the song. " There are many inflexions of sound and a good deal of shaking. He who by a quicker motion of throat can now suspend the song for a while, now protract and now interrupt it with groans and laughter, or can imitate the bellowing of a bull, or the tremulous voice of a kid, he will gain universal applause."

" One of the singers rattles a gourd filled with maize seed to the time of the music. The people sing of warlike expeditions, slaughter, spoils of the enemy, and burning with depopulation of the Spanish colonies."

Summary

Head hunting, so the evidence suggests, is a practice which has spread as a modification of some basic idea relating perhaps to human sacrifice as a means of fertilising Mother Earth. The facts are not accounted for by supposing the custom of head hunting to be a perfectly natural one, just a spontaneous expression of an instinct tending to cruelty and pugnacity.

The war dance is one which, in more or less intense form, can be traced throughout the world, though I have not read of it among tribes of very rudimentary culture such as the Punans of Borneo or the Veddas of Ceylon. Eskimos have their blood feuds, but evidence of a war dance, though such may exist, is not prominent in the writings of investigators. Can it be that at one time there was a golden age of peace and prosperity when all men led the simple nomadic life of collectors and hunters? Is warfare an artificial product of definite stages of civilisation?—a phase of self-assertiveness, the temporary peevishness of a rapidly growing child—

or must we agree to the doctrine of an instinct of pugnacity operating in all the ages through which man has toiled from a simian ancestry?

Whatever may be the answer to these queries the purpose of the war dance is definite in giving cohesion and unity of purpose, either for attack or defence. The wild displays described have saved the community and preserved social solidarity, while they have had an important secondary function in stimulating sexual feeling and aiding a natural process of mate selection.

CHAPTER IV

SEX AND SOCIETY

There is in modern dancing of men and women a powerful sex influence of a refined kind which was present even in the modest dances of a century ago. Between present day dancing and that of primitive races, Oriental peoples, and classical antiquity, there is little in common. In primitive society the dance has an importance entirely lost in modern times, while dancing of men and women in pairs is unknown in Oriental society, and not frequent in primitive groups.

SEXUAL SELECTION

Choosing a mate ever has, and always will be, the most interesting event in the life of a man or woman, and the value of a right choice to society is no less important than it is to the individual.[128] There are many ways of selecting a partner, and the serenade and valentine are amusing examples of a primitive method surviving into modern society. The Melanesian boy smears himself with " girl medicine " supplied by the local witch doctor, and so fortified goes by night to play his Pan pipes or " Jew's " harp outside the home of the girl he desires. Or a girl may make shy advances through a third party ; and it is well established that tattooing both of girls and boys has an important sexual significance.[129] Tattooing of boys is an indispensable sign of manhood, and on the other hand no woman of the Kayans or Kalabits of Borneo, or the Roro of New Guinea, would be thought marriageable without the customary tattooed designs.

These are displayed with pride at public festivals, and though some of the matings may be of a tentative kind, many are permanent, so that external aids ultimately prove useful in assisting racial survival. Women who choose the most energetic and enduring dancers are unwittingly assisting biological processes of a helpful kind.

Agricultural dances, performed once a year, are an appeal to the gods of fertility, who are invoked by a troupe of male dancers, each carrying a drum decorated with long streamers. From the heads of the performers long waving strings of plaited leaves are flying, and the hair is festooned with brilliant flowers. On arrival at the ground the dance begins with a peculiar crouching movement which is changed quickly in response to a sudden cadence in the note of the drum. Without warning, a troupe of girls appear, mingle with the men for a few minutes, then suddenly depart. These girls wear mats round their waists in such a way as to leave a glimpse of beautifully tattooed thighs, which are exposed with every swaying of the skirt in response to music of bamboo drums. The tattooing is a symbol of eligibility for marriage, and no doubt in this dance there is a process of sexual selection invoked in addition to any appeal which may be made to the deities presiding over agriculture.[130]

In the islands of Torres Strait the game that combines agility, endurance, skill, and emulation to the greatest degree is that of dancing. These dances have considerable value in keeping muscles supple and assisting general development and deportment ; while in case of abdominal dances for women the pelvis is enlarged and the internal organs are massaged so that parturition is made easier.[131] During the secular dance, or Kap, girls usually lost their hearts to the young men whose activity and stamina they admired. A youth who was a good dancer would find favour in the sight of the girls, a fact which occasions no surprise to those who have seen the active, skilful, and fatiguing performances of these people.[132]

Movements of grass petticoats appear to have attracted the curious attention of several European observers, mostly men, who seem to share the susceptibilities of the more primitive brothers they went to study. One ethnologist says : " The rhythm of these dances is further exemplified by the movements of the girl dancers, which consist essentially of a slow rocking movement of the pelvis on the thighs, each leg being alternately slightly flexed and the heel being lifted from the ground. The muscles of the back give a rotatory movement to the pelvis, causing the petticoats to swish from side to side. When dancing in columns the movement is usually slow, but in solo dances so violent that the strips of the petticoat, tied over the right hip, fly up in a spray of fibres allowing the tattoo on the buttock and thighs to be seen."[133]

Roro and Mekeo girls often intermingle with the men in the same lines, but frequently they form up at the end of the group. " They sway their bodies at each step with a side twist of the hip, rather like some of the movements of Arab and other Eastern dancing girls, but quick instead of slow, which makes their grass petticoats at each step swing round and upward, first on one side and then on the other, sometimes almost as high as their shoulders."[134]

The love song is perhaps a more highly developed and more artistic form of sex attraction than the dance, for the former relies on intellectual effort rather than physical charm. Some of these love ditties are quite charmingly expressed ; thus the Shan youth of Upper Burma sings : —

" Thou fairest and best, more precious than rubies
Thou choice of my heart, I pray thee now listen
While I weave in fit measures, the smooth flowery cadence,
My tender sweet song."[135]

Perhaps the lady does listen, attracted by such poetical effort, but it is certain that she would not do so if the singer were not artistically tattooed, for such is the hall-mark of manhood.

The Maoris, like all other Polynesians, have fine intellectual qualities, now shown in Parliament, but formerly displayed at the installation of a chief, at a war dance, or in composing a love lyric of sad plaintiveness.[136] In fact, love songs form a large section of Maori poetry which has been handed down orally. An old tattooed dame said : " Listen O stranger ! this is the love song handed down among our people, which Tutankai composed for a flute song." She wagged her close-cropped venerable head and imitated the sound of the nose-flute and at same time the nasal long-drawn singing of the ballad.

" Aye, my well beloved !
Oh that thou would'st come for me !
Then searching, slowly paddling,
Thy willing bride would'st find
And both would flee together.
Here on this lovely resting place
Like grey night owl,
I sadly crouch and wait,
Would that I were in my dear home
On Whitirer's threshold there above !
I'd greet thee fondly, and embrace
Thy lordly form with chief's tattoo adorned.
O lover mine."

So said a maiden on a lonely rock, when she found
she could not launch a canoe to paddle to her lover.
Another favourite love song ran :—

> " Oft the spirit of my love returns to me
> To embrace in Reinga land
> This form of mine.
> Though far away, I ever dream
> Fondly of thee ;
> And a sweet pain is ever in
> My bosom, O my love ! "

Even the inhospitable climate of north east
Siberia does not so " freeze the genial current of the
soul " as to exclude love songs from the repertoire
of the Kamschatdales, who were carefully, though
somewhat unsympathetically studied, so far back
as 1764. " Their dance is in this manner. Two
women kneel opposite on a mat in the middle of the
room holding a little tow in each hand. At first
they begin to sing very low, moving slightly their
hands and shoulders. By degrees they raise their
voice and increase the motions of their bodies till
they are quite out of breath and fatigued. This
strange, uncouth entertainment, as it appeared to me,
seemed greatly to delight the Kamschatdales, so
strongly is every nation prejudiced in favour of its
own customs. In their love songs they declare
their passion to their lovers, their grief,hope and other
affections. The women generally compose the ditties
and have clear agreeable voices. Though they do
not want an inclination for music, yet they have
no musical instrument except a simple flute, and
upon that they cannot play any tune."[137]

The Abipiones of Paraguay, now a remnant of
the flourishing people visited by Martin Dobrizhoffer,[138] sometimes strike a drum loudly to announce
the nuptials, but the strange custom described would

make more lively music a sad irony. The bride is covered with a screen, and Gumilla relates in his " History of the Orinoco," that in one nation old men were married to girls, old women to youths, so that age may correct the petulance of youth. For they say that to join young persons equal in youth and imprudence in wedlock is to join one fool to another. The marriage of old and young is a kind of apprenticeship, which, after they have served for some months, they are permitted to take a mate of their own age.

The omission of violent dances shows a nice discrimination of the fitness of things, for it would be a sorry sight to watch extreme age capering after frivolous youth in a merry-go-round lasting from sunset to dawn.

Among some Peruvian tribes the love scene is enacted by a man dancing in a circle to the time of his own flute music, while a woman follows him about.[139]

In jungles of the Amazon still unexplored the love dance is executed by gaily feathered men, and girls whose chief dress consists of gaudily painted thighs, the designs on which often represent the zig-zag patterns on a snake. When the girls form in single file, each with her hands on the shoulders of the one in front, and the line writhes and twists, a very life-like display of snake movements is produced.

" The dance commenced with a swaying line of gaily painted but otherwise unadorned girls slowly advancing and retreating into the little palm-encircled clearing. The men linked arms and advanced into the arena to the accompaniment of wild cries.

" Catching hold of the hands of their partners they began a curiously monotonous series of weird contortions of the body. Those with the dancing sticks stamped the ground with their feet as well as with long poles, and everyone chanted and shrieked, while

the older women sat on the ground, beating a kind
of tom-tom.   When it was over the girls walked
about in their finery without the least embarrassment,
but never could one say that their conduct savoured
of indecency or vulgarity.''[140]

The most amusing incident ever recorded in
connection with a wedding dance comes from
Persia.[141]   While the bride is dressing the family and
their guests dance a circular measure in the compound.
From time to time the exhibition ceases to allow a
servant to hold up in turn each article of the bride's
trousseau which has been supplied by the bridegroom.   The guests applaud and the men at the
tom-toms redouble their efforts.   One hopes that
the bride is not overlooking the compound from her
window.

The use of satirical songs, which are of a disciplinary nature, is common among the Yakuts, who
will cause merriment by singing of the inability of
their neighbours to drive and manage teams of dogs.
Domestic incidents may provide a subject for some
bard who accompanies himself by strumming on the
'' balalaika.''   A young wife, whose husband had
not returned from market at the usual time, was in
grave anxiety, and at once organised a large search
party, which very shortly discovered the unconcerned
truant quite near home, just a little delayed by a
heavy snowfall.   Within an hour the village bard
had improvised a humorous song descriptive of the
incident, which caused great amusement to a local
audience.

In the opinion of the Rev. J. Weeks,[142] '' The
dance is the real centre and expression of the social
life of the village,'' and the topical songs, in which
persons may be held up to ridicule, are greatly
feared as a disciplinary measure.   '' Is there a
death ?   Then relatives and friends will show their

sympathy by dancing their best and chanting the praises of him who has so lately gone to the mysterious ' longa,' where all spirits find their home for a time. Is there a marriage? Then relatives and boon companions of the old bachelor days are invited, and after the feast a dance is arranged, and although some of the legs will be unsteady, through too much sugar-cane wine, yet all present will be in a jovial mood. On moonlight nights the drums will be brought out, reed rattles, ferret bells, and anything else that will tinkle will be tied round the ankles, the men and women will form lines opposite each other, and for hours the dancers will jump, twist and wriggle to the rhythmic drum. All distinctions are forgotten, and for a time skilled and unskilled, rich and poor, slave and free, are all mixed in indistinguishable confusion." With the advance of civilisation, dancing appears to become an ever-diminishing expression of communal sentiment and social unity, and it is not without regret for the decadence of village dances, that one reads of Mr. Cecil Sharpe's researches into the subject of Morris dances and their appropriate songs, which formed such an artistic, free, and natural expression of social life in rural centres.

Satirical songs may be a powerful factor in influencing conduct. The greedy man, the thief, the coward, the worker of black magic, and the incestuous, are made the subjects of songs sung at village dances. Such chants are a great factor in influencing natives by inciting them to reckless bravery or deterring them from committing crimes. "Village songs inspire brave deeds, brand and shame cowards, or restrain rascals. Natives hate to be held up to ridicule in a village song."

The songs and chants of the Ainu of Yezo run in no scale, so the airs cannot be written down, in fact the so-called singing is often a monotonous recitative

H

Some of the women and girls have rich pleasant
voices and when singing in unison they have a fulness
of tone and accuracy of tune. " They can make up
pretty tunes in which to recite recent acts and
experiences." The Rev. Bachelor says he has often
listened to the servants who have returned from
town chanting their doings for hours at a stretch.
Friends who meet will tell in this way of births,
deaths, marriages, and other local events. Still
there is nothing which can be described as metre, or
verse accurately measured into syllables. This
recitative singing,found in every primitive community,
is a social asset which belongs to backward races
only; its universality suggests that it represents
some definite stage in the unfolding of musical
ability. The recitative verse, as we have seen, may
be satirical, laudatory, either of the singer himself,
or a patron, descriptive of hunting, war, or the
most menial tasks. Sometimes the song is prepared,
more frequently it is spontaneous, just an impromptu
outflow of the thoughts and emotions. The only
analogy one can think of in medieval times in Europe
is that of the troubadour poet who :—

> " Poured to lord and lady gay
> The unpremeditated lay :
> In varying cadence, soft or strong
> He swept the sounding chords along :
> Each blank, in faithless memory void,
> The poet's glowing thought supplied."

THE WELCOME DANCE AND PUBLIC FUNCTIONS

The corroboree brings into relief the lighter and
more attractive characteristics of Australian social
life,[143] for the musical performance is essentially of
a convivial nature, and usually there is the intention

of paying a compliment to some visiting tribe.

Spencer and Gillen describe the corroboree as the natives only form of social enjoyment. On these occasions the men have a chance of appearing at their best before women and children, who always form an admiring audience. Night after night for two weeks the Arunta of Central Australia will continue a corroboree which, to an observer, is a wearisome repetition of songs and dance movements, the only variety being introduced by a change of decorative design, which usually consists of patches of coloured down stuck to the body with human blood.

For many days prior to the commencement of this dance men busily clear a ground situated a considerable distance from the camp, and it is to be noted that the ceremony is still of a somewhat sacred character, for women and children are kept away from the scene of preparation. Phonographic records of the music show that although the words differ for each corroboree, the music tends to uniformity throughout, beginning on a high note, and falling gradually until it fades into silence, the effect being just the same as that of a number of people chanting as they travel along until their voices are lost in the distance.

As a rule twelve performers participate, and the dancing, which is of a very simple nature, consists of moving in a line which wheels backward and forward in front of the audience, every movement being characterised by a prancing high knee action. The lines alternately approach and fall back as in lancers, then they pass through one another, while for marking time each performer carries a stave which beats to control rhythm of muscular movement. The dance is varied at times by a single performer charging at great speed towards the others, who fall backward before him with a peculiar side-stepping motion accompanied by wild yelling and prancing. At this point women and children retire hastily, while men continue their wild gyrations round an enormous fire whose uncertain glare casts the wildest and most fantastic shadows. Corroborees are passed from tribe to tribe as a mark of friendship and social feeling, so it comes to pass that the words and movements are performed hundreds of miles from their place of origin, and it is remarkable that the tribes should be able to memorise accurately songs whose words have no meaning for them. A corroboree when given to a friendly tribe is seldom performed again by the donors.

A very striking feature of the music of Australians is the great uniformity of procedure among all tribes, and a description of a corroboree held among the central tribes would need little modification to make it applicable to people of Queensland or South East Australia. W. E. Roth,[144] when speaking of the Pitta Pitta tribe of Queensland, describes the audience as seated row upon row, and in some instances men are separated from the group of women and children. Time is beaten by striking two boomerangs flat on flat, while the primitive opossum skin drum stuffed with feathers is again in evidence.

Corroborees mark the conclusion of peace. They are also held after initiation ceremonies, when tribes from widely separated areas unite in order to submit their pubescent boys to a series of tests, and a course of instruction which results in their inception into tribal councils. Thus the dance, with its accompanying songs and simple use of percussive instruments, may be regarded as an expression of social emotions and tribal sentiment. Social tendencies have been of paramount importance in the development of musical expression by song or dance among primitive and erudite peoples. The simple nature of religious ideas among Australian aborigines precludes the extensive use of music as an adjunct of religious worship, though dancing is in common use at magico, religious ceremonies, and the simple " bull roarer ", constructed from a string and thin slat of wood, is reverenced, because when rapidly whirled it produces a shrill weird noise, regarded by the Yuin of South East Australia as the voice of a god Daramulun.

Thomas Worsnop [145] says that the corroboree is not a sacred ceremony, but only a play which may imitate movements of animals such as the emu, kangaroo, or wild dog. The blacks are very observant and great mimics, exhibiting a skill and dexterity to be gained only by long practice. From the day an infant was able to stand and walk alone its education in the movements of the corroboree began, a fact which supports the suggestion that this dance is social and not sacred, for young children are excluded from what is sacred.

There are of course dances at which women and uninitiated boys are not allowed to be present, for example those invoking rain or food. But the welcome dances at present under discussion are free expressions of joy on the return of some of the clan from an expedition. Australian dances cannot be easily explained, for after some of them peculiar marks are made on the trees near the dancing ground, and little bundles of sticks bound with vines are left behind hanging on the trees ; the significance of these is not understood.[146]

Natives of New Britain are particularly fond of action dances which they usually perform as a mark of respect to visitors, and it is interesting to note that such dances are often the peculiar property of a particular village which may sell them to neighbours. The people who sell the dance visit the purchasers and spend a considerable time in teaching correct movements, during which process they are treated with every respect and consideration, while, as a final act of grace, a grand fete is organised as a prelude to distribution of presents to the performers by the village chief.[147]

The natives of Urama, New Guinea, gave a welcome dance to Frank Hurley.[148] Warriors attended in gala attire, and women and children were ordered to the jungle until the festivities were over.

During social dances at Hall Sound, New Guinea, each group supplied its own orchestra, which was nothing but a drum and chant without conductor to give the key and tune. Hence there were seven different tunes and keys going simultaneously, so producing a bedlam of happiness. Hour after hour the beating of tom-toms and drums continued to the same chant which hourly grew hoarser. Daylight broke over the mountains, but this was not regarded as a signal to cease dancing, although the exhibition had been in progress for ten hours. A tired remnant of revellers continued to dance on the ground, now becoming heated by the rising sun. Leaves were strewn to make the ground more comfortable, and the weary dancers showed a readiness to come away and have their photographs taken. The village club house looked like a theatrical outfitter's establishment, gay with huge feather head-dresses hanging round the walls. Under the house lay twenty-three pigs with their legs fastened together so that a pole could be passed through. The eldest son of the chief was master of the ceremonies, and it was his duty to kill the first pig by a blow on the side of the head; then he performed the first cutting up, after which other men might assist. Small portions were given to women and children, but the best parts were reserved for the men.

MEKEO MEN IN DANCING DECORATIONS.

(By permission of Messrs. Seeley Service and R. W. Williamson)

This social function was to celebrate the wearing
for the first time of some beautifully embroidered
garters, which women had made for their sons as a
sign of manhood. The adornments had been privately
placed in position before the dance and remained
covered with bark-cloth during the ceremony. The
five youths afterwards paraded to receive compliments
which had, however, to be paid for. " Naime, you
do walk grandly, mine is a wallaby " ; and later
Naime would have to kill a wallaby and present it
to the man who praised him before others. Another
admirer says " You do handle the drum well," and
" I like fish," so that Naime, who has a busy time in
prospect, would be honour bound to go fishing for
his friend.[149]

Dancing among Roro and Mekeo people, though
an amusement, is generally associated with ceremonies
which are now, or were originally, connected with
some religious and superstitious belief. One of many
occasions is the erection of a club house or the repair
of an old one. A Roro village ceremonial dance was
seen by Williamson near a club house which had
been partly rebuilt and redecorated. Local chiefs
had a few days previously visited neighbouring
villages with presents of areca nuts, the symbols of
friendship, carrying invitations to the dance, for
which a goodly company was expected. The village
was lighted up with coco-nut flares and bonfires, and
a small amount of informal dancing was in progress
to entertain early arrivals. Roro people dance in
groups, the movements consisting merely of slow
paces, almost goose-steps, by which a group progresses
very slowly along the village enclosure. During the
unveiling of the club house dancing ceased, coconut
flares were held in front of the building to light it up,
and all assembled before it. Concealing curtains were
torn away, so revealing for great admiration the

new front. The head chief of the village stepped on to the club house platform and made a speech, in which he was followed by others. " The main tenor of the speeches was the importance and valour of the people of the village and especially of the speaker (this being a matter on which each of them seemed to dwell long and lovingly). Some friendly compliments to visitors and the beauty of the club house concluded the address.

" Real dancing began. The dancers were all fully decorated, their faces and bodies were painted and stained a shining red, to which were added on their faces, bands of other colours. Their necks, chests and backs were heavily ornamented with necklaces, pendants of shell, beads, dogs' teeth and other things. Wrist bands, leg bands, and anklets adorned their arms and legs, and bright-coloured leaves were inserted in these to enhance the decoration. Head ornaments were huge erections eight to ten feet high, made of cane. It is a marvel that men can dance so many hours in these heavy structures.

" The night was so dark that dancers were dimly seen except when passing fires. More coco-nut flares were brought out, and the men carried these close to the dancing party in front and behind to light up the groups ; so closely were they held that the flame sometimes almost swept across the dancers' faces and they were constantly stepping with bare feet on burning fragments, this not seeming to incommode them in the slightest."[150]

In Tonga the Hea dance of ancient type described by an observer [151] in the early part of the nineteenth century was a mark of social distinction. " As among the ancient Greeks it was thought inconsistent with the character of a gentleman not to know how to strike the lyre, so among the Tonga people it would be considered a mark of great ignorance to be unaccomplished in the graceful, manly, and expressive movements of the dance."

The movements were very difficult to execute, and only chiefs and superiors learned them. The display was accompanied by a chorus provided by ten or twelve chiefs, in the middle of whom sat a conductor beating time on a loose, flat piece of hard wood three feet long and one and a half inches square, fastened only at one end on another similar piece. This wooden bar was struck by two small sticks which the operator held, one in each hand. The difficulty of the dance arose chiefly from the rapidity of the movements, especially near the end, but these specially trained chiefs kept perfect time carrying out a rapid series of movements with their arms and heads, and adapting their facial expressions to the character of the rhythm.

Among the Muruts [152] and other tribes of North Borneo the social dance as a welcome is well developed, though there is nothing remarkable about it from the artistic point of view. Intoxicating drink made from rice circulates freely, and faster becomes the rhythm and louder the gongs and shouting. The dance is important, for it brings together in friendly converse natives of districts once hostile to each other. In the dance *berunsai* the chief performer is a girl celebrated for what is commonly known as "back chat." There are perhaps two or three other girls and twenty to thirty men present. All move slowly round in a circle with hands on each other's shoulders, taking a few steps forward and one backward in unison. The leading-lady in a shrill nasal voice asks questions in a chant to which the men reply. As night wears on the fun grows fast and furious, questions and replies become of a more doubtful character, and the more respectable prefer to leave wives at home or send them to bed. Most

Dusun dances are extremely crude performances for the reason that by the time the dancing stage is reached everybody is drunk. Muruts take dancing more seriously, and every Murut house has a dancing floor. A company of men and girls wheel slowly round in a circle with little variation of grace or skill. In the long,dimly lit house beneath a roof black with the grime of ages, there is a cluster of smoked heads. Below is a fire flickering on the central hearth and throwing weird shadows across the half-naked bodies of shrill chanting women and deep voiced men.

The Wapisianas are the poorest musicians of all South American tribes, and such poor efforts as they are able to make have been borrowed from the Macusi. The borrowing indeed is not any great infringement of copyright, for the singing consists of only two nonsense syllables, " hai-ya ", which they repeat in the rhythm of the dance with little variation of pitch, so making most monotonous music. When they exercise these poor efforts the occasion is of some social importance, such as the arrival of a friendly tribe, the conclusion of a hunt, or the building of a house. One man sings a solo, the words of which are to some extent improvised, then all men and women swell the chorus. To emphasise the rhythm rattles are attached to their legs and hands. A solitary musician will often amuse himself by playing a flute made from a section of bamboo or the leg bone of a jaguar ; both varieties of flute are engraved with intricate designs. For the dance a great trumpet is made by coiling together long strips of palm-leaf, so providing an instrument which gives a low hoarse tone that marks the changes of rhythm.[153]

Music frequently provides an accompaniment for gambling games, one of which is generally played by two sets of people, who arrange themselves in opposite rows. Each side possesses a pair of bones, one of which, the trump bone, is distinguished by a binding of sinew. The bones are passed from hand to hand, and the opposite side have to guess which of their opponents is holding the trump. During the course of play the side holding the bones sing their gambling songs, which are accompanied by beating of drums. The instruments are merely sounding-boards placed on the ground, and the music is produced by striking in cadence with shot rods.[154]

The kindliness and hospitality of backward races is a well-established fact which is illustrated by a dance given by the wealthiest and most aristocratic young men of the tribe. This function has for its object the benefit of a widow whose husband has recently been killed in tribal warfare. Performers are clad in breech-cloths made from quills of the eagle and raven, while for purposes of marking time each carries a rattle in his right hand, and the medicine man is close by beating a drum and joining in the song at the highest pitch of his voice. The widow sits near the door of her wigwam ready to receive the gifts which never fail to be rendered by spectators, whose sympathies are appealed to by the so-called " beggars' dance," in which the Great Spirit is invoked by song to make generous the hearts of all onlookers, who are assured that the supernatural powers will be kind to those who assist the helpless poor.[155]

INITIATION DANCES

With primitive people entry into tribal life is not merely a gradual physical and mental development which by hardly perceptible stages merges the youth or maiden into the adult stage. On the contrary, there has to be a special ceremony, or maybe a long

series of ceremonies, which give the novice a decided
start, in fact a new birth. Puberty and tribal fellowship for boys and girls is recognised and prepared
for in various ways, including tattooing or scarification, seclusion, food restrictions, physical suffering
by beating, heat, exposure to cold, moral instruction
and silence for a long period. Then there follows re-
introduction to society, the novice is born again and
is no longer known by his old childish name.

In New Guinea assumption of the perineal band
marks the arrival of puberty, and a special dancing
ceremony is held for both boys and girls, who are
dealt with several at a time. Each child is heavily
ornamented with strings of dogs' teeth round the
forehead and waist. A pig has to be provided by
each family sending a child to the ceremony, and the
youngster has to stand on the pig provided by his
people while a special feather head-dress is adjusted.[156]

In the Western islands of Torres Strait seclusion
of girls is a most important part of pubertal training
and the duration and character of the preparations,
vary greatly from one island to another. There are
food taboos, prohibitions against the novice seeing
daylight, also against contact of any kind with males
and against her feet touching the ground. At Saibai
the girls repair to the bush, where they remain for a
fortnight under the shade of a tree, around which
other girls and adult women perform dances. During
this period an old woman does the cooking and feeds
the novice, who is not allowed to handle her own
food.[157]. At Yam and Tutu the young girl is blackened
all over with charcoal, after which she is accompanied
to the bush by a married woman. The advance of
womanhood is made impressive by ceremonial dancing,
food restrictions, and an occasional beating from the
old dame.[158]

Initiation of girls in Africa is always accompanied

by dancing, and as a rule there is scarification, fattening, and possibly clitoridectomy.

Among the Makua, when girls arrive at time for reception into tribal life, the drums begin the festivities by striking up in that peculiar cadence which no African traveller can forget, and in response to the throbbing a closely packed body of people form up for the dance. Round they go with steps something like those of a water wagtail moving rhythmically, gliding and rocking round two central posts at which three old hags, who have instructed the girls in the bush, stand grinning in anticipation of their reward.[159]

Among the Yao there is seclusion and instruction by a " cook of the mysteries ". The girls are anointed with oil mixed with medicines and their heads are shaved after they have been dressed in bark cloth. Toward the end of the ceremony the girls carry over their heads a roof or model of a house. Thus they symbolise their future position as pillars of the home. The whole proceeding is called *being danced* into womanhood.[160] Anyanga ceremonies of a similar nature occupy one day only, during which the girls are kept in seclusion with an old woman. Men disguised as animals dance with the girls, who gyrate round figures of animals drawn in the sand. The meaning of this dance is not known ; possibly it is a fragment borrowed from some ancient cult of animals just an isolated act from elsewhere introduced into Anyanga ceremonies.[161]

With the Nandi tribe there is circumcision of girls, who dress as men. If they are courageous they receive presents from warriors, who stand a long way off during the ceremony. The girl has to balance a ball of mud on her head and one on her great toe. She is said to be a coward if these are displaced. Following the dance which succeeds this ceremony

the girls retire to their mothers' houses, where they
remain under certain restrictions.[162]

In Southern tribes of California the seclusion of
girls is in a pit near the fire.   There are symbolic
acts such as showering grain on the girls to make them
prolific.   Sweating in the pit expels demons, and
during the ceremony old women dance, sing and wave
branches to drive away these evil spirits.[163]

" For girls of the North West Amazon region
there are secret lodges in the bush under the protection of older women of the tribe.   The novices
learn to dance,sing and paint themselves for festivals.
Life in the dense tropical forests of the Amazon is
a fruitful field for ethnological research, for the
people,partly on account of their hostility to strangers,
partly by reason of their elusive habits, have never
been studied with the same thoroughness as primitive
peoples of Africa, New Guinea, and Australia.[164]

In addition to tribal initiation of girls there are
in many parts of the world special dances connected
with the dedication of girls to temple service.   This
widespread custom of keeping a retinue of young
women as concubines of the gods was known in
ancient Egypt, Persia, Peru and Mexico, and these
priestesses have their more primitive representatives
in Formosa and the Celebes.   In fact, woman has
among backward peoples a higher status than has
generally been supposed.

Kaikolan musicians of Coimbatore believe that
at least one girl in every family should be set apart
for the Hindu temple, where she is instructed in
music and dancing.   During the tali-tying ceremony
the girl is decorated with jewels and made to stand
on a heap of paddy (unhusked rice), while a folded
cloth is held up before her by two dancing girls.
The novice takes hold of the cloth, and her dancing
master, who holds her legs, moves them up and down

in time to the music. Instruction is given in music
and dancing and the *ars amoris* before the girl goes
through a form of marriage to a sacred object. Dedication may be accompanied by tattooing or branding
with the sacred marks known as the " chank " and
" chakra ".[165]

Dancing is indispensable for the initiation of
boys, and is resorted to even by very primitive
people like the Andamanese[166], who have no musical
instruments. Three men and a young woman all
decorated with clay of various colours to impress
the novice dance round him at the ceremonial feasts
when pig and turtle are eaten. This dance, with
the exception of the peace-making dance, is the
only one of a special kind within a given tribe, a fact
which shows the native opinion of the dance as an
adjunct to initiation. At one stage in the ceremony
the novice is anointed with red paint and fed on
turtle fat, while on the fourth day preparations are
made for the great dance. An older man takes his
place at the sounding-board, near to which sit the
women, while near the centre of the dancing ground
the novice is placed in company with six men. The
man at the sounding board sings a song for which
he beats time with his foot. Usually the ditty relates
to hunting the turtle, and the women help by singing
the chorus and clapping their hands on their thighs.
Each dancer flexes his hips so that his back is nearly
horizontal, then with bent knees he leaps from the
ground with both feet, showing great energy in
keeping time to the sounding-board, which moves
with great rapidity. At the conclusion of the dance
the novice receives a new name, and henceforth it
is considered insulting to use his boyish title.

The Wilyaroo[167] dancing ceremony is one connected
with making cuts along each side of the spine in the
Urabunna and other tribes of Australia. There is

an interesting myth to explain that these marks are made in honour of the bell bird which once saved the blackfellows from a hawk. No doubt there are many local differences which have led to a variety of opinion among eye-witnesses. If a young man is too familiar with the women of the tribe old men catch him and tie string round his arms and thumbs. They open their own veins and pour blood over him. A circle of fires is lit round him while women dance about in a circle close to the fires. Outside them Wilyaroo men dance in the opposite direction. After two or three circlings the women retire and light another fire, just sufficient to warm the ground, which is cleaned and the ashes are swept away. The women sit with their heads between their knees, so they may see nothing. The men dance up leading the young man. The leader swings a bull roarer, which is covered with ashes until warm, then it is jerked out and again hidden. The young man is ordered to take one of the women. "You take 'em this one go away." The strings are cut and the blood is rubbed off ; then Wilyaroo marks are put on his back by the young Wilyaroo men. After this he goes to the bush with his appointed woman for a week or even three weeks. The men are proud of their marks, for they are a distinguishing sign of manhood and tribal fellowship.

DANCING IN SECRET SOCIETIES

Secret societies have in all parts of the world, and at every phase of human development, caused anxiety to guardians of law and order. It is true that the society itself claims the prerogative of maintaining a moral and political standard, as in the instance of the present day Klu Klux Klan of the Southern

States of America. Witches of medieval Europe had
their cult of the devil, secret meetings, tattoo marks,
songs and dances. Tattooed criminals of Italy and
France have been found to belong to secret organisa-
tions working for social upheaval or private vengeance

In primitive communities of the present day
secret societies are seen at their best, or shall we say
their worst, in the Bismark Archipelago and most
parts of West and Central Africa.

During initiation into a secret society of Torres
Strait the youths for the first time witness the sacred
dances and learn some of the legends of their tribe.
After this they are gathered together and attacked
by armed men dressed up to represent spirits, and
often badly hurt. The mask of the front dancer
has no eye openings, so the second one has to guide
him with a piece of rope. In dancing each foot is
raised high before it is brought to the ground, and
there are long pauses between the steps. Dancers
emerge from a sacred house wearing masks, and dance
into the horseshoe group of men, then back again into
the house, repeating the performance twice. When
returning, the dancers kick out as if trying to drive
something away.[168]

At Las in Torres Strait initiation into a secret
society appears to be part of the cult of two heroes
Bomai and Malu, the former being a patron who is
called on in times of danger, for example during
serious illness or the capsizing of a canoe. Malu, the
personality behind the present day cult, is represented
as a shark-headed man who is the main interest in a
cycle of hero stories. In all probability the animal
dances connected with this cult come from New
Guinea, where totemism is still a strong social and
religious factor. In the dance witnessed by Dr.
Haddon[169] there were " pigeon " men and " dog "
men. The former advanced in double file with their

elbows flexed. Their forearms and hands were held vertically, then with their bodies and knees well bent they lifted high their legs, and as if uncertain of their step dwelt long upon each foot as it rested on the ground. The men of each dancing pair then approached and whispered " pigeon talk." They wheeled so as to face the sea, where they took three or four rapid steps, leaped into the air, striking their breasts with the palms of their hands in imitation of the flapping of pigeons' wings. Drum beating accompanied this dancing, and decorated stone headed clubs were used.

The cult appears to have developed into a religious fraternity or secret society which took upon itself disciplinary functions ; indeed it is very similar to some of the secret societies that are found in Melanesia. The dance was performed on the sea-shore at Las the day after the masks had been shown to initiates. Women and children were allowed to witness it from behind a bamboo fence which separated the village from the sand-beach. Old women were engaged in heaping up food, and after the dance a great feast was given. Dog men performed the first dance. They formed in two rows, facing one another on hands and knees, then advanced until their heads nearly touched. Afterwards they retired three times and lay prostrate.

Secret Societies are prevalent among many tribes of British North America, and among the Haida, Tsimshian, and Kwakiutl mystic dances are held. During these ceremonies masks are worn by performers who represent beaver, bear, or cannibal spirits. Mimetic dances are indulged in, and the shrill blast of the medicine whistle is heard in imitation of the voices of spirits.[170]

Dancing in connection with initiation into tribal life is common in Africa. Novices of the Bagesu, who

live near Mount Elgon to the north of Lake Victoria
Nyanza, are led from place to place by an experienced
man who teaches them songs, and as he does so
instructs them in matters of importance to the clan.
There is no tune in the songs, which are drawled out
in a recitative manner, while the boys, painted with
red ochre and rubbed with oil, dance to the rhythm,
meanwhile waving aloft reeds of charred bamboo
which they hold in their hands.[171]

Among the Bagos of North West Africa there is
recorded a " Juju Nkali Feast " in honour of the
members of a priestly secret society. The members
carried as many masks as there were dead to mourn
for. " Then one fine day this band would come
suddenly dancing into the village toward evening
with fearful shouts and cries, and constant yelling
of ' Juju Nkali ! Juju Nkali ! ' whereupon all took
refuge in their houses. But someone, usually a slave
or an old man, was seized and carried off to the bush
by the masqueraders. What there befell him nobody
could tell, but it is certain that a few days later the
masked band returned to the village with a finger,
a toe, a bit of skin, or some other part of the captive
fastened to a pole. This pole was then brought before
every house occupied by a young man who wanted
to be received into the priestly association. The
sequel was that young people went off into the forest
singing and playing music, seeking thereby to drown
their own fear. Then a few weeks later was heard
once more the howling of the masqueraders, who were
this time followed by the novices of the society
painted white. These carried first a shrouded object
and advanced to the middle of the village. The
dancers dragged forward a long post or pole, to the
top of which each of the young men attached the
free end of a piece of string, the other end of which
was twined round his neck. The shrouded object

was the decayed head of the victim who had been seized on the first day of the maskers' appearance. The head was stuck round with feathers, so that it looked like a hedgehog. A fire was kindled and the maskers began a furious dance, wildly yelling ' Juju Nkali! Juju Nkali! ' This continued until it was assumed that the young men with ropes round their necks were dead. Then the pole and young men, were carried off to the forest. It was explained that the Spider had seized the souls of the young men but that would not matter, since the priests had the pole with the strings. The souls of the young men continued to live on the strings until they reappeared in their tribe after an absence of two years, to be greeted as quite distinguished people."[172]

There is evidence to show that the secret societies of Sierra Leone,[173] which have proved so hostile to European discipline, include dancing among their ceremonies for admission of new members.

The " Bondu " secret society belongs exclusively to women, and among the Mendi exerts considerable disciplinary power, so much so that whole districts may be terrorised by blackmail and murder. Headquarters are situated in the densest part of the bush, at a point known only to members of the society, and here girl novices undergo a period of initiation. Young girls are ornamented with bracelets of palm-leaf fibre, and their simple dresses of white cotton are freely decorated with small iron plates, which jingle merrily as the owners dance to the beating of drums and the twanging of a guitar. The faces of all performers are smeared with animal fat, and the " devil " is clad in thick, black, fibrous matting, which gives the appearance of a shaggy animal. Huge masks of stained wood hide the identity of performers, and severe penalties are inflicted if a mistake in dancing and ritual is made.

EXHIBITION DANCING

From the social psychologist's point of view exhibition dancing is not so important as ceremonies which express the history and strivings of a primitive community. There is however in displays of skill by one person, or a small troupe, an example of a definite stage of decadence in the social importance of the dance, though the skill of the few people concerned may be a subject of admiration.

Dancing is primarily expressive of every department of social and religious life, but a definite stage of devolution is witnessed when an exhibition of skill takes the place of communal effort. In India, Burma, Turkestan, Persia, China, Japan, and Java dancing is not a form of expression for the community as a whole, as is the case among the aborigines of Australia, Papuans, Melanesians, most African tribes, and native Indians of South America.

A correct impression of these special displays of skill, which in many Asiatic countries have usurped the original function of the dance, may be gained by considering a few examples from Africa, Central Asia, Persia, Burma, and Tibet.

Whip dancing is a test of physical endurance in bearing pain, and when I saw the ceremony at a Sudanese village some two hundred miles south of Khartoum it was performed to musical accompaniments provided by an orchestra of women, who beat tom-toms with their hands and wrists, while others were standing and clapping in rhythm.

Three Sudanese dancers stood in line, while a fourth circled around them in time to the music, flourishing a whip of rhinoceros hide with which ever and anon he threatened to strike. Presently the lash came down over the shoulder of one of the three men standing in line, but for the twitch of an eyelid, the blow, which stripped off the skin and drew blood, might as well have fallen on the trunk of a tree, for it absolutely failed to elicit any sign of emotion. Each of the three men in line received in turn a blow, after which the striker took his place in the line and was replaced by one who had already suffered. So amid much clamour and energetic thumping of drums the whipping dance continued, until each of the four men had delivered a blow to each of his fellows. The dancer who happened to be circling round with the whip would pause suddenly as if about to strike, then with a cunning smile would wheel about and continue his dance. Women and girls among the spectators showed the keenest appreciation of this performance, and the scars obtained are honorific marks.

Further south the Lango have such a dance, the blow being given so that the whip curls round the body, leaving a great weal and not seldom drawing blood. Each of the small dancing party endures three such blows, sometimes from the same person, or perhaps from different people. As an eye-witness of a similar ceremony I readily believe Driberg's statement that if allowed by local custom the recipient leaps into the air, and after the last blow gives a tremendous bound. The men I saw made no movement, but one when struck gave a painful grin, which was loudly applauded as a derisive smile. Among the Lango the leap is permissible after the stroke, but when the blow is actually given the victim must on no account flinch or in any way show that he felt it, for if he did so he would be shamed before the women and counted as a coward. Tradition says that the women instigated the practice, so that they might choose brave husbands.[174] If this is so we have an interesting instance of a crude form of sexual attraction, previously noted in a more refined way in Papuan dances, when the girls admire and choose the nimblest and most enduring young men.

The Arawaks of Guiana had a musical performance, now possibly obsolete, which was a test of physical endurance and power to withstand pain. Male dancers, each of whom carries a whip, stand in opposite rows, and when the music begins the whips are waved rhythmically in unison. From time to time a couple of dancers separate themselves and face one another, prepared for the ordeal, which consists of lashing each other's legs with a whip of hard fibre until one yields to his opponent.[175]

Hammock dancing in Sierra Leone is indeed a perilous exhibition of the art, and it is no unusual thing for the performer to dance and drink himself into a state of hysteria before commencing. An ordinary grass hammock is stretched between two poles raised to a height of twenty or thirty feet above the ground. The orchestra in attendance produces a considerable volume of sound, both vocal and instrumental, and when at last the performer has danced himself into a frenzy he quickly scales one of the high poles and begins a hazardous gymnastic dance in the hammock. Time after time he pretends to fall, then quickly recovering his balance hangs by one leg or rolls up in the hammock and makes it revolve, a performance highly exciting and continued until the dancer is completely exhausted.[176]

The Mandingoes of Sierra Leone have a peculiar habit of combining dancing with rowing. The oarsman places one leg on the bottom of the boat while the other is raised to a seat. Paddles are vigorously plied, and at the same time a rapid leg motion is followed. At times the oarsmen " lift themselves on the seat with both legs, and while still rowing each throws one foot backward and upward into the air, balancing on one foot and not relinquishing the oars."[177] Rhythmical and united movement is preserved by chanting a song, which, though mournful in cadence, seems very inspiring to the boatmen.

Certain animal dances performed by the Ibos of Nigeria have lost their significance, if such they ever had, and are now mere gymnastic feats in imitation of the movements of guinea fowl. The physical strength required is tremendous, and leads to a great development of the lumbar and abdominal muscles. The motions of the dance are free, so after practice they produce no sign of stiffness.[178]

A scene near Blantyre in South East Africa introduces us to the strolling player, who is always a welcome guest. The master of the ceremonies was the principal dancer, but took no part in the vocal music. He wore a calico turban, a leather belt gaily ornamented with huge feathers, a large cloak of catskin, and numerous anklets in the form of dancing rattles. Six drummers made the chief contribution toward an orchestral accompaniment, and of these, one beat a large drum which was raised from the ground by three short legs, and the other musicians beat with their hands on drums suspended round their necks. The players did not confine themselves to drumming, but danced with great energy throughout the whole performance. Two young boys contributed special dances, and in conclusion a collection of beads and fowls was made from the audience.

Werner[179] gives a further account of dances executed by Yao people, and it appears that although in some instances the performance is reserved either for men or women, there are ceremonies in which the sexes unite and a selection of partners is made. At a dance witnessed at a Yao village near Blantyre the principal part was played by a woman with a baby six weeks old. This dance was similar to one which generally precedes the birth of a woman's first child, the chief difference being that casual spectators and men were present. Eight or ten women took part in the dance, led by the principal performers, all of whom were freshly anointed and decorated with their best calico, beads, and a dancing rattle on one leg. Three men held drums against their chests and struck them with their hands, while a boy had a four-legged standing drum which he beat with two sticks. The women stood in front of the band in a semi-circle, marking time, then formed in couples, marched round in single file, bent forward from the hips, and concluded by dancing together in a kind of jigging step.

Asiatic countries show a survival of the religious dance in the form of elaborately equipped processions, but oriental peoples are, above all others, patrons of the exhibition dancer, and the performance of the sexes together is almost unknown.

A dancing girl of Mandalay goes through an early course of vigorous training until her body becomes as supple as india rubber. Her movements are natural and graceful even though they are exaggerated so as to become contortions. A girl will bend backward until her lips touch the mat on which she stands and pick up rupees. Or she may double her head and limbs into a space represented by her head and trunk; so neatly folded is she that a small portmanteau will contain her.[180]

Through Persia and Turkestan the most popular dancing is that provided by strolling players. I do not think dancing could in any sense be included among national games affecting the people as a whole, in other words the social importance of the dance is almost negligible. At Bokhara the principal instruments used were a kind of guitar forty-six inches long with a sounding board nine inches by

four, which could be played either with the thumb
or a bow. Another instrument resembled the
flageolet but gave notes like those from a bagpipe.
Two dancers dressed as girls wore bracelets studded
with tinkling ornaments. Small cymbals and
tambourines were played by the dancers to mark the
rhythm of their movements which were of an immodest kind.[181] At Kitab four dancing boys wore
red flowing robes and loose white trousers, their feet
were uncovered and the hair was allowed to grow
long. In the first dance these performers walked
leisurely round keeping time with the clappers, but
in the next dance their pace increased as round they
went singing a love song to the time of their hand
clapping. A third dance provided an opportunity
for the boys to answer the questions they had asked
in their first songs, while as a grand finale they
turned somersaults and went through violent antics.
When these *batchas*, or dancing boys, were putting
themselves through contortions intended to be graceful, two men carrying candles dodged about nimbly
holding their lights close to the dancers so that
their good looks and movements might be admired.
The candle bearers added to the amusement by their
facial contortions and clownish actions. One of their
nonsensical actions was to take advantage of a pause
in the dance in order to sit opposite to one another
making grimaces and moving the skin of their faces
like a rabbit. Next followed a Persian song and dance
which the *batchas* accompanied with whistles, snapping
their fingers, and beating time by striking together
a pair of wands. Central Asiatics do not dance for
their own amusement but show keen appreciation
of a performance such as that described, for which
a large crowd gathered. A rich man will keep
a troupe of trained boys solely for his own
amusement.[182]

A typical entertainment of Persia is given by four girls and a buffoon ; the latter sings while all contort themselves, meanwhile keeping up a patter of indecent conversation which appears to amuse the audience. The girls may be any age from twelve to seventeen years and their well developed figures and sparkling dark eyes would give a pleasing impression were they not marred by an excess of facial paint. Their dance had little skill to recommend it for they spun round with heads held erect while their fingers were snapped as loudly as castanets. Frequently the feet were motionless while the body was wriggled and contorted, every muscle being made to quiver, and the trunk being bent back until it almost touched the ground ; in some dances tiny cymbals replaced the finger snapping to punctuate the rhythm. As equilibrists the girls showed some skill, for they were able to balance lighted candles and glasses full of water on their heads or hands while going through strange posturings. The buffoon retired for a time then returned in most remarkable disguise which made him appear scarcely four feet high with a face like a full moon. This grotesque visage was carefully painted on his bare abdomen, and to shut off the upper part of his figure a black shroud was used. He had cleverly made a pair of arms and adjusted these in right relation to his false face, so presenting the figure of a dwarf with an enormous countenance of pathetic stupidity. Then followed clever, though crude belly dancing, in which the abdomen was wrinkled so as to make the artificial face grin and droop alternately. Coins were showered in appreciation of this display which concluded by the girls mingling with the spectators and becoming personal in their attentions.[188]

Tibetan dancing of the devil-mask type has degenerated into a public entertainment, though on account of its original function of exorcism it is more correctly dealt with in a comparison of magical dances. Exhibition dancing in Tibet is appreciated in all parts of the country, through the difficult passes of which itinerant performers find their way over surprisingly long distances.

Landor, and other bold intruders into the wastes of snow covered rocks, give accounts of these strolling mountebanks. Possibly there are not more than two performers, a man and a boy. Landor saw two such musicians, the man wearing a peculiar four-cornered hat made of skin, and carrying a two-stringed instrument which he played with a bow. The child danced and went through many clumsy contortions, now and then giving himself a rest by going round with his tongue thrust out, to beg from the audience. At times the man changed his musical instrument for a club and sword which he used in a martial dance, pausing occasionally to apply the club to the boy's back to encourage his terpsichorean efforts, a pantomime which drew roars of laughter from the spectators.[184]

The inhabitants of Lhasa are fond of songs which they accompany by a guitar, flute, or bell, while men or women dance on planks or sounding boards a measure with movements like those of a hornpipe. Theatrical performances, including dancing, are given in courtyards, perhaps at the expense of a wealthy patron. There are mystery plays, a very common one being a representation of the birth of Buddha.[185]

Strolling mountebanks may include women, who give a miserable shuffling performance consisting of postures and slow steps. The programme, poor as it is, seems to create a thirst, for the bedraggled creatures frequently drink to excess and have to be turned out. In singing the women took alternate verses describing mountains, Buddha, temples, and

affairs of every day life. Some of the dancing movements are borrowed from the Chinese, notably those
in which one performer while swinging the arms
and body, dances round the others in a slow shuffle.[186]

Summary

Among backward races dancing is of the greatest
importance in helping men and women to choose
their mates, for there is in the display a physical basis
of charm, grace and endurance. On the intellectual
side music on the pipes, or self-composed love lyrics,
are another important adjunct to love making. All
these arts and artifices are natural and spontaneous,
comparable in fact to the display of birds and other
creatures during the mating season, which is an
indefinitely extended period with human beings.

Recitative music is something very primitive,
and psychologists will be interested in comparing
this form of self-expression with that of our own
young children who frequently chant to themselves
concerning toys and trivial events or pleasures, not
making verse it is true, but keeping up a monotonous
though not unpleasing rhythm. Topical songs are
a moral influence of a mild disciplinary kind,
these certainly do, like folk lore stories, influence
the general standard of conduct.

The social dance shows the community at a
maximum of concord and happiness, at which strangers
are entertained, or tribesmen welcomed to their
homes.

Dancing at initiation of boys and girls is part
of the general launching out into tribal life and the
performances though not as a rule public, are of a
social character, that is they serve a communal
purpose. The dancing of novices in seclusion may be

to test their powers of endurance before circumcision or other main event of puberty rites. Or the dances taught may be those of a secret society to be performed in future only on important public occasions.

Exhibition dancing does at times make an appeal to sex instinct by arousing in women a desire for the man who shows the greatest agility in the display; or affection may turn to the man who shows himself proof against pain, as in whip dances. This side of the dancing of small troupes is perhaps only of secondary importance, for to the student of devolution of custom, exhibitions represent a definite decline in the importance of the dance on its social side.

When, as in all Asiatic countries, display dancing takes the place of dancing as a national pastime we have a definite step toward modernism. A youth or girl no longer joins spontaneously in a dance connected with sex, food supply, magic, or worship, but in sedate and deliberate manner is content to pay for a sight of the contortions, gymnastics, puppet shows, theatricals, and other degenerate forms of what was at one time, not an accessory of communal life, but its very essence.

CHAPTER V

MUSICAL ABILITY AND INVENTION

ACCESSORIES OF THE DANCE

The amount of time and energy devoted by primitive peoples to dancing is beyond computation ; it would be interesting to see the equivalent in terms of hunting, agriculture, and fishing. Among the Papuans dancing of an informal kind takes place every night but the opening of a club house or less notable event, evokes a special effort.

A big dance is talked of for months and messengers carry the glad tidings by stating that so-and-so is beginning to fatten pigs. To ignore the porker as an accessory of the dance in Papua and Melanesia would be a great injustice. He is indeed accessory before and after the fact. In early stages of the ceremonies pigs are carried round with their feet tied to a pole, and in the glare of the firelight a glimpse is given of the good fare awaiting an exhausted company. The animals are then left tied to the poles under a house close by, from which quarter grunts and squeals punctuate the festivities throughout the night. Occasionally the already lively proceedings are brightened by a pig hunt when an intended victim makes a dash for liberty.

In the Nicobar Islands a regular part of the proceedings is a series of contests between men and wild boars, which have been imprisoned in pens for several days. A man sits on his haunches and holds the

143

tusker at bay by the ears. Naturally enough, gashes are sometimes received from the animal's tusks, but a spearing party stands by to deal with a boar which proves too strong for his antagonist. There seem to be long odds against the pig.

Near the dancing ground fires are lit, and in the uncertain light may be seen groups of performers. Here a wife is painting lines and patterns on her husband's face. There a few girls are having their grass petticoats trimmed so as to give the desired swing. A young man is blowing oil over the body of a friend, whose muscles gleam in the firelight. All along the line old age is advising and criticising with many a reminiscence of famous orgies, while all are chattering in gay anticipation of the shrill whistle which will sound the rally.[187]

Preparation of ornaments is undertaken in a serious spirit. Family heirlooms are brought out and polished, and no small amount of skill and time are expended in fabricating new decorations. In the picture there is a long necklace of canine teeth representing the execution of forty dogs (1). The necklace extending round three sides of the photograph is expressive of much patient effort in grinding small cowrie shells flat before they can be strung (2). The discs, or *koios*, of which one appears in the centre and four on the left, consist of a dark pattern made from the real turtle shell, which is moulded into a saucer cut from white shell. The cutting and paring require great skill, for the implements used are generally a boar's tusk, shark's teeth, or an old nail. *Koios* are made only by people near Hall Sound, New Guinea (3). *Toeas*, or shell ornaments for the arms, are highly prized, and a native earning only £12 a year will willingly pay £5 for a good specimen (4). The half-moon pearl shell is worn on the breast, and no marriage ceremony is complete without one

(*Upper*) ORNAMENTS FOR MALE DANCERS, HALL SOUND, PAPUA; (1) DOG'S TEETH
NECKLACE; (2) NECKLACE OF COWRY SHELLS; (3) ORNAMENTS CUT FROM
TURTLE SHELL (KOIOS); (4) ARMLETS (TOCAS); (5) PEARL SHELL BREAST
ORNAMENT; (6) PENDANTS OF WALLABY TEETH; (7) TURTLE SHELL
EARRINGS; (8) NOSE STICKS.

(*H. M. Dauncey, London Missionary Society*)

(*Lower*) DANCING CLUB, SANTA CRUZ GROUP.

(*By permission of Trustees, British Museum*)

or more of these changing hands (5). Two nose
sticks of long heavy pattern have been carefully
cut from a clam shell and ground into shape (8).
Large pendants made from wallaby's teeth are
worn on the breast, and to these are attached dry
husks which rattle with every movement of the
wearer (6). Seven small turtle shell earrings are
shown, and of this variety of decoration some women
will wear as many as twenty in one ear (7).

Each person who accepts an areca nut from the
messenger has pledged himself for the dance, and
for important occasions three thousand nuts may
be distributed. A later message sustains interest by
announcing the number of pigs which are to be killed,
an item of news which sets all hands busy for some
days getting their feathers in order and polishing
ornaments.

Tattooing has a significance of a religious and
social kind much deeper than the ornamental function;
but this is not to be altogether neglected.[188] We
have seen how careful the girls are to have themselves
tattooed, and what pain the boys will stoically
endure with the same end in view. In dealing with
displays of tattooing at dances, attention was called
to the part this decoration plays in sexual attraction,[189] when grass petticoats swing and uncover
beautifully tattooed designs.

When considering the subject of body marking,
Joest[190] laid too much stress on the decorative and
sexual aspect of the problem, for a brief consideration
of the ritual and prohibitions connected with tattooing, likewise the historical facts showing great
antiquity and extensive migration of the practice,
dispose of the too facile " decorative " explanation.

Among the Long Glat women there is an elaborate
system of tattooing which commences at the first
menstrual period ; the backs of the fingers are marked

K

with concentric circles, and a year later the designs are carried over the backs of the hands to the wrist. The feet also are tattooed during the same periods that the hands are being treated, and about the age of eighteen or twenty the fronts of the thighs are covered with designs. The ladies believe that after death those who have been tattooed with the orthodox designs on hands, feet, and thighs will be able to bathe in the heavenly river Telang Julan, and in consequence of this they will be able to pick up the pearls which lie in the bed of the river. Partially tattooed women will remain on the banks of the river to watch their more fortunate sisters reap a rich harvest, while the untattooed women will not be allowed to approach the banks of the mythical treasure stream. These beliefs are not confined to any one tribe, but are universal among the Kenyahs, the Klemantans of the Upper Mahakam, and the Batang Kayan.[191] Tattooing must not be done at seed-time or harvest, or if there is a death in the house. There are food restrictions and other prohibitions.

These well-elaborated beliefs are quite easy to understand, and appear natural enough when considered in the light of the general beliefs concerning heaven.

Hawaiians had divine patrons of tattooing whose images were kept in the temples of those who practised the art professionally, and every application of their skill was preceded by a prayer addressed to them that the operation might not occasion death, that the wounds might soon heal, and that the designs might be handsome.[192]

An association of religious ideas and body marking might be carried out by collecting a number of instances having reference to corporal decoration at times of spiritual revival, as for example during dedication ceremonies of adults or children, or at times when the religious sentiments are aroused and expressed by a pilgrimage. Then in addition to these points there are the questions of the operation being performed by priests, sorcerers, and the like, under conditions which suggest that there is some association of the tattooer's art with magical and religious rites. " In Fiji tattooing was carried out by priestesses in secret recesses of the forests."[193] Many Marquesan signs have a decisive and arbitrary character highly suggestive of a hieroglyphic system, the interpretation of which is confined to the Tuhunas or priests, now very few in number.[194] Among Taiyals and Paiwan of Formosa, tattooing is always done by priestesses. A newly married couple on return from their honeymoon build a hut where the bride has her face tattooed with the insignia of matronhood. The design, which extends from lips to ears, is always pricked in by a priestess, who also unites the blood of bride and bridegroom at the wedding ceremony.[195] The weight of evidence reviewed as a whole is in opposition to the view of Marquardt, who says " Ich bin mit Jöest der Ansicht dass die Priester zunachst mit der Sache (i.e., tattooing in Samoa) garnichts zu thun hatten."[196] But Jöest wrote on tattooing in 1886 before anthropological method was developed, and his work is concerned more with details of technique than psychological and sociological considerations.[197]

Turner speaks of two patron goddesses of the tattooer's craft, namely Taema and Tilafanga,who set out to swim from Fiji in order to introduce their art into Samoa, repeating as they swam a formula inviting the inhabitants of Samoa to tattoo the women, but not the men. The fatiguing journey caused the goddesses to muddle the formula, and they arrived chanting " Tatu the men, but not the women."[198] Mr. G. M. Brown's version of the story is more

elaborate for, after remarking that Taema and Tilafanga were worshipped as deities presiding over the
tattooers' art, he gives legends concerning the origin
of these deities, and concludes by relating the story
of the swim from Fiji to Samoa, during which the
two goddesses became interested in diving for clam
shells,and so arrived at a reversion of their message.[199]

Dr. Tylor has a similar story relating to the
mythical origin of tattooing, which attempts to
explain why some people tattoo their women, while
others mark only their menfolk.   A messenger was
sent from Fiji, where the women are most generally
tattooed to Tonga, where the practice of tattooing
men was most common until a few years ago.   The
messenger landed safely in Tonga repeating " Tattoo
the women " but not the men.   After accomplishing
his long swim without mishap he stumbled over a
tree stump when landing, and was so disturbed that
he inverted his message, arriving at the chief's house
repeating, " Tattoo the men, but not the women."
A work recently published in Germany deals in detail
with the subject of tattooing in Samoa, where,
contrary to expectations, Marquardt found that the
ancient art is still flourishing.[200]   Even now, all the
men, and from sixty to seventy per cent. of the
women, are tattooed most elaborately in the ancient
manner.   This persistence of habit and exact reproduction of design is very remarkable when one considers
the civilising influences which have been brought to
bear on the Samoan people, and the admixture with
races for whom tattooing would have very little
attraction.   The illustrations given in Marquardt's
work show that the most elaborate designs of the
artist are inscribed on the thighs and buttocks, which
are usually covered.[201]   If ornament only was the
object of the body marking, it seems natural to
suppose that after years of contact with Europeans

some other form of decoration would have been substituted.

THE MUSEUM COLLECTION

Primitive musical instruments are made in a most ingenious manner, and their variety and distribution are surprising. Their scientific classification is a task of great difficulty, partly on account of numerous allied forms, and the confusion which has arisen through difficulties of terminology ; the words " harp ", " piano ", " banjo ", " fiddle ", and so forth being used with special connotations known only to those who employ them. Clearness of definitions, acceptable to ethnographers generally, would be of great advantage in the further elucidation of problems connected with the evolution and distribution of primitive musical instruments. The archives of the British Museum are stocked with every variety of percussive, wind, and stringed instrument which primitive man has invented, and, in addition to these, there is a large and varied assortment of masks and ceremonial dresses which have adorned savages of every country. Here are hideous masks worn to add to the impressiveness of witch doctors, whose dances aim at the exorcism of demons of disease. There, are bright-coloured streamers, tiaras, and crests of gorgeous feathers, along with a vast array of fibre petticoats, shoes and mocassins beautifully beaded ; in short, every form of accessory which could contribute to the impressiveness of the dance.

Drums there are in abundance, varying in size from a small tom-tom, to be carried under the arm or round the neck, to a huge wooden cylinder five feet high, covered at one end with a sheet of lizard skin. Magical drums whose music is supposed to transport a Siberian Shaman to the world of spirits are to be

found, and in appropriate place are weird instruments
decorated with human bones. Thigh bones were
used as drumsticks, and the melancholy beating of
these uncanny instruments from Ashanti has oft-
times summoned victims for human sacrifice. Friction
drums from various African tribes, for example the
Ba Tetela, Bu Shongo, Ba Kete, and Kwilu, are of
special interest on account of the method of manipulation. A rod, covered with resin or like substance,
projects from the lizard skin membrane covering the
upper end of the wooden cylinder. The operator
strokes his hand up and down this rod, which by
communicating the vibration to the membrane,
produces a note. So that, although the instrument is
of drum-like form, the sound is produced by vibration,
not percussion. From Melanesia and the Malay
States are large wooden drums without skin membrane,
the vibration being caused by beating the edges of a
slit in a wooden cylinder with a heavy mallet.
Signalling drums, consisting of hollow wooden
cylinders, are representative of the Congo Free State,
Polynesia, and many regions of the Amazon Basin.
Such drums, suspended from the bough of a tree, when
beaten with a wooden mallet, can be made to emit
various notes, each of which has a definite meaning,
and so, under suitable atmospheric conditions,
messages may be sent a distance of fifteen miles.
A chief among the Boro and Okaina people of South
America stands between two signal drums, which he
beats with rubber-headed drum-sticks, sending out
a call for war or social festivities. The drums are
male and female, the latter having pendant breasts
inside.[202], [203]

Trumpets and horns, made from wood, shell, and
antlers, are very common. A particularly gruesome
fetish horn from a juju house, Andoni Country,
Southern Nigeria, is ornamented with human skulls.

(1) DRUM SOUNDED AT HUMAN SACRIFICES, W. AFRICA.
(2) " PIANO " WITH RESONATOR, BABANGI TRIBE, BELGIAN CONGO.
(3) FRICTION DRUM, BAYAKA, KWILU RIVER, BELGIAN CONGO.
                    (*By permission of Trustees, British Museum*)

The Maoris of New Zealand, likewise the Indians of
Guiana, have contributed flutes made from the leg
bones of a fallen foe, while from the Congo Free State
(Ba Bangi tribe) is an instrument with a keyboard,
provided with a resonator manufactured from the
calvarium of a human skull. So it comes to pass that
a non-musical tribesman may contribute very directly
to the music of his people.

Rattles, drums, and whistles are all common in
the collections representing the music of North
American Indians, and from the Eskimo are drums
and tambourines. Representative instruments of
South America are trumpets of wood and bark, drums,
and flutes of Jaguar bone. A very interesting, single,
stringed instrument, played with a bow, comes from
the Gilyak tribe of North Eastern Siberia, and from
the same people are wooden jews' harps, rattles, and
fish skin tambourines used by the Shamans or
medicine men. The Ainu people of Yezo, Japan,
are presumably of no great inventive power, for their
only musical instrument appears to be a small bamboo
jew's harp. From Tibet are whistles constructed from
bamboo, and the bones of an eagle's wing; there are
also banjos and guitars with three or more strings.
In addition to these are drums, conch shell trumpets.
flageolets, and cymbals, all of which have played their
part in the mystical Lama's ceremonies of unexplored
Tibet. Tibetan masks are without doubt the most
frightful productions of their kind, though those of
Ceylon vie with them. The Tibetans have a " Jew's "
harp, in addition to a cunning contrivance of three
bamboo harps of different tones, which are held in
the left hand and played simultaneously. Several
musicians play in unison, and the instrument is
carried in a case of bamboo, prettily decorated with
chevron-shaped carvings and bands of coloured
quills. The long Tibetan oboes and their lugubrious

sound will long be remembered by those who heard them in London when the Everest film was exhibited.

The Veddas of Ceylon have no musical instruments, neither have the Fuegians. With respect to the Fuegians, it may be said that, wandering almost naked on the cold inhospitable shores of Magellan Strait, subsisting on a diet of shell-fish and berries, can hardly be provocative of mirth and a desire for the merry sound of musical instruments. The Andamanese possess only one musical instrument, a sounding-board, usually beaten with the foot to keep time during dances and solos. A similar contrivance is used by the Punans, a wandering jungle tribe of Borneo. How is it then that the Andamanese' near neighbours, the Nicobarese, have bamboo flutes, in addition to two kinds of palm-wood fiddles played with a bow ? Have the Nicobarese a stronger innate musical tendency ? or are they better off in respect of materials and leisure ? The explanation is that the Nicobarese have been more directly influenced by forces operating from Southern India and the Malay States, so benefiting from a culture contact which has escaped the negritos.

The Burmese are expert makers of brass gongs of excellent timbre. The Shans use these instruments, though they do not make them, and in the house of a chief are always to be found at least three gongs whose tones harmonise. In every household there is one of these instruments which is struck as an " Amen " after reading of Buddhist scriptures. The sonorous gong is frequently sounded in a chief's residence to indicate that he is about to eat, sleep, or pray, and must not be disturbed.[204]

Australian aborigines have few contributions to make to an ethnographical collection of musical instruments. Their utmost effort, directed toward the production of musical sounds, consists of beating

a stretched skin, or clashing two boomerangs. Gongs
are found in all the Pacific Islands except Santa
Cruz and Florida. From New Zealand one observes
trumpets of wood and conch shell, flutes of wood and
bone, likewise gongs. Some of the flutes, like specimens
from Fiji, New Caledonia, Formosa, Malay Peninsula,
Borneo, New Britain, and New Guinea, are made to
be played with one nostril. Gongs from the Admiralty
Islands, have been used as a special signalling
apparatus in addition to fulfilling the ordinary musical
function of an instrument of percussion. New Ireland
has contributed a peculiar musical instrument consisting of a block of wood with four projecting tongues,
which give out different notes as the fingers are
drawn across them.

Naturally enough, the collection of primitive
musical instruments from Africa is of colossal propor-
tions. Mohammedan influence appears to have caused
a very wide distribution of some form of fiddle, and
there is every probability that Egyptian culture
assisted the development of African instruments,
which are drums, flutes, pipes and harps in endless
variety. Stringed instruments are present to represent
the musical culture of such Nilotic tribes as the
Dinka, Mittu, Achloi, and Ja-Luo, while from the
Nandi are friction drums and the zither. Zulu
tribes contribute drums, rattles, xylophones and a
species of piano with iron keys. Xylophones are by
no means confined to Zulu tribes, examples are
provided from areas occupied by the Bu Shongo,
Bakete, and Kwilu peoples. Friction drums are
present in collections representing the musical life
of the Ba Tetela, Bu Shongo, and Ba Kete ; and nose
flutes, which are met with in the Malay Archipelago
and Melanesia, appear to be commonly in use with
the Ba Huana. In the Congo Free State stringed
instruments are rare except among the Ba Teke,

Azandeh, and Abarambo.   When speaking of
West Africa one may say that drums are found
everywhere except among the Buhe, while harps are
numerous from large areas such as the Cameruns
and Liberia.   The island of Madagascar has contributed drums, flutes, clarionets, shell trumpets,
and cymbals.

The course of evolution through which any
primitive instrument has gone is the special study of
ethnographers, who are able to show how the gong
may have developed into the bell by the insertion of
a pellet which produces a rattle.   Perhaps in the
first instance a small piece of metal became accidentally
detached in the casting, and eventually this scrap
of metal has become the swinging clapper of a bell.
Rattles may, in the first place, have been suggested
by the rattling of dried seeds in a gourd, a natural
form of instrument, which, improved upon, leads
to the rattle made of raw hide containing several
pebbles.   The natives of North Western Rhodesia
use a musical instrument which illustrates possible
early stages in the development of the xylophone,
for the essential features are a series of slats of wood,
each capable of emitting a distinctive note when
placed across a gourd, which acts as resonator.
Burmese xylophones illustrate the evolution of a
continuous resonator used instead of separate gourds,
which, by the way, were ingeniously attuned to give
different notes by making the top edges of various
thicknesses.   There is evidence to show the evolution
of the friction drum from bellows, and the two
are often tribally associated.

In my collection a small instrument from Southern
Nigeria, having many varieties of wide distribution
in West Africa, illustrates the ingenuity of primitive
man when manufacturing an instrument which
requires a resonator, and keys of different vibrating

lengths. The sound-box has been shaped from a solid block of wood measuring $4\frac{1}{2} \times 8\frac{1}{2} \times 1\frac{1}{10}$ ins., and over this is fastened with wooden rivets a thin lid having a thickness of $\frac{3}{10}$ in. In the middle of this thin lid is a rectangular aperture one inch long and $\frac{1}{10}$ in. wide. The keyboard consists of nine strips of cane, the upper extremities of which rest on a thin cylindrical piece of wood. Under the middle of the keys is a second strip of wood which serves the purpose of a violin bridge, inasmuch as it lifts the vibrating portions from the resonator. The nine cane keys are held firmly to the resonator by a binding of rattan, which is arranged so that the keys may be pushed to and fro in such a manner as to alter their vibrating length. The tips of the cane keys are highly polished by the fingers of the operator, who, after stroking them, allowed them to be released with a twang. His fingers then came into contact with the resonator in which slight smooth depressions have been formed.

Such an instrument is used on special occasions for the amusement of chiefs. A native performer will improvise complimentary verses in honour of his chief, or white master, and will often, for his own amusement, stroll along twanging the cane keys of this little instrument.

Nose flutes are used by people of the Malay Peninsula, chiefly Sakai, Semang, and Jakun.[205] In Formosa the nose flute is played by men only, and is, among the Taiyal and Tsuou tribes, of a sacred character, being used only in celebration of victory or other special occurrence. "Not even a priestess will play on the nose flute."[206] The mapping out of the distribution of this instrument in South East Asia, including Borneo and the Philippines, likewise through many Polynesian and Melanesian islands would, if accompanied by careful comparisons of

structure and methods of use, lead to interesting facts
respecting culture contact and migrations of peoples.

MODERN METHODS OF RECORDING
PRIMITIVE MUSIC

The illustration shows Mr. Frank Hurley recording
Papuan songs which are rendered into the trumpet of
the instrument in the presence of an interested crowd
of natives. The human voice, like a photograph, is
regarded by backward peoples as a concrete part
of the person, something which can be used by an
enemy to the detriment of the owner, as for example
nail-parings and hair are used in working aggressive
magic. But a tactful investigator is able to gain the
confidence of his subjects; perhaps he does so by
giving them his own photograph so they can if
necessary work counter magic.

The phonograph, rhythmograph, metronome, pitch-
pipes, tuning forks, and a cinematograph should
form part of the equipment of a scientist who intends
to investigate the music of primitive people. Records
can be taken by a person of slight musical ability
whose data may be worked out by musical experts
at home. This method was followed by Dr. Seligman,
who collected phonographic records of Vedda music
from Ceylon. The details of these wax impressions
were later studied and reported on by Dr. C. S.
Myers.[207]

Phonographic apparatus must include wax
cylinders, recorder, reproducer, pitch-pipe, and spare
parts in duplicate. At times long tedious journeys,
for example across Central Australia, have to be
accomplished, so it is advisable to secure an instrument
weighing not more than 20 lbs. When recording, the
best results are secured when the operator is working

SCIENTIFIC METHOD OF STUDYING PRIMITIVE SONGS, DANCES AND FOLK LORE IN NEW GUINEA.
(*Frank Hurley's " Pearls & Savages." By permission of Messrs. Putnam's Sons*)

in a temperature of 60 to 70 degrees. Blanks require careful packing in separate tin cases lined with oiled paper, a precaution which should render the wax proof against the damp heat of some tropical countries.

The rhythmograph is a special drum-like apparatus which records the beats of the drum, stick, or rattle used by natives for marking time during dancing and orchestral music. Beats made by the operator are communicated by a kind of lever which scratches on a rotating smoked surface. Immediately below the scratches are a series of marks made by a pendulum every half second. Varnish, and specially prepared sheets of paper, are the only accessories of this simple instrument, which is obtainable for the sum of five guineas. Operations begin by smoking the paper over a stove or paraffin lamp, then fixing it by a gummed edge to the cylinder of the rhythmograph. The clockwork is wound, and the levers which mark the movements of the drum and pendulum respectively are placed lightly on the rotating surface of the cylinder. At the time of recording rhythm, full notes should be made concerning the general nature of the performance, its social significance, duration, whether carried out by people of all ages, and both sexes, together with any other data which serve to render the music more intelligible ; there may be for example a dramatised story connected with the music and dancing.

Records of solo and orchestral music are easy to take, though in case of the former there may be some difficulty in getting the operator to sing into the trumpet, especially if he knows that the voice can be reproduced.

All emphasis in vocal music should be carefully recorded, likewise the use of tremulo, falsetto, glissando and the average range of voices among any particular tribe. Such data should, of course, be collected in suitable categories headed " range among adult males," " females ", and " children below the age of puberty ". The music of primitive man is an unrestrained and quite spontaneous means of expressing emotions, so the observer should make full notes concerning evidence of grief, sadness, joy, exultation and irony. The general structure of tunes, frequency of part songs, refrains and solos should all be noted, while a constant watch must be kept in order to detect sacred whispered words, use of obsolete and archaic language,[208] also examples of poetical licence. As a rule primitive man is quick to learn the music and words of strangers. Ability in this direction forms an interesting line of musical and psychological study, during which the grafting of native words to European tunes, or vice versa, may be detected. Tests of ability to reproduce successive notes of varying pitch, and observations respecting primitive man's preference for certain intervals, are all worthy subjects for investigation, and data suitably tabulated might be very enlightening to a trained musician concerning himself with origins and evolutionary theories.

A study of the technicalities of dancing should invariably be accompanied by queries respecting the origin and purpose of the function. In our own time and country dancing is merely a means of expressing aesthetic, sexual, and social emotions, but among primitive people the dance is a more integral and expressive form of the whole social life. Custom is adamant among savage races, and in dancing, as in other departments, there are often stereotyped movements from which no individual dare depart. The secret " Dukduk " society of Melanesia prepares its novices for a social function in which complicated dances play an important part, and during the novitiate young men have daily instruction in dance movements which are severely criticised when the performance is given in public. At such times older members look on and show their disapproval of a mistake by shooting arrows at the offender.

The cinematograph is a most valuable asset when recording dances of any description, but, in addition to a pictorial representation, the inquirer should endeavour to give accompanying tunes, under the notes of which are written symbols " l ", " r ", " h ", to denote left foot, right foot, hop, and so forth, underlining (*r*) being used to denote particular vigour or stress of the performer. Careful notes should be made concerning the dress and accessories of all performers, also with respect to any leaders or principals who appear to function as masters of the ceremonies. It may be necessary also to note the presence of some paid professional who has travelled a distance in order to teach new words and movements.

Musical instruments should be purchased if the natives can be persuaded to part with them, not an easy task when an instrument has acquired a sentimental value through repeated use at tribal festivities through a prolonged period. Moreover certain instruments, especially drums, acquire sanctity through association with magico-religious ceremonies. Examples of this are the use of drums for helping the Shaman to gain access to the world of spirits ; use of the " medicine " whistle in North America, or the " Flute of Heaven " in exorcising demons in the Ba Thonga tribe of South Africa.

The emotional promptings of primitive man may never have led him to construct a musical instrument, but nevertheless he is ever ready to express himself in dancing. Even the Andamanese, who know no musical instrument save the sounding-board, have weird expressive dances carried out in the glare of firelight which casts strange leaping shadows. There is a little clearing in the jungle where more than a hundred painted men and women have assembled. A combined audience and orchestra of women sit on one side of the clearing, prepared to keep the rhythm of the dance by vigorous hand clapping ; the composer of the dance theme is stationed where he may be seen by all, and with one foot on the narrow end of a sounding-board he poses, resting his weight on a spear or bow. The dancers race into the arena and perform their parts with passion and energy, unerringly keeping time to the sounding-board in a series of hoppings and genuflexions which carry them to and fro across the arena. There is a sudden shriek, a helter-skelter of performers, and the student of primitive music is left alone to watch the fantastic and spectre-like shadows cast by flickering embers.

PROBLEMS OF MUSICAL ABILITY

In the dense jungles of Central Africa or Brazil, in the burning sands of mid-Sahara or Central Australia, and along the surf-beaten coral shores of a thousand Pacific Islands, there are musical evidences of a homogeneity of emotion which, in spite of the disrepute into which the term " psychic unity " is falling, clearly show a common basis of aesthetic taste varying only in complexity and form of expression.

Before surveying the broad field of primitive man's ability in dancing, instrumental music and song, the reader should have in mind the problems, not of detail, but of broad basic principles which are likely to arise.

If we considered musical ability in relation to geographical position, climate, and biotic factors generally, we might hastily conclude, and not without some justification for doing so, that musical expression among Tasmanians, Australian Aborigines, Veddas, Andamanese, Fuegians and Eskimo is undeveloped, in some instances because of unfavourable environment; for maybe the whole energy is absorbed in hunting for the immediate necessities of existence. This conclusion will not remain tenable when one considers that Pygmies of the dense Ituri forests of the Congo, and Bushmen of the Kalahari Desert are good musicians, for the precarious conditions of their lives are inimical to progress. The Australians have no musical instruments except a drum improvised by stretching an opossum skin across the knees, but they have an elaborate social system and are clever workers in stone, while their spear throwers and boomerangs are ingeniously made. The Eskimo have only a drum, perhaps more correctly a tambourine, and a bone-whistle, but they have found leisure for expert carving in bone and ivory.

One must avoid begging the question from the start, but the reader will, as evidence accumulates, find himself trying to answer the biological conundrums : What are racial characteristics ? How were they formed and stabilised ? And in what manner are they perpetuated ? Can these racial attributes be entirely eliminated by adverse conditions or by social and religious repression ?

We must, however, consider impartially this question of musical ability in relation to racial heredity, geography, and social custom. The musical ability and poetical sense of the Polynesians can in a measure be understood by considering their long romantic migration from Northern India right through the Pacific to Easter Island and northward to Hawaii. But the negro, most musical and ingenious of all undeveloped peoples, has no exceptionally

L

inspiring history or environment, and his religions are somewhat dull and depressing.

Alluring plaintive music of the " Paradise of the Pacific " speaks of moonlit sands and swaying palms. The natives of Hawaii have hereditary and highly honoured bards who compose and perform songs which are recitative of the deeds of famous ancestors, while in the improvising of dirges and love songs they are equally expert. To quote from the words of Mr. W. F. Blackman[209] such songs " have in their syllables the dash of the surf, the cry of the wind, and the warmth of the tropical sun," a statement which expresses the very feasible idea that natural surroundings determine the emotional life which finds its truest and most forcible expression in song and dance, especially during some communal or individual crisis. Thus Lo-Lale, a poet of Hawaii, wrote at a time of mental stress, caused by the desertion of his wife, the lines :—

> Farewell my partner on the lowland plains.
> On the waters of Pohakea.
> Above Kanehoa.
> On the dark mountain spur of Maunaina.
> O Lihue, she is gone !
> Sniff the sweet scent of the grass.
> The sweet scent of the wild vines
> That are twisted about by Waikoloa.
> By the winds of Waiopua (the brook).
> My flower !
> As if a mote were in my eye,
> The pupil of my eye is troubled.
> Dimness covers my eyes. Woe is me.

Blackfeet and Sioux Indians are in the habit of making ceremonial inter-tribal visits, on which occasions appropriate songs are rendered, while a chief, riding through the camp on a magnificent white horse, keeps time for the singing by shaking a string cf bells. Walter McClintock[210], a recent investigator, states that on first paying attention to Indian vocal music, he was not favourably impressed by the untrained voices of the women, who sing an octave higher than the men ; but later the opinion was modified, for the author states : " Having learned several of their airs, and having mastered the peculiar intonation and different voice vibrations, so that I could join in the singing, the wild beauty of their music dawned upon me. Their music seemed so thoroughly original in its conception, and so unique in the method of expression, that I became filled with a desire to do something for its preservation. Development through past ages has been independent of all sources of inspiration or colouring other than those provided by the natural environment of mountains, forests and plains. Their stimuli have been a wild life of hunting and warfare, their sun-worship, and those emotions and passions which are common to the human heart the world over." The quotation suggests that Indian vocal music is a free, spontaneous means of expressing emotions, which result, not only from innate tendencies, but from physical surroundings of wild rugged grandeur, which have power to mould the psychic life of primitive men.

Mr. R. W. Williamson[211] was interested in the different degrees of musical ability shown by the adjacent Mekeo, and Mafulu mountain people of New Guinea, and this point he considers in relation to geographical position and evidence of artistic skill and taste.

The ideas of artistic design shown by the Mafulu people are simple and crude in the extreme, for they are quite unable to represent any object living or dead, and cannot even draw a symmetrical curve. Melanesians of the Pacific, for example Solomon

Islanders, are able to make life-like pictures of animals and men. Possibly the Mafulu are representatives of an early Pygmy race who occupied New Guinea before the arrival of the Papuans and Melanesians. Poverty of art among the Mafulu may be due to absence of totemism which encourages portrayal of animals supposed to be associated with the genealogy of the people. " On the other hand, the Mafulu are a distinctly musical people, thus conforming to what I believe to be a general rule that music is more indigenous to hill country than it is to plains." This hypothesis opens up an extensive inquiry; perhaps the truth is that mountain dwellers, through isolation, retain their music, just as they do their speech and ancient dances, because they miss the main streams of migratory influence. The Mekeo are an artistic people, and it is strange that they have never been able to pass their skill to the Mafulu.

The points emerging from these facts are that one branch of aesthetics, for example decorative art, can be developed to perfection, while another faculty, say music, remains dormant. Perhaps Williamson is right, there must be some strong social or religious motive and compelling force behind aesthetic expression of any kind.

The Mekeo people certainly place a high value on their songs and dances, and a cause of quarrel may be that visitors presume to perform a cassowary dance which is looked upon as the exclusive property and copyright of the hosts.[212] Apart from dancing, there is the question of accuracy of pitch to be considered, and in speaking of people of Rubiana giving a concert it has been said : " The old man certainly had a true musical ear, for he never once made a false note during quite a long continuous song, neither did he drift out of the original key by a perceptible fraction of a note."[213] Bamboo flutes were played, but these hindered rather than helped his accuracy, for little connection appeared to exist between the instrumental and vocal sounds.

MUSICAL ABILITY IN AUSTRALIA. TASMANIA AND THE PACIFIC

In dealing with musical ability in the Pacific, there is, in considering Australia, an interesting instance of dancing being well developed along with vocal music, while musical instruments are entirely absent. The map will make clear the positions of islands mentioned, but the terms Papuans, Melanesians and Polynesians may be more difficult to understand. Melanesia includes part of New Guinea and the neighbouring islands, also the Chain of Archipelagoes that extends from the Admiralties to New Caledonia including Fiji. The primitive stock appears to have been a very dark coloured and invariably woolly-haired people, to whom the name Papuans can perhaps be best applied. They form the majority of the inhabitants of New Guinea and the basis of the populations of the Melanesian Archipelago.[214] The original home of the Polynesians was in Northern India, from whence they made voyages as long and romantic as any achieved in the world's history.

Among many primitive people musical compositions are produced only by bards, but there is no such restriction among the natives of Australia, any of whom have the right to invent a corroboree which may take the form of a simple dramatic performance in which recent events are reproduced. Great care is always taken to avoid any mention of names of the dead, for ghosts are said to be easily disturbed by the living who are incautious enough to mention the deceased by name. Scenes depicting daily occupa-

tions, such as gathering honey and climbing for
opossum, are popular ;   so also are dramatic performances representing the saving of a person from
drowning.   Thus the corroboree in some instances
illustrates the foundation of dramatic art.   The
commercial value of music is of some interest, and
W. E. Roth[215] states that the copyright of the
performance may be sold to another tribe who make
payment in kind.   This tendency to barter, combined
with the extensive wandering of all tribes, results in
the spreading of songs and dances over very extensive
areas, so much so that a tribe may be totally unaware
of the meaning attached to the words in use.

The Tasmanians, who became extinct in 1870,
had many dances and good vocal ability, but no
musical instrument.   They could sing well, all joining
in concert and sweet harmony.   They began say in
Key D or E, then went sweetly from note to note,
and so gradually that it was a continuation of harmony
but very melancholy.   This is merely a general
impression, for no records were made.   They had
dances in imitation of animals, which they mimicked
by leaping and running round a fire, pausing now and
then to squat on the ground and beat it with their
hands.   The exercise was violent, and many performers
dropped out exhausted.   An early observer says that
their principal amusement was the corroboree, which
was sometimes   held in the   daytime but   more
frequently at night. " They light a large fire, round
which quite naked they dance, run, and jump, keeping
time to their own singing,which is far from unmusical.
These songs are various, each having its own peculiar
dance intended to illustrate some action or effect
from causes.   In the kangaroo dance they give great
leaps, sing and shriek until their frames can stand
it no longer, and they give up in the uttermost state
of exhaustion."[216]   Some of their dances are lascivious,

others medicinal; at times the tribes assembled at full moon and gave a kind of bestial *bal masque*, in which the performers looked like demons dancing in the firelight bedaubed with grease and red ochre. Large tufts of bushy twigs were entwined round their ankles, wrists and waists, and these completed their toilet. The significance of Tasmanian dances is guesswork, but some had a sacred character, for women and children were excluded.[217]

During the dance their minor tones and monotonous voices were accompanied by playing upon greasy Kangaroos' rugs, which were rolled up so that when struck with the open hand they gave the sound of a muffled drum. Other people joined in the rude concert by beating time with two sticks with a precision adapted for an orchestra, so providing rhythm for a dance in which females were " unadorned and genuine as when they were imported into this world."[218]

In entering into New Zealand we have to deal with a highly cultured type of Polynesian who conquered the islands in the fourteenth century A.D.

The Maoris of New Zealand possess intellectual qualities of a high order, and with the advent of educative influences have proved themselves capable orators and statesmen. It is not surprising, therefore, that they should give evidence of musical talent combined with dramatic power. In the old days of relentless warfare, dancing was the means of arousing warriors to frenzy, and should this stimulus prove insufficient resort was made to a drug which threw the nervous system into a state of violent excitement. At such times warriors indulged in a prolonged gymnastic dance imitative of the conflict about to ensue. Imaginary foes were slaughtered, and the conquerors made their performance hideous by the most grotesque facial contortions. Shortly before conflict Maori women danced in front of their men, and there is no doubt that Maori dancing was employed to arouse the most violent aggressive emotions connected with conflict. Such dancing, along with the cannibal festivities marking the conclusion of successful raids, represent the grosser and least admirable aspect of Maori talent. Vocal music was generally of a sad plaintive variety in the minor key, characterised by the use of small intervals and a scale not employed by modern musicians. Australian music, along with the primitive mimetic dances of now extinct Tasmanians, may be considered as a separate technique ; but on the other hand the music of the Maori bears a relation to the musical culture of Polynesia, and in all probability Maori dances and musical instruments were derived from the region of Tahiti via Raratonga.

A missionary[219] of the early nineteenth century describes the South Sea Islanders as being peculiarly addicted to pleasure in the form of music and dancing, " to which they give nearly as much time as to all other occupations." Their music wanted almost every quality that could render it agreeable to an ear accustomed to harmony. It was deficient in all that constituted excellence, being boisterous, and with the exception of the soft and plaintive warblings of the native flute, the music of Polynesians was distinguished chiefly by discordant and deafening sounds.

In the night the silence would be broken by the beating of temple drums announcing that a human sacrifice would be made next day. At Maeva the people trembled, for each feared that he might be seized as the victim. The conch shell trumpet was important because of its use in temples and war canoes. Songs were of great antiquity, and contained trustworthy historical facts metrically expressed in their verses which gave the names and genealogies of priest-kings, and the names of war canoes with accounts of their journeys. Some songs were merely descriptive of everyday tasks, others were idolatrous and impure.

The possible origin of Maori dances in religious festivals of Polynesia is suggested by the attitudes of performers who, according to one authority, " posturise, wave the arms, and bend the body, as if before a shrine." It is not certain, however, that the dance was secularised when woman were admitted, for the Polynesians had their priestesses.

In connection with the musical abilities of Australian aborigines mention was made of the sacred " bull roarer " whirled at magical ceremonies, and among the Maoris too this simple instrument was employed at the death of a chief, whose body was protected from evil spirits by the shrill musical note of a circling slat of wood. With the Maoris, musical instruments were represented by the drum, conch shell trumpets, nose flutes of wood or human bones, " jews' harps ", and small reed instruments commonly described as " Pan pipes." The trumpet probably had a religious significance, for the evidence tends to show that it was employed by priests and chieftains, usually as a call to arms and a signal of alarm. Triton shells are well adapted to giving forth a voluminous note, made tremulous by the introduction of a tonsil into the mouthpiece, which was usually provided with a wooden appendage for causing the operator's breath to be forced through a narrow passage. Some shell trumpets are made to give forth two distinct notes by the boring of a stop hole, and from Taranaki trumpets provided with two, or even three stop holes, have been obtained. Such hybrid instruments appear to combine the structure and qualities of the flute and trumpet, so illustrating one of the difficulties confronting an ethnographer who desires an exact

and logical classification of musical instruments. Pan
pipes were not in general use among the Maoris, but
in the island of Tonga they were particularly well
developed, and instruments comprising from five to
twelve reeds were commonly employed, though the
scale of notes produced did not show a regular cadence,
and the intervals were not in correspondence with
any which are characteristic of our modern
instruments.

Maori musicians performed upon the most
elementary kind of drum known in Polynesia ; perhaps the instrument might be more correctly described as a gong, for it consisted of a suspended
wooden slab. The reverberation was of great
significance in religious ceremonial, though the Maoris
generally confined their use of the gong to purposes
connected with war, as for example the call to arms,
and the sounding of night alarms.[220]   During dances
Maori warriors preferred the use of their bodies
as percussive instruments rather than the employment
of gongs or drums. The dancer would strike his
chest with one hand,while the other was shaken over
his head ; feet were stamped heavily on hard ground,
and sometimes rhythm was marked by smiting the
right hand against the bent left arm. Samoan
dancers always clapped hands in order to keep time,
while the Tongans loudly snapped their fingers,
producing as much noise as might be emitted by a
pair of castanets, whose origin may be traceable to
this very simple source. Prominent among Polynesian
instruments is the nose flute, which in Tahiti is played
with the left nostril ; in New Zealand with the right.
A collection of Polynesian nose flutes shows a great
variety in the number and distribution of stop-holes,
consequently the notes produced vary in pitch and
interval. In many flutes from New Zealand only
one stop-hole is to be observed, but in spite of this
limitation the pitch of the note could be varied by

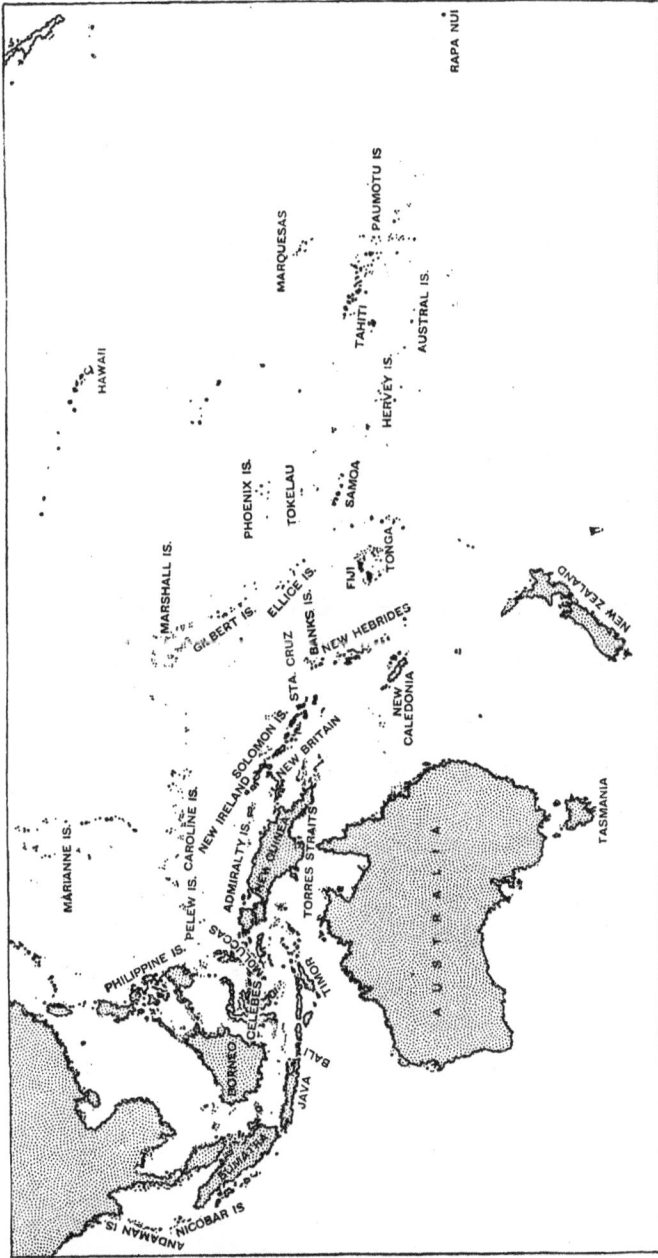

Oceania and Indonesia.

covering a large or small portion of the hole. One hand of the performer had to press the free nostril, hence the development of these primitive nose flutes is checked, and the musical abilities of the operator are prevented by mechanical difficulties from finding free expression.

The Tonga or Friendly Islands, so named by Captain Cook, who visited them in 1773, and again some four years later, are inhabited by a people who are physically and mentally among the finest of the Polynesians. To the student of music the Tongans are of interest because they seem quite unable to separate instrumental and vocal music from the dance, and in addition to this they show a remarkable aptitude for improvising songs based on European tunes and metres.[221]

Men who are about to take part in a musical performance arrange themselves in one or two straight lines and begin with a few slow stately evolutions, the time of which is marked by twirling light wooden paddles overhead. Three large wooden drums are used to mark rhythm, and around these are grouped the members of the choir. Vocal effort is restricted to a measured and wearisome reiteration of one or two phrases, though it is of importance to note the early stages of evolution in part singing, for while several voices maintain one note the others continue a melody. A simple melody may last as long as twenty minutes, relieved only by a crescendo from time to time, but this matters not, for all vocal and instrumental music is subordinate to the dance.

Sir Basil Thomson[222] describes a dance named the " Otuhaka," for which the singers generally sit in a single line, loaded with garlands and anointed with scented oil. The chief feature of the performance is the gesture dance, for which the performers usually remain seated. All parts of the body, even the toes, have their rhythm, and the precision of the gestures is extraordinary. The performance commences with a long solo on the drum, consisting of the same bar insistently repeated. After thirty bars the gesture dance begins in silence to the same monotonous accompaniment, until at last the leader bursts into a song, which is punctuated by drum rhythm, which never varies except to make a slight rallentando towards the finale. All performers sing, the leader taking the melody, and the chorus the second part. There is constant repetition of the same theme until the leader gives the signal for a change by striking a higher note, on which signal gestures change, the time quickens, and the chorus breaks into the coda ending with a long-drawn note, and a sudden dropping of the voice down the scale.

In Tonga we have the opportunity of witnessing a special evolutionary change resulting from contact of natives with colonising Europeans. The Tongan native composer will retire to the bush and improvise a complete composition—comprising words, gestures, and music—which is often founded on a familiar hymn tune, so that to European onlookers the performance is grotesque in the extreme. Pathetic lamentations are popular, especially when based on a hymn tune of long meter, and as rivals to these are boating songs and odes to nature. Major and minor scales are both in use, and frequently a good effect is produced by blending of male and female voices ; women are in the habit of marking time by moving heads and arms, while their bodies remain stationary.

Recent investigation brings to light some astonishing facts respecting the Tongans' aptitude for utilising European melodies, and among the tunes employed as a basis for native compositions are many well-known hymns, marches, and lines from Mozart's " Twelfth Mass."[223]

It appears that many natives can read tonic solfa notation, They have great aptitude for part singing, and already there are choral anthems very creditably performed. Evidently missionary enterprise has laid hold of a valuable innate faculty, which may be utilised for intellectual, social, and religious progress. Inhabitants of Tonga have a generous share of aesthetic taste, which is characteristic of the Polynesian race, and a very pleasing sight may be witnessed when a band of shy young girls, decorated with garlands entwined in their black hair, and accompanied by lithe, active young warriors, come dancing through the village. Neither is a touch of humour wanting, for old women, still young in spirit, make grotesque efforts to join in the dance in imitation of the graceful movements of their juniors.

Bamboo drums are the characteristic instruments of the Melanesian Islands to the South East of New Guinea, with the exception of Florida, and Santa Cruz, where, according to the observation of Bishop Codrington,[224] native drums are unknown. Usually the drum of Melanesia consists of a cylinder of hollow bamboo with an open longitudinal slit whose edges are made to vibrate by beating with a stick or mallet. Such drums are said to be resonant and well toned, consequently the music, produced under favourable atmospheric conditions, can be heard several miles away. In Banks Island there appears to be an innovation in the art of producing drum music, for two or three drummers, performing on the same instrument, can produce a sequence of notes very creditable in rhythm and tone. At Saa the method of combining rhythm is varied by having three drums of different size and tone which, in the hands of skilled performers, produce quite pleasing compound rhythm.

The drums of Leper's Island have the distinction of being exceedingly large, and so cumbersome are

they that handles have to be provided for transport.
Great care of these instruments is necessary in order
to shield them from sun and weather, and as the
huts do not provide sufficient accommodation a small
thatched house is built over each instrument.
Horizontal drums are most general in Melanesia,
but in Ambrym and the Southern New Hebrides
the instruments are made to stand erect, the base
being buried in the ground, and the tapering upper
portion is shaped into a human face. Bamboo
drums, when very large, are held by an assistant,
so that the operator is free to use both hands, while
on the contrary small instruments are carried by
dancers, who use the one free hand as a striker.
Improvised drums are readily made by beating with
the fists on a thin slat of wood stretched over a hole
in the ground, or the music may be produced by
pounding with the fists on a mat placed over the
top end of an upright hollow cylinder of wood.

With regard to wind instruments employed by
the Melanesians, it may be said that Pan pipes and
bamboo flutes are in common use. In Mota and
Florida, Pan pipes usually consist of seven or eight
reeds, which are sometimes arranged in a double
row, one pipe of each pair being open at the bottom,
the other closed. Pipes of Leper's Island consist of
three distinct reeds, and in order to supplement the
rather feeble notes the operator assists with vocal
sounds. The single bamboo pipe appears in Florida,
and when, during a dance, several performers play
distinctive tunes in unison, the effect is musical
to European ears. In Leper's Island a long bamboo
flute, sometimes having a length of three feet, is a
favourite form of wind instrument, and as four stop-
holes are provided a variety of notes may be produced
For accompanying dances the musicians of this island
use a double flute composed of two lengths of bamboo,

about two-thirds of an inch in diameter, united by a bamboo knot. Strong noises are not favoured during an accompaniment, so the performer regulates the volume of sound by pressing his fingers against the open lower ends of the pipes.

The " Jew's harp," common in the Solomon Islands, but unknown in the Eastern Islands of Melanesia, is a wind instrument, generally regarded as a toy, which can be made to produce a thin musical note by allowing the outgoing breath to play against a thin tongue-like projection of bamboo.

A most ingenious musical contrivance, employed by the Solomon Islanders, possesses features which are somewhat analogous to those of our own violin and zither. The essential parts of the instrument comprise a bent reed or bamboo a foot long, and half an inch in diameter, supported by a longitudinal bridge. Two strings, tuned to the same note, are stretched over the bridge, and the performer, while holding the instrument in his mouth by means of a projection in its back, strikes the strings with a small reed plectrum held in the right hand, while at the same time he uses the fingers of the left hand for manipulating the vibrating portion of the string.

Castanets, consisting of shells, nuts, and seeds, are worn on ankles and wrists during the dance, while in Santa Cruz dancing clubs, decorated with these, natural products are waved so as to produce a rhythmical jingle. Inhabitants of San Cristoval are in the habit of wearing castanets on their wrists while employed in nut scraping, and, in order to relieve the tedium of the task, they move their hands in time to a tune, so producing a musical tinkle in rhythm. In Banks Island a feast is incomplete without a multitude of big and little drums, to the noise of which is added that produced by shaking dry shells in a bag of matting.

When speaking of the Indians of Guiana we have to mention a form of instrument known as the aeolian harp, because of its operation by the wind. Far away in the Melanesian Island of Aurora are similar contrivances consisting of bamboo rods pierced with holes. These instruments are fastened in the tops of high trees in such a manner that the breeze passing over them produces weird musical sounds.

Popular superstition regarding the shrill musical note of the bull roarer has already been touched upon, and from Banks Island there comes a further instance of this small instrument being credited with supra-normal power. The inhabitants believe that the shrill piercing note has the power to drive away ghosts, and for this protective purpose the instrument is energetically whirled, while in Mota the music is an adjunct of the funeral feast.

Among the Mafulu people of New Guinea a boy is not allowed to manufacture a drum unless he has gone through a special initiatory rite.[225] The ceremony, which usually takes place when the boy is ten or twelve years of age, commences with the killing of a pig and a dancing performance in which uninitiated boys and girls are not allowed to take part. Sometimes the rite is performed for young girls of seven or eight years of age, but no matter whether the novice is male or female, he or she must stand on the dead pig and beat the drum after being shown how to do so by an elder of the tribe.

A youth who has attended the ceremonial climbs a tree from the wood of which his instrument is to be made, and there he must remain, sometimes made more comfortable by a small scaffolding stage, until the drum is completed. Food is brought to the base of the tree by the boy's wife or mother, who attaches it to a string which is used to haul up the provender into the branches. During process of manufacture the novice must keep the tympanic end of the drum toward the wind, for it is believed that during this period the wind endows the drum with its power to give forth a resonant musical note.

The Roro and Mekeo people make a number of boys retire together to a secluded part of the bush, where they remain isolated until the instruments are completed, and during this period several important taboos must be observed. Food consumed during this period has to be cooked in a small round pot, for the belief prevails that a boy who eats food prepared in a large pot will develop an abdomen so great as to prevent him from participating in the village dances. Water must be taken only from the axils of leaves, and fish must be avoided, for the puncturing power of the small sharp bones is thought to exert an evil influence over the membrane of the drum. No woman is allowed within sight of the drum during manufacture, and should a female see the instrument by accident, the boy who owns it has to commence work again.

In Banks Island, New Britain, The New Hebrides, and elsewhere there exist secret societies which act in an intimidating manner towards those who have not been admitted to membership. Young children, whose parents pay the fees, are admitted to an enclosure where they learn the songs and dances peculiar to the particular society which they wish to join, and when all are proficient a public ceremony is held in the village on a moonlight night.

Members of the society stationed in adjacent bush cause loud noises by bursting bladders. Enormous head-dresses, masks, and ceremonial paints are worn in order to give the affair an air of mystery, which impresses the spectators, so rendering extortion practicable. In some societies there is much torture and privation during the months of preparation, during which care is taken to acquire the dancing steps with perfect accuracy, for at the public ceremony old members of the society may stand near and discharge their arrows at a faulty performer. The leader of the band carries a bamboo drum with which he controls the ceremonies, while the rest of the troupe carry bows which are waved in time to the music. These dances have no religious or superstitious character, and may be regarded as purely social in function, serving as a bond of unity between members of the same society, who alone have the right to learn and perform them.

In the various islands of Melanesia there are considerable differences in the grace and elegance of popular dances. Women of Florida are heavy, ungraceful dancers who circle round stamping their feet, and swaying their bodies, while screaming an accompaniment. On the contrary, men of San Christoval perform a graceful dance, in which time is kept by waving beautifully carved clubs in time to the music provided by numerous bamboo pipes.

Every great man of Santa Cruz has a dancing ground of his own adjoining his residence, fenced round with huge discs of coral, and in Banks Island private dancing enclosures are ornamented with elaborate carvings. In the latter island, dancers, wonderfully adorned with glistening palm fronds, advance and retire in two lines, interlace in intricate curves, cross and recross, while stamping in perfect time, so causing a rattling of their anklets, which are constructed from empty nuts. A bamboo drum provides the music in Banks Island, while in Maewo and Aurora clapping of hands is the usual accompaniment of dancing steps.

In the Loyalty Islands everyone loves music, dancing and singing of tunes mostly in a minor key, which is sad and melancholy to Europeans.

"A peculiarity about these tunes is that no white man on the island, to my knowledge, is ever able to reproduce them." A few bards on Lifu, who composed and taught the songs which the people sang to the accompaniment of dancing, usually began the performance slowly, and continued with accelerated speed as the excitement increased, their steps keeping pace with the music until, becoming quite exhausted, they threw up their arms, gave a loud yell, and collapsed. There are songs for men, songs for women, duets, and solos, fighting songs, love songs, songs to sooth to sleep, but no comic songs.[226]

The story of Polynesian migrations in the Pacific is one which fires the imagination, and it would provide a romantic narrative for a novelist who had the historical facts and ethnological knowledge. Scientific people have adopted such terms as "The Mystery of Easter Island," and the "Riddle of the Pacific," when discussing the facts of migration and culture contact. In the far east of the Pacific is Easter Island, or Rapa Nui, discovered by the Dutch navigator Roggewein, who landed there on Easter Day, A D., 1721. The island is the furthest eastern outpost of the Polynesian race, and there ever arises the speculation as to whether these bold navigators crossed the stretch of 2,000 miles to the coast of South America. The origin of huge stone figures remains a mystery; what secrets of adventure, lost religions, daring voyages, and defunct peoples are symbolised by the grim stone figure in the portico of the British Museum we do not know.

The inhabitants of Easter Island appear to have been inferior to other Polynesians in musical ability, or perhaps they lacked the materials for making instruments, or decay of custom set in through too long isolation; though isolation as a rule tends to preserve original customs and artefacts, which provide useful material for the sociologist and antiquary.

In common with Polynesians the Easter Islanders had tattooing and many other customs. Their singing and poetry were primitive and monotonous, being of the slow recitative kind dealing with any event which had arrested their attention. The Easter Islanders had no bamboo instrument, neither had they the nose flute of the Polynesians with its two finger-stops. Like the Maoris they could have used human bone, but they had not even the bone whistle of that people, let alone the bone flute or flageolet. The only hole through which they ever whistled was a natural hole in the top of a three-foot high stone on the north coast. Nor had they anything that could be called a drum, apparently there was not sufficient timber to make a wooden sentry gong like that of the Maoris.

Throughout the Pacific, shark's skin drums are common, but although the Easter Islanders caught sharks and had hollow gourds which would have served as resonators, they do not appear to have thought of utilising the materials for drum making.

They had a kind of sounding apparatus made by placing a flat stone over a half-filled gourd which was sunk in a hole three feet deep. On this depressed stage an operator danced to give the time to two lines of performers, one on either side of the resonance pit. The conch shell was blown for a war call, and sticks were struck to mark time, but the general musical development as shown at the time of discovery and since observed is noticeably lower than that of the average Polynesian.[227]

On the whole the environment of the Polynesians and Melanesians has been favourable to musical development. There has been no lack of materials, for plant and animal life abound, and in addition to this the Polynesians have a long romantic history, genealogy, and religious system, all of which are powerful factors in stimulating musical expression and poetry.

MUSICAL ABILITY IN AFRICA

The musical ability of the negro is granted by all observers, and I have read of only a single exception, namely the Bushongo, who have a poor capacity for music. These people have, however, great skill as weavers, embroiderers, carvers in wood, and workers in metal, in which aesthetic crafts they have not their equals in the whole African continent.[228]

Here is an instance of one branch of artistic proficiency being developed at the expense of another, for one cannot believe that the Bushongo differ from their racial type by the absence of such a constant racial factor as musical ability, which is found all over the continent in conjunction with skilled work in pottery, metals, and textiles.

At a very early age negro children learn to dance even when so small that they are hardly able to walk, and of this juvenile effort Dudley Kidd[229] gives an amusing description, while Mr. N. W. Thomas has made a charming photograph of such a scene in Nigeria. Rhythm appeals to the Kafirs more than melody, and children prefer dancing to singing.

As regards ingenuity in making musical instruments the African is unequalled, and there would be great interest in finding to what extent he owes this achievement and skill to the knowledge of the Egyptians, among whom four or five thousand years ago stringed instruments and flutes were well developed. The musical ability of the negro is something racial, it cannot be accounted for by geographical surroundings of a very inspiring kind,

and his ancestor worship and fetishism is of a somewhat sordid type ; there is no great spiritual stimulus.

Bushmen of the Kalahari Desert have, in spite
of their nomadic existence, and primitive material
culture, evolved a system of aesthetics in which art
and music are prominent.   Bushmen rock paintings
are remarkable for their realistic representation of
wild animals such as the lion, hyena, elephant, and
eland, while portraits of human figures, though often
lacking in proportion, are well executed.

In speaking of the music of Bushmen, Dowd[230] says
that dancing takes place almost nightly inside or
outside the huts.   If the hut is large enough the
spectators circle the inside, while a bright fire blazes
near the entrance.   The performer places a rattle on
each ankle and dances until out of breath, when he
is relieved by another.   On moonlight nights the
dance is an open air function at which people form a
circle, which jumps and swings until limbs are
exhausted.   It is in fact a general truth that primitive
people consider dancing to the point of exhaustion
a most necessary part of a musical performance.
The drum is the chief musical instrument employed,
and this is made by stretching a hide over a wooden
vessel, the beating being accomplished by fingers
instead of drumsticks.   A kind of harp or musical
bow is improvised by attaching a gourd resonator
to the end of a bow, so that the sound given by
twanging the string may be amplified.

Another instrument of a vibratory nature is the
" goura," which is made by placing a flat quill in the
end of a bow, between the string and the rib.   This
quill when blown communicates a vibration to the
bow string, and a flute-like noise is produced.   This
is another form of musical bow to which more detailed
consideration is given a few pages ahead.

The consensus of opinion regards Africa as the

home of the most musical or primitive tribes, many of whom possess professional travelling minstrels, and everywhere there appears to be a gift for improvising songs, while many old traditional ones are perpetuated from generation to generation. Natives nearly always sing when paddling canoes, carrying burdens, or hauling a log, and with regard to my own experience among various Sudanese workmen in the province of Sennar, it may safely be said that manual labour in such forms as digging, pushing a cart, or hauling a stone, was never performed without the accompaniment of an unvaried refrain. Most Bantu music is peculiarly monotonous, droning, and minor in its sound, owing to the commencement on a high note and gradual descent in intervals not in use among ourselves. A Shiré canoe song illustrates the refrain characteristic of native vocal music, and at the same time shows the effect of Jesuit influence.

> [231]" I have no mother ; I have no father. I have no
> mother Mary : I have no father. I have no
> mother to be nursed by her : I have no mother.
> Thou art my mother, O Mary."

The few lines serve to illustrate the effect of imported religious ideas on native music and poetry, and in all probability the lines are the result of Romanist teaching in a Portuguese province. On the Lower Zambezi canoe men receive small pay, and their mistrust of traders who employ them is expressed in the words, " You cheated me of old " or, " Thou art slippery, slippery, truly."

No matter what African tribes are under consideration, the evidence is strong and unanimous in declaring the musical ability of negro races, and emphasising the importance attached to communal dancing as an expression of individual and social emotions. " The Baloki people of the Congo quickly acquire new tunes ; their voices are loud, clear, steady, and flexible ; they sing from their chests, and very few harsh voices are to be found."[232] Men and women unite in forming a chorus, the rhythm and time of which are preserved by beating a stick on a plank or clapping the hands. Solos are introduced, and as a rule the time is in recitative measure, preserved when canoeing by tapping a drum attached to the side of the boat. A boat's crew approaching without the usual song is regarded with suspicion, and no doubt music has served the very practical purpose of distinguishing friend from foe. Itinerant professional singers visit villages, where they settle temporarily in order to teach their latest compositions to the inhabitants. Topical songs, when sung in canoes, are useful as a means of disseminating news, and these combined with local songs, in which the daily events of village life are recorded, form the greater part of the Baloki repertoire.

A perusal of the literature concerning musical ability in West African tribes serves to corroborate the previously expressed opinion that the African native is probably the most musical of all primitive peoples. After a wide experience in Northern and Southern Nigeria, Major Tremearne [233] is of the opinion that the " natives have good memories and a wonderful instinct for rhythm ", while native words are quickly improvised and set to European music. Popular songs such as " Home Sweet Home ", " Auld Lang Syne ", and the " British Grenadiers " are quickly learned ; neither had Major Tremearne any difficulty in securing a native military band for the troops he was training.

Native musical instruments are varied and numerous, and among these the auto harp, which is widely distributed in the Eastern part of Northern

Nigeria, is of very ingenious construction. The instrument is made of stiff reeds, about eighteen inches in length, placed side by side and fastened in position with strips of vegetable fibre. Each of these reeds is cut into three strips, which are not totally severed from the matrix, but are left adhering at each end of the main fibre. A small bridge is inserted at each end of the fibres which have been separated, and a sounding board is provided by plaiting the fibre strings on the under side. The sounding-box contains dried seeds, which are shaken while the operator twangs the strings with his fingers. The notes are said to resemble those on the lower register of a piano, and variety of pitch is obtained by sliding rings of vegetable fibre up and down the strings. Among the Hausa, guitars in many forms are common ; xylophones abound in most parts of West Africa, though they are not in use among the head hunters of Northern Nigeria. The syrinx, and flutes of various shapes are numerous, and their manufacture is very simply accomplished by utilising hollow stalks of guinea corn. In many instances the notes emitted by these grass flutes are sweet and liquid, the favourite intervals being thirds and fifths.

Another authority on Nigeria[234] describes the musical faculty of the people, especially that of the Ekoi, as being wonderful, and the same author is impressed with the number, variety and ingenuity of musical instruments. Drums vary in size from a small tom-tom to the large communal instrument of the village. This large tambour, in honour of which many songs are composed, is to an Ekoi native what the quarter deck is to a sailor. In the absence of a chief the native, coming to the town as a stranger, salutes the big drum by bending before it until the tips of his fingers touch the ground. Drum language is used as a means of signalling from one village to another, and most natives are very expert in the production and interpretation of musical sounds which convey news of war, or call members of various units to a public festival.

An instrument described by P. A. Talbot very closely resembles the one detailed by Major Tremearne. This stringed instrument is made from a mid-rib of palm-leaf three to four feet long, from which strips of fibre have been loosened, save for two inches, which remain to preserve a junction at each end. Under these strips of fibre small bridges are inserted after the manner of our modern violin construction. Two musicians are required to operate the instrument, for while one strikes the strings with two slender wooden sticks, the other intermittently applies a small calabash, which acts as a resonator, and in addition may be made to produce " runs " by passing it quickly up and down a vibrating string.

As a compromise between percussion and stringed instruments there are friction drums. The " humming " drum is made by the Badjohn (elephant) people and may be observed further north among the Batetela. " This instrument of torture," says Mr. E. Torday,[235] " looks like an ordinary drum two feet high and one foot in diameter, prettily ornamented with carved designs. There are two membranes, and on one side of the drum is a hole into which a funnel-like calabash is fixed with rubber. Toward the narrow end of this horn a hole is covered partly with webs of spiders. When the drum is beaten air is forced and sucked alternately through the web-mesh, and a sound like that given by a droning aeroplane is produced.

The friction drum does not appear to find favour with European observers. Karl Weule, describing such an instrument, says that a blade of grass passes through the middle of the diaphragm and, " by rubbing a moistened finger down this stalk, as the little wretches are perpetually doing, a noise is produced so excruciating that even my carriers, who are not precisely sufferers from nerves, take to flight when they hear it."[236]

Throughout British Central Africa the professional dancing man is a familiar figure. He usually carries a one-stringed fiddle with gourd resonator attached, the striker being a bow which cannot be separated from the instrument. A more elaborate instrument has six strings strung on a piece of wood across the mouth of a large gourd, which is decorated with bits of jingling metal and shell, whose noise adds effect to the twanging of the strings by the thumbs of the operator. A similar instrument is the " pango," which resembles the " limba," except that a plectrum is used instead of the thumbs. The " Mtangala ", played by women only, is a slightly bent reed with a string uniting the two ends. One end of this little bow is held between the teeth of the operator, who uses her fingers for plucking the single string. An instrument known as the " Sansi " has a set of iron keys fixed on a wooden sounding-box and is played with the thumbs. It has a piece of metal fixed on the front of the box, and to this are attached discs cut from the shells of snails, which clash when shaken. Flutes, about a foot long, are made from bamboo, cut near the joints, so that the instrument is closed at both ends. The stop-holes, three to six in number, are bored in the side of the flute, so that the operator may produce a variety of notes which are very sweet in tone. Whistles, constructed from the small horns of goats and antelopes, are used for calling and signalling, while the almost universal wind instrument known as " Pan pipes " are found in some form throughout Central Africa.

Various kinds of " piano " are in common use in

Central and Southern Africa, and although the use of the word " piano " may be somewhat misleading it is difficult to find a more correct substitute, though perhaps the name xylophone would be an improvement.

The " Timbila ", well known in the region of Delagoa Bay, is portable, and has wooden keys fixed on a flat frame, which is sometimes made in the form of an arc, so that the performer can easily reach all the keys when the instrument is hung round his neck. Resonators are provided by hard shells and gourds, which are attached under the keys. A more cumbersome form of the same instrument, known as the " Njanja," is constructed from two logs of soft wood, each a yard long, laid on the ground in such a way as to support the " keys ", or crossbars of wood, which may be as many as ten in number, merely laid on the supports or fastened thereto by wooden pegs. Musicians of the Ronga Tribe carefully tune their instruments by cutting away the under-side of the keys in order to make them give a variety of sounds of different pitch. The instrument is played by striking the keys with two sticks, and in this respect it approximates to the xylophone. At some performances two of these instruments are employed, and on such occasions the players cause one to give leading tones, with which the secondary instrument is made to harmonise.

Drums vary in size from mere toys of four inches in diameter to huge cylindrical logs five feet high covered at the top end with goatskin or ox-hide. Some small drums, which might be more correctly described as tambourines, are covered with snake or lizard skin, and the functions of these instruments may vary from a summons to human sacrificial rite, or a call to arms, to a merry rumble which signifies the commencement of a village dance. Truly this instrument gives expression to a variety of emotions, and its various tones have power to awaken unmitigated terror, pugnacity, strong self-assertion, or the lighter feelings which prompt the organising of a communal merry-making.

Trumpets made from gourds, horn, and ivory have a very wide, probably universal distribution among African natives, and in order to enliven the dance and mark rhythm rattles are extensively employed. The commonest rattles are made from hard-shelled fruits, about two inches in diameter, which are allowed to dry, so that the seeds become hardened inside. Dancers are in the habit of fastening these instruments to their ankles, or of carrying several attached to a stick, which is shaken throughout the performance.

The most popular Thonga wind instrument, frequently used as a toy by children, is made from the hard shell of a kaffir orange, through which two holes are drilled. An operator blows through one hole, while he uses his fingers alternately to close and open the other. A very simple flute, the "nanga," is used by boys, who are able to produce two notes, and a more elaborate wind instrument, provided with a mouthpiece and three stop-holes, is made to produce very pleasant tunes. Associations of musical instruments with magical practices are known all the world over, and it is not surprising to learn that the Thonga have a magical flute described as "The flute of Heaven." [237] This instrument is manufactured from a hollow bone five inches long, covered with skin and filled at its larger end with black wax; inside is a vulture's feather which is said to keep the flute clean. Three lucky beans are inserted in the wax substance which is manufactured from the pulverised heart, eyes, bones, feathers, and flesh of the vulture. A native musician who sees a thunder-

storm approaching blows into the flute and shouts :
" You ! Heaven ! go further, I have nothing against
you, I do not fight against you," an action which is
supposed to divert the storm in another direction.

Probably in the construction of this magical
flute there is an idea of sympathetic magic, by means
of which the powers of flight possessed by the vulture
are communicated to hostile powers.

A " Bunanga," or band of specially trained
musicians, is to be found in every clan of royal descent,
and admission to this select company of performers
is gained only after specialised training and com-
petition in a musical contest. The trumpets used
are manufactured by specialists, and each musician
carrying his own instrument waits near the big drum
when a performance is about to begin. When the
large drum beats slowly the musicians march in a
circle, playing while making grimaces and wild
gesticulations. Actions vary with the sounding of
the big drum, and when a particular soft note is
produced the trumpeters form into line and carry on
a slow perambulation. Gradually the pace of the big
drum accelerates, in response to which the trumpeters
begin to quicken their movements until a maximum
velocity is attained, and the performance, as is the
rule with primitive peoples, continues until complete
fatigue and shortage of breath cause a termination
of the festivities.

M. Henri Junod,[238] a Swiss missionary well
informed by years of residence among the Ba Thonga
tribe, gives us to understand that these natives of
Portuguese East Africa attach great importance to
the part which music plays in their national life, and
no important occasion, be it birth, marriage, death, or
war, is allowed to pass without an appropriate dancing
festival. During these dances rhythm is usually well
marked both by stamping and instrumental music,

while spears are often brandished as a further assistance in keeping time. Singing is common throughout the tribe, and few natives are totally devoid of musical sense, as custom demands from everyone ability to take part in national or tribal festivities. Frequently these songs are sung in a minor key, and the general rule is to start on high notes and descend with gradual diminuendo until the voice dies away. Short ditties are very popular, and people on their way to break quartz sing :—

> " Stones are very hard to break
> Far from home in foreign land " ;

words which are undoubtedly true, and not devoid of pathos. Sailors' songs, which accompany the actions of rowing or pushing a boat, are sometimes harmonised in two or three parts, and in addition to the songs of everyday life there is a bard who goes from one village to another singing and dancing. These professional musicians compose new songs and dances, which bring in a livelihood when they are performed before an audience, or taught to the best dancers of every village visited.

A most ingenious stringed instrument is made by the Ba Thonga, who attach a calabash or sound-box to the lower extremity of a bow. The performer holds the bow at the lower end and produces notes by beating on the lower third of the string with a little stick, and here it may be noted that the usual method is to tap, and not stroke, the strings of a primitive musical instrument. So far as my reading goes, there has been no definite statement concerning the stroking of a string in the manner adopted by a violinist, though on the other hand there are numerous examples of producing musical sounds by tapping a string with a bow. The Thonga musician acquires great flexibility in his fingers, and not only can he grasp the bow at its lower extremity, but in addition to this, he manipulates the vibrating length of the string, and so, of course, controls frequency of vibration and pitch. The large drum is regarded with a certain amount of reverence, so that when a skin cracks no one is permitted to look inside, and a specialist is requisitioned to do the repairs. This big drum is the signal for war, for announcing a fatality, and among some people there is a belief that the instrument contains the skull of a powerful enemy.

The A-Kamba have a great variety of musical instruments, and among these Mr. C. W. Hobley notes, " a one-stringed harp or fiddle with a piece of gourd or calabash to act as a sound-box.[239] This instrument, played with a tiny bow, is said to be the only one of its kind in East Africa.

The A-Kamba make bamboo pipes with a gourd attached to the end in order to magnify the sound, and many natives are adept in the use of this instrument, as they are with trumpets made from antlers of the eland and koodoo. Pipes and whistles, fabricated from the horns of a buck, are used for signalling, and expert use of these has often saved the A-Kamba from a disastrous and unforeseen attack from their warlike neighbours the Masai, the most truculent race of Kenya Colony. For use during the dance, a small drum open at one end and beaten by the hands is most popular. Similar small drums, suspended horizontally, and beaten with both hands, produce music which is regarded as having a special magical potence for driving away the *aiimu* or evil spirits which have taken possession of the sick. The largest drum of all consists of a hollow wooden cylinder, four inches in diameter, and four feet long. The open lower end is made to rest on hard ground, so that great resonance is obtained from the earth, which acts as a sounding-board. Over the upper end is a membrane, and the whole contrivance may be carried by means of a large wooden handle.

Thus far we have tested negro proficiency in music and invention by an itinerary touching all points of the compass, but we have not yet penetrated the densest glades of the Congo forests. The Wanandi are not true Pygmies, but they are sturdily built people of small stature, who work a little then dance a lot before working again. Their type of dance is similar to that of the true Pygmies, in being made up of close rings of men and boys who dance round three big drums hung on posts in the centre. The outer rings are formed by short sturdy women, many of whom will dance while carrying babies on their backs. There is a great difference between the energy displayed by women and men, for the former shuffle along very slowly, wagging their heads and twitching their bodies, while the men show great spirit and zest. The master of the ceremonies from time to time leads small parties of boys and girls, all blowing shrill whistles, to the centre of the uproar, where there is violent jumping, pantomime, and facial contortion. These were the antics which so amused the Pharaohs of Egypt three thousand years before the Christian era.

A small present of salt to the Semliki Pygmies is sufficient inducement to start a dance. Drums are rapidly hitched up to a post and the fun begins; even little children bedaubed with red and black pigment pat their small protruding abdomens and dance round in imitation of their elders.[240]

The skill of these small people with the bow and poisoned arrow is a terror to their neighbours. Christie does not think the poison would kill an elephant, possibly the stories of it having done so

N

are exaggerated ; but precision of aim is the wonder of all observers. There are several conjectures respecting the origin of these Pygmies. Are they the remnant of an ancient race which peopled Africa in ages past when the continent was entirely covered by forest ? Are they refugees of a one-time well-developed people who have been stunted by ages of seclusion from the sun.[241] They are not particularly ape-like, but show considerable intelligence and are masters of gesture language. The illustrations in the South Kensington Museum of Natural History show two of these pygmies who were brought to London, and Schweinfurth has a drawing in his " Heart of Africa."

The Pygmies celebrated the arrival and departure of a big game hunter with dancing of the type already described, performed in the glow of the firelight and accompanied by the most melodious music the traveller had ever heard during extensive African exploration. Instrumental music came from a species of Pan-pipes and a small drum. " The forest dwarfs I put down as the best native musicians in Africa."[242]

Among the many instruments mentioned as illustrative of African ingenuity none is more deserving of attention than the musical bow, which in its earliest stage was the temporary conversion of the archer's bow into a musical instrument as described in the old legends of Greece. The Bongo of East Africa make such a bow of string tightly stretched and struck by a slender strip of split bamboo. The sounding-board is not made of a calabash, but resonance is given by placing one end of the bow to the open mouth of the performer, while one hand is left free to tap the string. This is a common pastime with boys when herding goats, and the lads seem to apply themselves very earnestly and with obvious interest to their musical practice. " The ingenious use to which they apply the simplest means for obtaining harmonies testifies to their penetration into the secrets of the theory of sound."[243]

The Damara of South West Africa, seeking temporarily to amuse himself, converts the bow used in hunting into a musical monochord, which serves to while away his spare time. When required for music all that is done is to add a little string bracing toward, but not at the centre, of the bow, so drawing the bow-string to the bow. This not only tightens the bow-string and raises the notes producible, but also divides it into two unequal lengths giving different notes. Mr. Balfour[244] shows the transition to stages where the bow is a musical instrument only, and he maps out its distribution in Africa, North India, Cambodia, Borneo, Timor, New Guinea, the Solomons, the New Hebrides, Hawaii, the Marquesas, Mexico, Brazil, and Patagonia.

In describing the music of the Niam-Niams, Schweinfurth used a phrase which adequately summarises the musical abilities of African peoples in general : " Music rejoices their very soul, and the harmony they elicit from their favourite instruments seems to thrill through their very nature."

MUSICAL ABILITIES OF AMERICAN ABORIGINES

The stoicism and reserve of primitive people of North America is a popularly entertained idea, and from earliest days we are led to regard the " Red " Indians as the most unemotional of primitive races. Although this conception has some foundation in fact, there is considerable evidence tending to show that Indians, in common with most primitive people, can abandon all reserve and give free expression to emotional excitement, more especially at times of social crisis, and at periods when tribal welfare demands the intervention of a supernatural power, which is evoked by music and dancing.

The explorer George Catlin,[245] who was well acquainted with most Indian tribes, remarks, that musical instruments were few, and those examined, chiefly rattles, drums, whistles and lutes, were found to be of rude and imperfect construction. Rattles are of very simple construction, usually consisting of bags of raw hide, which have been thoroughly dried and sewn up with several pebbles enclosed. This instrument serves the purpose of a metronome in marking time during singing and dancing, and in addition it may function as a drumstick, which is used for beating a primitive instrument readily improvised by stretching taut a hide held by two members of the orchestra. Drums are of an elementary kind ; often they are more of the nature of a tambourine, consisting of a single piece of raw hide tightly stretched over a hoop or empty wooden keg. In some instances the drum is more complete, for a hide is stretched over each end of a wooden barrel, and drumstick rattles are employed in beating time. The object of the performer appears to be the production of a maximum amount of noise by a vigorous use of his rattle drumsticks, which in some instances are replaced by strikers having small hoops covered with buckskin in order to soften the sound.

Catlin was of the opinion that the mystery whistle, employed by medicine men in magical performances connected with veneration of animal emblems, is ingeniously constructed on a principle entirely different from that of any wind instrument known in civilised nations. Even when a careful observer watches an Indian performer he is unable to reproduce the notes, neither is it an easy matter to produce any

sound whatever. The notes produced are said to
be peculiarly sweet and liquid, and in this respect
they differ essentially from the sounds emitted by
the war whistle. This latter instrument, which is
highly prized among all Indian tribes, is usually
manufactured from slender bones found in the foot
of a deer, or in the legs of wild-fowl. Whistles so
made are generally six or nine inches in length, and
are ornamented with porcupines' quills of various
colours. No chief or leader goes to battle without
one of these instruments suspended round his neck.
Two notes may be produced, one extremely shrill
is employed as a signal for the attack, the other less
piercing note is a call for retreat ; the operator
changes the note by blowing into the other end of
the whistle.

A deerskin flute provided with three, four, or six
holes, as stops, is in common use, and the tones are
said to be not unpleasant, although the intervals are
quite different from any produced by the wind
instruments of civilised races. Undoubtedly the
intervals are very irregularly graduated, but the
criticism which states that the performers have very
little taste or ear for melody is too harsh in view of
modern research, which tends to show that primitive
man has his own codes and ideals respecting rhythm,
scales and intervals. His standards are not the
same as ours, and to assert that he has no music, is
equivalent to stating that he has no logic, no religion,
no morality and no social life, merely because his
principles, premisses, and ideals differ widely from
those to which civilised man has adhered. The deerskin
flute has its amorous uses among numerous tribes of
the Mississippi valley, where the young Indian
suitors seek to further their cause by playing the
instrument near to the wigwams of the ladies they
desire.

As a means of emotional expression, dancing appears to be more fully developed than its twin sister, musical accompaniment, for whereas the latter is usually employed merely for the purpose of marking time and rhythm, the former is capable of expressing many complex social and religious sentiments. Vocal accompaniments of the dance are in general of a very crude nature, consisting of harsh guttural chants interspersed with yelps and barks given out in perfect time not unaccompanied by a certain method and harmony. Music and singing too have their function as a private recreation, and often at eventide the Indian will lie by his fire singing in a plaintive subdued voice to the soft accompaniment of measured beats from the drum. Dancing is of the gymnastic variety, in which four principal steps may be noted, but in spite of the restriction so imposed, figures and scenes, especially those which are imitative of animal activity, are of great number and variety. Some movements are merely grotesque and laughable, others, as for example in the scalp dance,[246] are terrifying in their realistic production of the fiercest emotional tendencies.

In these times of modern ethnological research the music of North American Indians has been carefully studied and analysed. Songs are more important than instrumental music as anthropological studies. Indians have respect for tradition, so that there is a greater stability of songs over a long time. In song and rituals there are archaic forms of language which may have been obsolete for centuries in the spoken tongue, and these express the innermost thoughts of a social and religious kind. " Whatever phase of life of the people we choose to study, we find additional light through the songs which have come to be associated with it. Songs are the property of religious or medicine societies, or of any ritual group, and are sung with recurring seasons. Some persons of considerable musical standing have, without any profound knowledge of it, condemned Indian music as hideously lacking in melody, form, and variety. On the contrary, there is a beautiful melody of surprisingly intricate form which is unappreciated because the critics are fettered by tradition. Composing songs is a general practice among Indians, and it is not confined to a few specially gifted members of a tribe ; everyone sings, and has songs of his own composition.

The Eskimo are fond of dancing and song, but their efforts are of no great excellence. Their only musical instruments are the drum and a bone whistle.

Among Coppermine River natives the only musical instrument is a tambourine, but children, and even adults, at times produce a scale of notes by flipping their finger-nails in succession against their upper incisors, beginning with the little finger. There can, of course, be no fixed intervals in their scale, but different notes are made by the different fingers through modifications of the cavity of the mouth, though the movement is difficult to detect. The drum of these people has a rim of poplar wood from Great Bear Lake, curved to a rough oval and having overlapping ends riveted with iron nails. The membrane is a scraped caribou skin lashed round the rim with codline. The Eskimo never tune their drums to any particular note, but if the instruments show signs of slackness and loss of resonance they rub a little water over the surface.[247]

The Shaman's drum used in séances is perhaps better left for description in connection with various forms of music and magic. Such a drum is in use among the Chukchee of far north-east Siberia, and these people have a somewhat cleverly made whistle. The instrument is fabricated from goose quill or wood and has a thin tongue of whalebone which vibrates from time to time, so producing a sound called the eider duck's voice.[248]

The Amazonian region presents boundless possibilities for research work, and no doubt a careful investigation among Indian tribes in this imperfectly explored country would bring to light many points of interest connected with the musical ideas and ideals of primitive man. Sir Everard im Thurn[249] has recorded a number of interesting details relating to the musical instruments and performances of Arawak and Carib Indians of British Guiana, among whom the social importance of musical festivals is fully recognised. The drum is accorded a prominent place, and along with rattles and flutes is employed in most musical performances.

The first step in the manufacture of a drum is the selection of a suitable tree, usually a palm, from the trunk of which a cylinder of wood is obtained. In order to secure more resonance and a note of higher pitch the walls of this wooden cylinder are considerably thinned, after which membranes are stretched over the open ends. Pieces of jaguar or monkey skin, having been previously extended and dried on a wooden frame, are fitted over the ends of the cylinder. Placed diagonally across one end of the drum is a thin cord provided with a slip-knot, into which a sprig of hard wood is inserted, in such a way that it lies at right angles to the string. The object of this attachment is to cause the ends of the drum to give forth notes of different pitch, for the end of the drum to which string and splinter are attached gives out a more metallic note, possessing a higher pitch than the note which results when the other end of the drum is struck. When selecting the skins of howling monkeys for use as drum membranes the Indian is actuated by the idea that an instrument provided with such a skin will be able to give forth the rolling, roaring sounds characteristic of the howling monkey. This idea suggests a belief in so-called sympathetic or contagious magic, which is commonly found among savage races, who maintain that the qualities of a person, animal, or substance may be transferred by taking portions of such person, animal or substance, and transferring them to new surroundings. Possibly it is thought that the animal itself is present. Thus an Australian native who wishes to be alert and wakeful during the night will suspend round his neck the tail of the bandicoot, which is a wakeful animal, and highly sensitive to impending danger.

One variety of drum extensively used among the Indians of Guiana is formed by stretching the skin of a monkey over one end of a hollow cylinder, which in this instance is made to produce its note by striking the uncovered end ; the hard ground on which the instrument is placed acts as a sounding-board.

Flutes are readily constructed from hollow bones of a jaguar, deer, or even of a human being, though flutes made from the last named are now somewhat rare. By way of decoration, incised patterns coloured red and black are engraved on the bone implement, which is further adorned with tassels of white cotton. A variety of notes is obtained by piercing small circular holes in the hollow bone. Other common wind instruments are wooden trumpets, flutes of wood made from bamboo stem, and Pan pipes, which have an almost universal distribution.

Aeolian harps are very ingeniously made by taking a long leaf stalk of the aeta palm, from which fibre strips are severed along their length, but allowed to remain fixed at the two extremities. Thus the strings of the musical instrument are provided, and in order to give the wind free play over their surface a small bridge is inserted below so as to lift them clear from the leaf stalk, which acts as a kind of resonator or sounding-board. The instrument is then secured in the top of a high tree in such a manner that natural music is produced by puffs of wind blowing over the fibre strings.[250]

Dancing is indispensable at wedding ceremonies, preparations for war, the funeral feast, and receptions given by the head man of a village. The participants are always highly ornamented with paint, bright feathers, teeth, beads, and seeds, while most of them come to the dance provided with sticks to which seeds are attached, so that when the dance is in progress time may be marked by striking the stick against the ground. Other performers beat time with hollow bamboos covered at one end with a membrane so as to form a little drum. Like the dances of so many primitive people, these performances of the Indians of Guiana prove to be extremely monotonous, though in many instances the participants move their bodies in a very stately manner, then, extended in a long line,link arms and move toward a corresponding number of women similarly grouped. For hours, to the accompaniment of song, flute, drum and rattle, these lines will continue to advance and retire until the spectator becomes utterly weary of the monotonous refrain. Time is preserved by a rhythmical stamping in unison on the hard ground, and so vigorous is the exercise that much refreshment is imbibed in the form of " paiwai," a native beer.

Many times our attention has been called to the historical value of songs, and Amazonian tribes treasure the songs of their fathers, which records they will utter in a language they no longer understand. We have had to note the same preservation of archaic language in songs when dealing with the Malay Peninsula, Java, and North America.

Accessories of the dance are great feather head-dresses, necklaces of tusks and beaded girdles. Invitation is given to the dance by signal drums, between which the chief stands and pounds out the message in sonorous notes. Children practise dancing assiduously in the forest, so anticipating the time when they will join the throng. " Out of the silent trackless bush scores of expectant guests all painted and feathered pour into the clearing until some hundreds are gathered." Fires blaze, while bone flutes, pan-pipes and drums make for jollity, which is maintained by imbibing enormous quantities of liquor.[251]

There is among many tribes of Guiana a great ability to extemporise, and with trifling modulation of voice they sing about deeds in war and the chase, or they give way to a flow of sarcastic humour and satire. The singers always conclude with a noise like the barking of dogs by which spirits who rejoice in other's misfortune are driven from the neighbour-hood.[252]

Along the banks of the Rio Paraguay the Indians have not much ear for harmony, and their small flutes and whistles are of a primitive kind, the former being made of bamboo with only one slit, the latter of bone. The drums are constructed by stretching a wet skin over a cooking pot, and from seeds in a dry gourd they make a rattle for beating time to their songs. These, with one exception, have no words, and they are all brief compositions in a minor key. The theme is repeated indefinitely until the singer loses his breath ; primitive people are never half hearted over their music, they always dance until they drop. The Lengua women are not allowed to dance, but their deprivation is not great, for in this tribe only one dance is practised.[253]

The Bororos have hunting songs, war songs, love songs and recitative verses sung in harmony. Vocal music is far in advance of instrumental performance, for the people have only primitive flutes and gourds filled with pebbles. The songs contain progressions in chromatic intervals, embellishments are added as the theme proceeds, but the groundwork is always traditional. Some notes have undoubtedly been suggested by the songs and calls of birds, or by the cries of wild animals, while sounds of crashing trees and storms are well imitated.[254] Such observation takes us back in fancy to the beginnings of vocal music; the Bororos never receive instruction, they just imitate Nature's sounds and copy from one another.

Summary

The review of musical ability and ingenuity in inventing instruments shows the Negro to be the most musical of all undeveloped peoples, and his faculty is something racial, for there is nothing in the environment physical, social, or religious which is specially inspiring. The Polynesian, also naturally musical and poetical, has experienced through wide migrations in the Pacific an environment of stimulating beauty from sun, sea, ocean breeze, and charming islands of the volcanic and atoll types. His religion, social life, history, and genealogy have all supported and developed an innate musical ability from which the Melanesians have benefited by contact.

Indians of North America are well advanced in song and dance, which express their social and religious life, but their instruments are extremely crude and rudimentary in comparison with those of Africa. South American Indians are dancers and vocalists, but their instruments are of a simple kind.

Australian Aborigines have complicated dances,

their vocal music is simple, and musical instruments are entirely absent. The Andamanese are good dancers and original songsters, but have only a sounding-board. Apparently these people, likewise Veddas of Ceylon and now extinct Tasmanians, passed through the early stages of musical development, namely song and dance, which are sufficient to express their social life, but the march of progress in instrumental music never touched them ; they remain, fortunately for the ethnologist, as examples of the early history of man.

The biologist wrestles with questions of the origin of racial characteristics such as stature, head form, and pigmentation of the skin, trying to account for the origin and stabilisation of these factors. The psychologist has scarcely got to work in trying to explain mental differences, though some experimental work has been done in testing acuity of vision and hearing ; while intelligence tests have been made in order to inquire into racial differences between negroes and white people, the experiments being devised to test intelligence as a natural endowment, quite apart from education and environment. Musical ability might be tested by power of discrimination in pitch and sense of rhythm, but the experimental work which has been done among the Veddas of Ceylon and the islanders of the Torres Strait is not sufficient for any general conclusions to be formed. I think a comprehensive survey would reveal racial differences of innate musical ability whose origin in the present state of our knowledge is no more explicable than are the physical differences.

CHAPTER VI

MUSIC, MAGIC, AND MEDICINE

We know that in the Aurignacian period of the old stone age, man had begun to speculate with regard to a life after death, for he buried with the deceased pieces of red ochre which may have symbolised blood and a new life. Flint implements were thrown into the grave for use in a spirit world, and later, in the Neolithic Age, pottery containing food was added. Cave paintings of animals are not the results of a mere pastime ; magic is old, far older than history, and its earliest applications were probably those of appeasing ghosts and increasing the supply of game by special ceremonies including dancing and the painting of animal portraits. The facts of this chapter bring us face to face with problems ever present, but no nearer settlement than they were in the stone age. Primitive man has his own methods of dealing with these grave problems of survival after death, bringing pressure to bear on spiritual forces, casting out devils, and propitiating ghosts. There have lingered into mediaeval and even modern times examples of these crude methods of dealing with a spirit world in order to avoid punishment, gain reward, escape from pain, cause the sun to shine and rain to fall, or to make animals wax fat and multiply.

A few of these modern survivals of dancing and magic provide an interesting point of departure for a journey, which will take the reader into the strange company of medicine men, wizards and sorcerers in all parts of the world, and though the appearances of these practitioners differ, and procedures vary, the essence of their work is always the same, namely a control of vague, ill-defined powers, forces, and even personalities, which lie outside the ordinary everyday life of man.

DANCING OF WITCHES

In England there used to be witches' dances to promote fertility.[255] There were several forms of ritual dance, varying apparently according to the kind of fertility required, whether of crops, animals, or human beings. The jumping dance seems to have had for its object the growth of the crops, for the higher the performers jumped the higher the crops would grow. The so-called obscene or indecent dance was for promotion of fertility among animals and women, the dance was for the increase of such animals as were represented by the disguises of the performers. When the dancers were undisguised the ceremony was to ensure fertility of women. The ring dances were usually round some object, sometimes a stone, and sometimes the devil stood or was enthroned in the middle. In a trial it was said that "Thomas Leyis, with a great number of other witches, came to the Market Fish Cross of Aberdeen under the conduct and guiding of the Devil, who was present with you all in a company, playing before you on his kind of instruments. Ye all danced about both the said crosses and the meal market, a long space of time." Thomas was the foremost and led the ring. He danged Katherine Mitchell because she spoiled the dance and ran not so fast round as the rest. Margaret Og

was indicted for going to Craigleauch "on Hallow
Even last, and there accompanied by thine own two
daughters and certain others your devilish adherents
and companions ye danced altogether about a great
stone under the conduct of Satan your master
a long space."

Beatrice Robbie was indicted as a notorious witch
for " coming under the conduct of the Devil thy
Master with certain others, thy devilish adherents,"
and at Craigleauche " dancing about a great stone
the devil your master playing before you."

Jane Bosdeau, who confessed freely and without
torture and continued constant in it in the midst of
the flames in which she was burnt, said that she
had been to a witch meeting and danced in a circle
back to back. In the follow my leader the Devil was
the " ring-leader." The Devil's second in command
was at the rear to keep up laggards, for pace was
important, and it was a punishable offence to lag
behind, hence the origin of the phrase " Devil take
the hindermost."

At North Berwick, Barbara Napier met her
comrades at the church where " she danced endlong
in the Kirk yard, and Gelie Duncan played on a
trump, John Fian led the ring, Agnes Sampson and
her daughters and the rest following the said Barbara
to the number of seven score persons."

The Devil was very real in those days, for we
read that one night going to a dancing on Pentland
Hills the Devil went before us in the likeness of a
rough tanny dog playing on a pair of pipes."
A further indictment reads, " At St. Catherine's Hill,
Aberdeen, under the conduct of Satan, present with
you and playing before you after his form ye all
danced a devilish dance." " The dance is strange and
wonderful, as well as diabolical, for turning themselves back to back they take one another by the arms

and raise each other from the ground and then shake their heads to and fro, and turn themselves as if they were mad."

Music at assemblies was vocal and instrumental. English trials hardly mention music, but Scotch and French trials prove that it was an integral part of the celebration.[256] The Devil himself was the usual performer, but other members of the society could supply the music. Pipes were in general use, also trumps and Jews' harps. At Tranent (1659) eight women and a man named John Douglas confessed to having many meetings with Satan, enlivened with music and dancing. Douglas was the pyper and the two favourite airs of his majesty were " Kilt thy coat Maggie and come thy way with me," and " Hulie the bed will fa'."

The Devil invented ribald songs. One who was the Devil's piper confessed to a minister that at a ball of dancing " The Foul Spirit taught him a baudy song to sing and play as it were this night, and ere two days past all the lads and lasses of the town were lilting it throw the street."

Such glimpses of medieval credulity, only three centuries ago, gives us a more sympathetic insight into the fetishism of Africa, the Shamanism of Siberia, and sorcery, divination and prophecy all the world over.

ECSTATIC DANCING

The Flagellants[257] used to whip themselves through London streets at times of mental strain due to fears of epidemics, a truly primitive way of trying to appease demons of disease. According to Herodotus (ii. 40. 61) it was the custom of Egyptians to beat themselves during the annual festivals in honour of

o

Isis ; in Sparta, children were flogged before the Altar of Artemis—in fact, flagellation of a communal kind carried out while the victims were making a dancing procession through the streets has a very long if not honourable history. Such facts as these make the self-mutilation and tortures of Indians during the Sun Dance more understandable, for all this kind of self-abasement results from a single idea of propitating unseen powers by voluntary sacrifice. Indeed, there is a probability that all physical punishments forming part of religious ecstasy are derived from the single generic practice of sacrificing a human being.

"Dervish" is a Persian word meaning "a seeker of doors", that is a beggar, and so is the equivalent of the Arab's word "Fakir". The Turkish orders of this fraternity of mendicants have recently been suppressed, but they still thrive in Persia and many parts of Africa, more especially in the East and North East parts of that continent. Howling dervishes, when in ecstasy through dancing and drug taking, cut themselves with knives, eat live coals and glass, handle red-hot iron, and swallow snakes. When a dervish is in a state of ecstasy he is supposed to be unconscious of the actions of his body, for his soul has gone far away to the region of spirits. This temporary separation of spirit and body is a phenomenon often encountered in observation of the performances of medicine men, who will allow their souls to go to learn the will of the gods, or they may set their spirits free to overtake the souls of the sick and injured.

At the Mohurrum Festival which is held annually in Persia, processions of men and boys parade the streets headed by fanatics robed in shrouds and covered with chains, horseshoes, and daggers. The leaders work themselves into a frenzy bordering on

epilepsy and cry,"O Hasan ! O Husein " ! meanwhile
gashing themselves until they fall exhausted.[258]   The
dervishes of Bokhara live in a settlement outside
the town.   They wear long hair so they can be readily
distinguished by their fellow men.   The dervishers
are vowed to celibacy and swear obedience to their
chief, who sends them to beg all over Afghanistan
and Persia.   " It is strange how much respect the
people have for them, considering what a wild and
worthless lot they are."[259]

MIMETIC DANCES

These pantomimic displays giving a realistic
imitation of the movements of animals have been,
and are still, reported from all parts of the world.
The Tasmanians were experts in mimicking animals
in their dances, and the aborigines of Australia at the
present day show similar skill in their corroborees,
and totemic ceremonies.   Many such dances are at
the present day mere play, but a large number still
retain their original purpose, namely an increase of
food supply.   Such performances take us back to
early stages in the development of hunting tribes,
and there is a probability that all these mimetic dances
are traceable to totemism, which is concerned with
a magical increase of animal life, and a veneration
for ancestors who still visit the earth in animal
form.

Dances given in honour of animal spirits are still
popular, but cannot be fully understood without a
proper appreciation of the Indian's belief in the
potence of spirits connected with animal helpers.
The majority of Indian tribes are divided into clans,
each of which takes some animal, for example, the
fox, bear, lynx or squirrel, as its special emblem.

Human ancestors are believed to dwell in these creatures; which are consequently interested in the welfare of the clan, whose well-being may be preserved by suitable recognition and reverence for the spirit parts of the so-called " totem " animal.[260] Carvings of these animal patrons of the clan are made on lofty totem poles which, among the Haida, Kwakiutl, and other tribes of British North America, are placed near the houses and over the graves of chiefs. The assistance thought to be derived from being " en rapport " with spirits of guardian animals is further exemplified by the selection of a personal or individual totem. Every Indian boy is subject to a rigorous course of training, which entails much physical hardship before he can be admitted to adult councils of his tribe. When reduced by fasting and excessive exertion the youth goes to sleep in some secluded spot, where he remains until a guardian animal appears to him in a vision, which is the signal for the boy to arise from his stupor and kill a specimen of the animal, so that a portion of the creature may be carried in a " medicine bag " suspended round his neck. Henceforth the animal is his own special totem, entering into complete understanding with the wearer, so that herd movements warn him of impending danger, and give directions for success in the chase.

Drums are sounded, and various members of the " Brave Dog Society ", famous with the Sioux, assemble for a ceremony in honour of their clan and individual totems. Blankets are laid aside, brilliant war paint is assumed, and soon the naked performers, girt only with skins of the grizzly bear and plumes of eagle feathers, are ready for the honorific dance. Each holds between his teeth a " medicine whistle," the shrill sacred notes of which are heard at frequent intervals through the ceremonies. A principal performer, " Grey Wolf," enters the arena, gaily decorated with paint and the scalp of a large grey wolf, while in his hand he carries a rattle for vigorous use during the singing and dancing which is to follow. Those dancing in honour of wolves are covered with white clay relieved by streaks of black under the eyes and a black circle on the back. Firmly grasping their white spears, decorated with eagle feathers, the "wolves" dance round the other members of the company, in imitation of a pack of wolves surrounding a herd of buffalo. While this is in progress other performers are taking the part of grizzly bears, sitting with drooping paws, or suddenly attacking and dispersing the other dancers by pushing their way to the centre of the throng. On the conclusion of these ceremonies all the "Brave Dogs" march through the camp singing "Let every one be quiet to-night, because the sacred woman is going through her ceremonies."

A further beneficent use of singing, dancing, and the playing of musical instruments is found among the Mandan Indians of the Upper Missouri. The explorer George Catlin,[261] who travelled extensively among Indian tribes, relates his experience of the buffalo dance, executed with a view to exerting an influence over those animals by a process of sympathetic magic.

Young men of the tribe, having searched the country in vain for a herd of buffaloes, return to camp and relate their sad tidings to a council of chiefs, who forthwith declare that a grand buffalo dance will commence, and be continued without interruption until the animals appear. As the dancing may continue for as long as three weeks, without cessation day or night, there are many relays of performers, so arranged that one set may at once replace exhausted dancers, who continue in the ring until a state of complete collapse has been reached.

Runners and criers herald the people, and before long the great dance has commenced in a clearing before the mystery lodge, the dwelling place of tribal medicine men. Each dancer is clad in a buffalo robe complete with head and horns, and in addition he must carry bow, arrows and a lance. Drums are violently beaten, rattles shaken, and during the whole ceremony there is continuous singing accompanied by mimetic dancing in imitation of the movement of buffaloes. The greatest confidence is placed in this means of appealing to the Great Spirit, who directs the course of the herds, and at the commencement of the dance sentries are stationed near the camp, with orders to report by waving their buffalo robes when a herd appears.

Fast and furious becomes the dancing, until exhausted performers, bending beneath the weight of their robes, would fain retire. This, however, may not be done except by a special formal method sanctioned by custom. An exhausted performer halts suddenly and bends low beneath the weight of his equipment, at which point an onlooker draws his bow and pretends to shoot the tired dancer, who falls to the ground simulating the death agony of a buffalo. Knives are drawn by several spectators who rush on the scene, go through the motions of skinning the animal, and finally bear the exhausted performer from the arena. Presently a herd approaches within view of the scouts, and without delay a hunt is organised. For a few weeks there is a surfeit of provisions, feasting and dancing are the nightly order, and at such functions thanks are rendered to the Great Spirit who blessed the magic of music and dance in order to give his people food.

The importance of vocal music and dancing is illustrated to a remarkable extent by the religious ceremonies of Sioux and Blackfeet Indians, whose

(*Upper*) BUFFALO DANCE, MANDAN INDIANS.
(*Lower*) BEAR DANCE, SIOUX INDIANS.

(*After Catlin.*)

worship is dignified by chanted psalms in honour of animal life and the mystic forces of nature. Each part of the religious ceremony is characterised by the employment of dances and songs in praise of the spirit counterparts of well-known animals on which tribal existence depends. In addition to this there is a clear recognition of spiritual forces actuating the whole process of nature, from the production of sunlight to the propagation of animal species. A prominent chief, "Mad Wolf," began the worship of beaver spirits by chanting seven songs, each of which was repeated four times, to the accompaniment of hide rattles and a rhythmical swaying of the performer's body. The beaver is compared to a strong medicine man willing to exercise his powers for the physical welfare of Indian people, while eulogy and supplication are expressed in the chant[262] :—

> " The heavens provide us with food
> The heavens are glad to behold us,
> The earth loves us,
> The earth is glad to hear us sing
> The earth provides us with food.

During these chants dancers are circling round in imitation of the movements of beavers when building dams, and on hearing the signal of the shrill medicine whistle, all performers disperse quickly in imitation of the sudden alarm of a colony of beavers. The beaver spirit is directly approached in the prayer " Pity us, grant us your wisdom and cunning that we may escape all dangers. May our medicine provide us with food, may all of us be blessed." Ceremonial beaver robes are unrolled and waved aloft in imitation of the movements of beavers swimming, while a prominent chief chants, " When I go out from the lodge and see an enemy, I dive

down under the water where no one can harm me."
Then again the shrill medicine whistle blows, and
all performers disappear with the celerity of beavers.
Great care is taken to avoid letting the beaver skin
fall or touch the ground, as such an incident is regarded
as a bad omen, and a further precaution is preserved
in chanting conciliatory words when the beaver robe
is handed from one person to another. The dancer
parting with the skin says, " I do not give you away
my child the beaver, because I am tired of you, but
because the son of the woman is sick, and she prays
that he may be restored to health."

The reproduction of these ceremonial songs,
prayers, and dances in honour of the beaver spirit
is carried out with the strictest accuracy of detail,
for on correctness of ritual depends the entire success
of supplication.

Other animal spirits are extolled and approached
in the manner adopted for the beaver ceremonial.
Thus the buffalo ceremonial commences with the
lines : —

> " The buffalo likes to live in the mountains during the autumn
> He comes down from the mountains to the plains.
> The mountains are his medicine."

The word " medicine ", so frequently employed
in these chants, is used vaguely to imply that which
is good, congenial, and beneficial. The supplicatory
portion of these ceremonies in honour of animal life
is dignified by the introduction of prayers addressed
to the Great Spirit who presides over all the activities
of nature. " Great Spirit in the sun, I am praying for
my people, that they may be able to have food and
survive the coming winter. May all of our children
grow and have strong bodies. May they live long and be
happy."

So the mimetic dances, interspersed with songs and prayers, proceed along the lines sanctioned by ages of unwavering custom.   During the " elk song, " female performers go through the movements of those animals when rubbing their antlers against the bark of trees.   In the " moose song " male performers simulate the movements of moose clashing their antlers, while the antelope ceremony is characterised by a graceful dance which imitates the movements of the animals in a most realistic manner.

Ceremonial songs and dances are also connected with the display of sacred pipes which takes place during these festivals of animal worship.   While a chief is unwrapping the pipes from their packing, two pipe dances are executed to the tune of pipe dancing songs accompanied by the shaking of rattles. The pipes are held toward each of the cardinal points, while the operating chief, with head bowed, offers to the great spirit in the sun a prayer for the recovery of the sick.

In accordance with other parts of the ceremonial, reverence for the weasel is marked by the introduction of songs, dances, and a prayer which, unlike many of the petitions, expresses a request for moral as well as material benefits, and in dignified terms the chief prays :—

" Great Spirit bless us all, men, women, children
 Sacred medicine bundle help us to live a straight life.
 Sacred medicine pipe bless us all, also the rivers,
 mountains, prairies, animals, and birds.
 Mother earth provide for us until we die."

Reverently the sacred pipe is filled by a chief who circles round in measured time holding up the pipe toward the sun and chanting : " Sacred Spirit in the sun, it has been a long time since you smoked with me."   Medicine whistles are blown as a signal for

men and women to form in a single file for the execution of a ceremonial dance following the apparent
movement of the sun across the heavens.

The " Smaitlas "[263] is a socio-religious function
observed by the Coastal Salish, who use their long
communal huts as a ceremonial dancing ground during
the winter. Solo dances are generally an imitation
of the movements and cries of the " totem " or
guardian spirit of the performer. These social
ceremonies are enjoyed immensely, and the appeal to
animal helpers is always followed by the capture and
storage of large supplies of animal food.

In Guiana, dances imitative of the movements
of animals such as the monkey or jaguar are quite
popular, though their function appears to be merely
to amuse, and they lack the solemnity and semi-
religious import of the mimetic dances described
previously in connection with the Sioux, Blackfeet,
and other Indian tribes of North America. At these
performances quarrelling is common, but the aggressive
dancer is generally hustled away and sewn up in a
hammock, from the depths of which he adds discordant
and muffled sounds to the revelry.[264] Many travellers
have reported animal dances which have no obvious
meaning.

The Ainu of Japan have a " senseless dance in
mimickry of the heron ", and there is no meaning
attached to the performance.[265] In Borneo certain
animals are humorously imitated, but in giving a
pantomimic display of the movements of the Macaque
monkey and hornbill there is no hidden meaning
connected with magic or religion. Dr. Charles Hose
thinks that the dances may have been at one time
connected with totemism of which there is evidence
among the Kayans and Klemantans of Sarawak.
These people do not dance in imitation of animals
they fear.[266]

In the tiger dance of the Macusi Indians we have
a game without symbolism. The biggest and strongest
men lead a procession of performers dressed as
animals whose movements they imitate. Each dancer
has to be removed from the group either by the
strength or strategy of two men representing tigers.
(It is not clear why the word " tiger " should be
used in connection with South America. Perhaps
the puma or jaguar is meant.) The dance takes a
long time to perform, and is continued until the last
person has been caught by the tiger, who would be
cheered as conqueror.[267]

The Chukchee hold elaborate dancing ceremonies,
having as their object the assurance of a good hunting
and fishing season. Heads of the walrus and seal
are preserved for a time after these animals have
been ceremonially killed just outside the tent where
the dance is to take place. Blood is sprinkled to all
parts of the compass, while drum-beating goes on
inside the tent and the women dance a rhythm
accompanied by tunes without words. The evening
and night are occupied by Shamanistic performances
inside the inner tent; these no doubt consist of
violent dancing which leaves the Shaman in a state
of collapse or trance, in which he visits the spirit
world to learn of future success or misfortune
attending the hunting season.

The ceremonial of boats is held in spring at the
breaking of ice which heralds the fishing season, and
in this rite only the boat's crew and family elders
take part. On the morning of the appointed day
these people go down to the beach, make a sacrifice
of meat to the sea, then take the boat from its whalebone supports and sacrifice again. It is considered
important that the woman who walks in front shall
be old and well versed in the details of the ceremony.
All the people who have taken part enter a house

close by where they sing, dance, and beat drums for several hours. The Shaman's performance is given in the evening, following which the boat is placed near the sea on its summer supports ; finally it is launched after a sacrifice has been made.[268]

The Eskimo of Baffin Land are anxious to secure the goodwill of Sedna who controls the weather, so a special Sedna Festival is held to " liberate the seals ". At this time marriage ties are lightly regarded, and considerable sexual liberty is allowed. The witch doctors or conjurors dressed as women go about among the people concealing their identity and representing themselves as the great power which gives fecundity to animals. All the men and women form up into two lines facing each other, and the conjuror sets off down the lane touching first a man and then a woman with his wand to indicate that they are to pair together, and be man and wife for twenty-four hours. The fun is fast and furious as much of the affair has been prearranged, and there is more eager anticipation than surprise as the unions are made, for many of the people have paid the conjuror to select the mate they wish to have. The whole idea is to increase the birth-rate of human beings and in addition to insure a supply of seals. There is a ceremony of killing Sedna, who comes to life again each year, so symbolising the return of the breeding season. As the mated couples walk away the conjuror dances round them, and they too must dance if he touches them when circling round. The chief Angakut or medicine man holds his séance, in which he becomes insensible after violent dancing, so that he can visit Sedna and compel her to aid the community.[269] A ceremonial dance in the Kagga or dancing house marks the commencement of the first deer hunt in spring.[270]

Bushmen dancers show great skill in the mimicry

of animals, and during the baboon dance cause great
amusement by making grimaces, gambolling, or
running on all fours. Musical accompaniments vary
with the nature of the dance, so that the " bee "
dance is executed to the time of a buzzing-like chorus,
and jumping frog dances are enlivened by a croaking
song. But there is no evidence to show that the
dances are held with the definite intention of
increasing animal fecundity.[271]

Songs of the Semang and Jakun of the Malay
Peninsula have a definite meaning, but this is difficult
to understand because the archaic language of the
songs is totally different from present-day spoken
dialects. The Semang, a negrito people, chant songs
descriptive of animals, reptiles, and birds, but there
is nothing actually mimetic in the performances.
Jakun songs and movements are distinctly mimetic
in character, obviously devised to increase the
kindliness of nature, and the people take great pride
in their pantomimic display.[272]

The shy Veddas of Ceylon are hunting peoples
of the jungle, where they have retained their racial
purity and primitive life. A glance at their rock
shelters, honey gathering, and simple rites, takes us
back to prehistoric times. Of their dances the
arrow dance is the simplest and oldest, its object
being to increase the supply of game. An arrow is
thrust into the ground, and round this the Vedda
males circle, meanwhile singing an invocation for
which they beat time by slapping their flanks with
open hands.[273] The movements of the dancers are
jerky and spasmodic, for they are made to the
accompaniment of a monotonous song which is
gasped out as the performers become short of breath.

At last a state of extreme nervous excitement is
attained, and the sweat pours off the dancers. Louder
and louder they beat on their stomachs until all fall

on their backs completely exhausted, but uttering
howls from time to time and trembling convulsively.
Suddenly all rise at once and the dance is at an end.
Sometimes the Shaman or witch doctor takes part,
and after dancing until he becomes possessed by
spirits he indicates where a deer may be found. This
ceremonial invokes the Yaku or spirits, and one
wonders whether such performances were given in
the caves of prehistoric Europe by these artists who,
toward the close of the Palaeolithic Age, painted
bison and reindeer with such faithful accuracy.

The Tasmanians[274] were a stone age people of
very rudimentary culture, ready it is true to perform
certain dances for Europeans, but secretive with
regard to those of deeper significance which were
kept alike from Europeans and their own women.
Dancing was their favourite amusement, and a
generous observer says that " their modesty is a
matter of opinion, and morals a question of taste."
The women beat time for the men when not dancing,
but there seems to be no clear evidence as regards
the ceremonies from which women were excluded.
All observers of Tasmanians have been impressed by
their realistic imitations of animal movements. They
used to leap in mimicry of kangaroos, and when
acting as emus the men slowly circled the fire,
throwing their arms about and nodding their heads
to imitate the movements of the bird when feeding.
Unfortunately the Tasmanians became extinct before
sufficient observation and inquiry had been made
into the significance of these mimetic dances.

Australian aborigines at the present day have
their totemic ceremonies at which symbolic dances
are given.   Performers decorate themselves in
supposed resemblance of animal ancestors and strut
about as these people were supposed to do when
alive on earth. The whole performance is carried

out to increase the supply of animals on which the native depends for food.[275]

In New Guinea, Mafulu dancers sometimes imitate movements of the birds of paradise.[276] The Mekeo people dance in imitation of the goura pigeon,[277] and the origin of the dance was probably due to observation of this bird. One powerful Mekeo clan has a tradition that they are descended from this bird, and that the ancestor of the clan, though himself a man, had all the power of movement of the pigeon. He used to dance with the birds and so learnt all their movements, which he taught to his people. This idea of animal ancestry is of course a fundamental point of totemic belief, but in this instance the people do not appear to think that their dance increases the supply of pigeons. The Mafulu, who imitate the bird of paradise, are a non-totemic people, who may have copied the dance from an adjacent tribe.

As far East in the Pacific as Easter Island the people, of Polynesian extraction, worshipped little wooden images of men, birds and fish. These they wore round their necks, and at times set them up in the open air and danced round them. The dancers could not explain their action, and in reply to inquiries said they merely did what their fathers had done.[278]

In the Western islands of Torres Strait mimetic dances were performed in a clearing in front of a screen, behind which the dancers retired at intervals for rest and refreshment. The ceremonies were performed after dark for six nights to the accompaniment of a chant, which made reference to the glassy surface of the sea during the calms of a North West Monsoon, when vegetation bursts into new life. The dancers were decorated with palm-fronds, but the performance was not undertaken for amusement, but magically to influence

fish and ensure a series of good catches during the
ensuing season.[279]   At ·Kiwi some of the dancers
imitated the movements of crabs, lizards, or pelicans.
In the pelican dance two men jumped in the air
and alighted on the tips of their toes. The dancing
became quicker in response to livelier drum-beats,
until the observers could hardly follow the movements.
When the performers were tired, other pairs carried
on the mimicry until all had danced.[280]   These
ceremonies are probably of the genuine mimetic
variety, having in view the definite purpose of
increasing the supply of animal life.

Primitive man has by no means neglected the
purely aesthetic value of music, song, and dance,
but he has at the same time a profound respect for
the practical utility of arts, which, according to his
beliefs, may be employed to bring him into closer
relationship with the unseen forces which mould his
destiny. Music stimulates emotional experiences, and
leads man away from his mundane surroundings—
a fact which primitive races have fully appreciated,
and utilised as a means of approaching the spirit
world, in order to bring non-human forces to bear in
a beneficial manner on their precarious existence.
Though present day observation leaves us in doubt
with regard to the meaning and object of certain
dances performed in imitation of animals, there still
exists sufficient evidence to make clear the original
purport of such exhibitions, which probably had their
origin far back in the childhood of man when he
employed magical ceremonies to aid him in securing
food by hunting.

AGRICULTURAL DANCES

After man had learned to subdue animal life by
magic and prowess in the chase, he made his conquest

of the soil. Perhaps we should be wrong in supposing that a hunting stage of existence preceded, and was clearly marked off from an agricultural phase of development all the world over. Only a general truth can be stated and that relates to the priority of hunting. Even at the present day Australian aborigines have no knowledge of agriculture, though they are expert hunters. Tilling the soil implies a more or less sedentary life and a careful watching of a sequence of events to which the hunter is not able to attend, for he must be mobile, following wherever the game is plentiful. Australian women have their digging sticks, but these are employed only in obtaining wild roots ; there is no domestic agriculture.

Just as there are ceremonies for increasing the fecundity of animals, so there are rites for fertilising the soil, making the sun shine, and rain to fall.

In the Ethnographical Museum at Madras there is a post, probably the only one of its kind in existence, to which human victims were tied when about to be sacrificed at the harvest festival. Possibly the idea of renewing the health of the soil with human blood is allied to the Egyptian custom of killing the king, so that his life might replenish all the depleted forces of nature.

Our knowledge of human sacrifice in India, where the custom prevailed among the Khonds or Kandhs in Bengal and Madras, has been derived from the reports of officers engaged in suppressing the custom. The sacrifices were offered to the earth goddess, Tari, to ensure good crops and immunity from all disease and accident. The Khonds argued that in cultivation of turmeric the plant could not have its deep red colour without the shedding of blood.

The victim, who was called " Meriah ", was acceptable only if purchased, or if he were unfortunate enough to be the child of a victim father. Grown

P

men were esteemed as victims because they were the most costly sacrifice. Children, after purchase, were sometimes reared in a kindly way for years without knowing the terrible fate which awaited them ; but when old enough to realise their impending doom they were fettered. Most of the children who were rescued had been sold by their parents ; adult victims were usually kidnapped, but criminals and prisoners of war were deemed unsuitable.

On the day of sacrifice there was feasting, dancing and intoxication. The sacrificial post was the centre of the dancing circle, in which the victim was carried while drugged and adorned with garlands. The people assembled, dancing to music, and all shouted to the earth : " O God we offer the sacrifice to you, give us good crops, seasons, and health." After this they addressed the victim, saying : " We bought you with a price and did not seize you, now we sacrifice you according to custom and no sin rests with us."[281]

Next day the victim was anointed with oil and again intoxicated ; part of the rite consisted of each one present touching the oil, then wiping it on his own forehead. After this the sacrifice was carried round to bounds of the village to the accompaniment of a marching band, and on returning, a pig was killed over a hole in the ground. Here the victim was suffocated amid loud noise from musical instruments. A piece of the victim's flesh was buried near the village idol as an offering to the earth, and a great dancing orgy was held.

Major-General John Campbell[282] was concerned in 1861 with suppressing this terrible custom in Orissa. He rescued a hundred victims and made the people swear : " May the earth refuse its produce, rice choke me, water drown me, and the tiger devour me and my children, if I break the oath which I now

(*Upper*) FANATICAL DANCE, ACCOMPANIED BY HUMAN SACRIFICE, AS PRAC-
TISED IN KHONDISTAN, 1864.

(*Lower*) KENYAH WOMAN DANCING AT HARVEST FESTIVAL, TINYAR
RIVER, SARAWAK, BORNEO.

(*Photo, Dr. C. Hose and W. McDougall, " Pagan Tribes of Borneo,"*
McMillan)

take for myself and my people, to abstain for ever from the sacrifice of human beings."

The Hos are a purely agricultural people, and their festivals are all connected with that pursuit. There is an ample quantity of home-brewed beer from rice which is boiled and allowed to ferment until it is sufficiently intoxicating, and its proper preparation is considered one of the most useful accomplishments a young damsel can possess. The Hos keep seven festivals a year. The first or principal Magh is held in the month of Magh or January when the granaries are full and the people, to use their own expression, are full of devilry, for they have a strange notion that at this period men and women are so charged with vice that they must give vent to their passions. The priest opens proceedings with a sacrifice of two black fowls, some flowers, and rice bread. He then prays that the year may be free from sickness, and evil spirits are driven away by beating the bounds of the village while singing a wild chant.

During the dancing the Ho people forget their mild decorous ways ; bad language is used ; there are obscenities ; and men and women who have formed temporary unions go away together. Such is the festival of harvest home characterised by amorous dances and a complete suppression of social inequalities which allows masters and servants to dance together, the latter addressing their lords as equals.[283]

Mr. Bradley Birt[284] says that the Munda girls have a harvest dance with instrumental accompaniments on drums and pipes. This is a ceremony illustrative of the various acts of cultivation. The dancers linked arm in arm first typify the sowing of the paddy, then its transplantation and reaping. The performance appears to be a modest survival of earlier crude symbolism of fertility.

In Assam the Nagas have their harvest " gennas,"

which include formal dances. Among the Semang
and Sakai of the Malay Peninsula there is a harvest
dance enlivened by much drinking of strongly fer-
mented liquor, and temporary exchange of wives,
though this appears to be a game only, and not a
real exchange, as among some tribes previously
described. These primitive people regard the dance
as having some sort of productive influence, not
only on the crops, but on all other contributing
sources of food supply. Among the Jakun, operations
of sowing and reaping are always accompanied by
a recital of charms, a custom said to have been
borrowed from the rice ceremonies of the Malays.
Periodical feasts with dancing and music mark the
time when the rice begins to bloom, also the beginning, middle and end of the harvest, when the
" rice soul " is brought home and suspended in a
house.[285]

Dr. Charles Hose[286] gives a humorous description
of the fun and frivolity of harvest festivals among
Kayans and other tribes of Sarawak, in North Borneo.
When the process of storage of rice is nearing com-
pletion the festival begins with preparation of seed
grain for the forthcoming season, selection being made
by women. The whole festival is a celebration of the
cult of the principle of fertility and vitality, including
that of the women no less than that of the rice. The
women make pads of the boiled sticky new rice and
cover it with soot from their cooking vessels. With
these they approach the men and dab the pads on
their faces and bodies, leaving sooty marks that are
not easily removed. The men give chase and return
the attention. For a short space of time a certain
licence prevails among the young people ; and
irregularities, even on the part of married people,
which would be gravely reprobated at all other times,
are looked upon very much less seriously. All join

in dancing, some of the women being dressed like men, while some carry padi pestles. At one moment all form a long line marching up and down the gallery in step to the strains of the Keluri. Some young men dance in realistic imitation of monkeys or hornbills, singly or in couples. The women also dance together in a long line, each resting her hands on the shoulders of the one going before her and all keeping time to the music of the Keluris as they dance up and down the long gallery. All this is kept up with good humour the whole day long while drinking " burak ". The women mingle with the men instead of remaining in their room as on other occasions. Before midnight a good many of the men are more or less intoxicated, some deeply so, but most are able to find their way to bed about midnight and are quarrelsome. The harvest festival is the time at which dancing is most practised, but the ceremony is not regarded as religious or of magical power.

At Kiwi, New Guinea, there is an agricultural dance before the commencement of the planting season, and this ceremony is connected with initiation of boys and girls into tribal life, another form of fertility cult. A large pole is draped with clusters of fruit and vegetables, which are given away to the spectators at the close of the ceremony.[287] In many parts of Melanesia and Polynesia the religious significance of these harvest dances is lost, though in some areas the old traditional beliefs remain, as for example in the Marquesas Islands, where men only are permitted to take part in the religious dances held at the time the bread fruit comes to maturity.[288]

Dr. A. C. Haddon[289] saw agricultural dances performed on the Hood Peninsula, Bahaka, and these exhibitions may assuredly be classed with well-defined fertility rites found in so many parts of the world. Seven recently tattooed girls walked in a row up and down the village showing themselves as the principals of the ceremonies, and giving some idea of their grace and charm. After some preliminary dancing and drum beating the girls ascended a platform of the club house, where they stood in a row facing the village square. Two men carried a pig tied to a pole and stood in front of the girls, who took off their petticoats and were anointed with coco-nut oil by an old woman. Drums were beaten as a signal for the girls to dress quickly and jump down. This is a ceremony similar in function to those of India, which have as their object restoration of fertility to the plantations. Next day the pig was killed and dancing was renewed. A similar ceremony was seen by Mr. R. E. Guise and reported in a scientific journal. Here we read that the girls, after taking off their petticoats, pelt the audience with areca nuts. Then each girl takes a knife in one hand and a yam in the other, and at each beat of the drum strikes off a piece of the fruit, so symbolising the increase of vegetable life. The girls are not ashamed and enjoy the fête, which seems to be of little concern to the men, few of whom trouble to watch, a fact which led Dr. Haddon to write : " I must confess to feeling surprised that the men took no notice of the girls."

These harvest dances may be found in any part of the world where the people depend on the fertility of the soil. In the North West Amazon region such dances may be seen when pineapples and manioc are ripening. Each performer carries a dancing staff, to which rattling seeds are attached to mark the rhythm, and the staff is ornamented with leaves and fruits from the crop which is being honoured.[290]

In Africa, too, many peoples have their harvest dances, while the professional rain-maker is ubiquitous. Canon J. Roscoe tells a good story of the professional rain-maker sent for by the king of his tribe, who made

SHILLUKS OF THE WHITE NILE, AVERAGE HEIGHT 6 FEET 3 INCHES.
(Photo by Major R. Whitbread   By permission of Sudan Publicity Dept)

the sorcerer eat salt until sufficient rain descended.
When the downfall was too copious the rain-maker
was immersed in a tub of water and pushed under
from time to time until the downpour ceased. The
Bagesu of Mount Elgon, Uganda, have a dancing
ceremony at their harvest festival, when there is a
liberal measure of beer for everybody and free love
is indulged in. At these harvest festivals, which are
generally held at new moon, the frolicking lasts
through the night, and it is during these nocturnal
dances that men and women arrange their
marriages.[291] In this instance there is again evidence of
a well-preserved fertility custom intended to influence
human fecundity as well as the fertility of the soil.

The Lango, a Nilotic tribe of Uganda, have their
rain-making ceremonies, for it is not much use to
expect fertility of the soil without arranging for a
downpour; and again the dance is essential for
success. A ceremonial weapon called the rain-spear
is held vertical with its point down in a calabash of
water. An old man chants " May the harvest be a
rich one, you spear of the rain bring good rain, fruit
and flowers, that our granaries may be filled and
the hands of the children will not be empty." Then
water is thrown from the spear to the east and west
during the chanting of an invocation for rain. The
gods Min and Jok are asked for a plentiful harvest,
while they are also urged to find out any people whose
hearts are so evil as to attempt the withholding of
rain by magic. All the people dance the bell dance,
a syncopated movement which is performed only at
this ceremony. There is no musical accompaniment,
but the dancers are formed into a circle, in the centre
of which a soloist stands leading a song, whose
refrain is taken up by everyone.[292]

With reference to the A-Kamba tribe of East
Africa, Mr. C. W. Hobley gives some interesting par-

ticulars concerning songs, music and dancing.[293] There
appear to be well-defined tribal laws and traditions
which preclude men from singing certain songs which
tribal etiquette demands shall be rendered only by
females. On the other hand, some songs are to be
sung by men only, and at a wedding feast or funeral
the verses are carefully allocated to men or women
according to the dictates of custom. The gathering
of crops is looked upon as a most important function,
celebrated by the performance of songs and dances
which may be executed only by elderly women, each
of whom must have borne more than one child. If
it is discovered that the mother of one child only
is taking part in the ceremony the dance breaks up
in confusion, and the offender is punished by being
deprived of all her property, which is immediately
stripped from the hut by an angry throng. An
explanation consistent with the general reasoning
and beliefs of primitive man is provided by the
suggestion that the A-Kamba regard the breach of
tribal law as a direct offence against the guardian
spirit of crops and harvest, in whose honour the
dance is inaugurated. Probably punishment is
meted out in a peremptory manner to the offender
by her tribeswomen, in order that the whole community may not suffer the displeasure of an outraged
deity. So far as I know Mr. Hobley does not suggest
that the A-Kamba are vindictive for this reason,
but in general there is among primitive men a rigid
code of tribal law, the violation of which is held to
incur the displeasure of ancestral spirits, or some
non-human power which may vent displeasure on
the community as a whole unless the culprit is
promptly punished. The dance under discussion is
a fertility rite which, so the natives think, would be
hindered rather than helped by the performance of
a woman who had borne only one child.

DANCING AND SUN WORSHIP

Dancing as part of the magical processes which are supposed to cause a rainfall and ensure the renewal of fertility would be incomplete without some recognition of dances in honour of the sun and fire. The Egyptians annually burned in their temples a wax effigy of Apep, who was supposed to interfere with the progress of the sun across the sky. The Egyptian God Re was recognised a giver of all life and the source of energy. The Persians were sun worshippers whose Zoroastrian cult is still adhered to by the Parsees. Sun worship was followed by the Incas of Peru, and the Inca himself was the sun. Aztecs of Mexico offered human sacrifices to the sun god, and many tribes of North American Indians practised on themselves most abominable cruelties and mutilations, such as swinging with skewers through their flesh and chopping off their fingers. Possibly such horrors are a survival of ceremonies at which a fire was lit on the breast of the Mexican victim whose heart was torn out with a stone knife and offered to the sun. In connection with these sun worshipping fraternities there were vestal virgins, who tended the sacred fires of the temples which were not allowed to go out.

It is of course a perfectly natural procedure to worship the sun, the obvious giver of warmth and life, but it is quite probable that methods of worship migrated all over the world, the sun cults are not necessarily of independent origin.

The Blackfeet Indians recognise a great annual festival known as the " sun dance," which McClintock[294] describes as a supreme expression of their religion. At this great ceremonial there are prayers, songs and sacred dances, usually performed by the medicine men in order to heal the sick, and in addition sacred vows are expiated by the infliction of self-torture, which individuals, usually young men, have taken upon themselves when in dire peril during the preceding year. At these annual festivals dances are organised with a view to testing the stamina and resolution of numerous young men, who dance round a burning tree which showers its sparks on their naked bodies. Or, as an alternative, the young people dance behind a leader, who clashes together two burning torches.[295]

Among the Dené and Salish tribes of British North America dancing is a recognised form of offering up petitions to supra-normal forces which are thought to control the destiny of man. With respect to the Salish, Hill Tout[296] observed that : " On these occasions they dance in a circle with hands extended, palms upward before them, swaying their bodies from side to side with rhythmic motion as they chant and dance, and as the dancing is about to end the master of the ceremonies bids the people raise their hands and cast their eyes skyward. They remain like this until the chief lowers his hands, then they do the same. In doing this they close them and put one over the other against their breasts, the action signifying that the request has been granted. This performance is usually repeated three times, at sunrise, noon, and sunset, and the spirit invoked in these instances appears to be the sun."

Eclipses of the sun and moon are natural phenomena much dreaded by the Dené, who regard the shadow as a scab resulting from a disease which may be communicated to themselves, and in order to ward off such a calamity special musical ceremonies are performed. Members who wish to participate assemble softly and silently in the open, where they arrange themselves in single file and begin a slow dance.

Each dancer bends forward and beats time by striking his right hand against his thigh, while he mutters a petition beseeching the demon of disease to keep away from him.

When Cortez first landed in America sun worship was a flourishing cult, and sacrifices of human beings were regularly made to the sun gods. As late as 1721 the Natchez of the Mississippi Valley preserved most of the Aztec rites, for they had their priesthood and sacred fires. Every morning one of their priests stood at the door of the temple facing the east and addressed the rising luminary. He prostrated himself and offered incense by smoking a pipe and blowing the fumes toward the sun, after the manner described by Sir Alexander Mackenzie as practised by the Assiniboines of the Lake of the Woods. The heads of families brought the firstfruits to the door of the temple, and grain was blessed there before it was planted.[297]

There was a festival connected with the solar calendar of the Aztecs, during which only bread and water were consumed, with intention of letting other food products rest. An image of Tlaloc was set up, and the worshippers performed a ceremonial dance clad in various animal costumes. An interesting feature of the ceremonies was the following: " In front of the image of the god was a tank of water containing frogs and snakes. Each of a number of men called Mazateca tried to seize one of these animals in his mouth without using his hands, and having succeeded continued to dance with it in his teeth. The custom has a strange resemblance to the snake dance performed by the Pueblo Indians up to the present time."[298]

Only twenty years ago Muichol Shamans of Mexico might be seen beating their drums in the temples of the sun god, where chairs were placed for the gods to occupy. While singing, the priest accompanied himself on a drum made from a log of oak, which had been hollowed and covered with a deer skin, and the belief was entertained that the drum was alive. Several times during the performance the membrane had to be tightened by burning resinous firewood inside the instrument. The Shaman, whose reputation was great, played with great enthusiasm to accompany a vigorous dance performed by men and women together. He became deeply intoxicated and sank low in his chair, so that only his hands could be seen beating their rhythm on the drum, but in spite of his inebriated condition he worked with undiminished vigour and kept perfect time.[299] Lumholtz also describes sacrifices of food made to induce Father Sun and Mother Moon to let the rain fall. Again the dancing was carried out for two whole nights, while the Shaman worked at his drum and sang a prayer to the unseen powers describing the beautiful refreshing effect of rain on vegetation. The Tarahumares assert that the dances have been taught to them by animals who understand magic and can assist in making rain. These animals are mimicked in the dance, which is described by the word " Nolavoa," meaning " to work " ; the exercise is not a pastime or pleasure, it is a ritual. The people say : " We pray by dancing and the gourd."[300]

Catlin has described the sickening rites of the Mandan Sun Dance with its accompanying tortures of devotees and in modified form ; perhaps without self-tortures, sun worship is found among nearly all North American tribes. The attendant cruelties were prohibited by the U.S.A. Government in 1883. Participants in the dance as performed by the Arapaho paint themselves with representations of the sun in many colours, and they use a sacred wheel fashioned like a serpent. Dances are performed to hasten the appearance of the sun, and in times of sickness vows are made to the sun. Thus a man will say : " In order that my brother may get well soon, let it be known to all spirits that early in the morning I shall cut seven pieces from my skin, and in lieu of my brother I will bury them," a vow which he fulfils at sunrise. The dancing movement is merely a swaying of the body with flexed knees, but the heels barely leave the ground. Thus the worshippers dance with slight intermission through most of the night. A blizzard raged, but the dance continued, although the performers were quite naked except for a loin cloth. The dance is accounted for in origin and purpose by numerous sun myths.[301]

The Kiowa sun dance of the Seri Indians resembles that of the Dakota and Cheyenne in its general features, but differs by the absence of self-tortures : even the accidental shedding of blood on such an occasion is considered to be an omen so evil that the dance has to be abandoned. Self-laceration was performed at other times, but not in connection with the sun dance. For four days the sun dance continued, and during this time no food, drink, or sleep were allowed. A captive always performed the most sacred ceremonial, so that a punishment for breach of ritual might be visited on him and not on the tribe.[302]

No one has yet worked out the connection between snake worship and sun worship, but the two are allied in some way, especially among the aborigines of North America. Bourke shows the dance proceeding, and the observer said : " I must repeat that no steps had been taken to render these snakes innocuous either by extraction of fangs, or by use of drugs." When the dancers held them between their teeth attendants tickled the reptiles with feather wands as the procession danced toward the temple. The ceremonies were accompanied by noises from gourd rattles and a large drum with sheepskin membrane, which in the hands of an energetic performer could destroy the peace of a whole neighbourhood. The old medicine man stood facing the lodge holding water and a feather wand, while all sang a refrain and danced a rhythmical accompaniment with the snakes held between their teeth.[303] Such was the snake dance of the Moquis in 1881.

THE DANCE AND FIRE WORSHP

A most interesting exhibit in the Pitt Rivers Museum, Oxford, shows frictional appliances for making fire, and apart from the study of these ingenious methods, there are the problems of origin of fire and the ceremonial use of frictional methods for lighting sacred fires, for example for sacrificial purposes, even after more modern methods are available. Perhaps a flash of lightning set fire to dry herbage or the sun's heat engendered a flame, or noticing that friction produced warmth, some primitive scientist persevered until a flame was produced. The Tasmanians are said to have carried fire about with them in clay vessels, and it is quite possible for a people to have used fire without knowing how to produce it artificially. Myths relating to the origin of fire are numerous, and there are fire dances and ceremonies of an ancient kind in honour of heat from both natural and artificial sources.

The Navajos of North Mexico prepare a huge fire around which they dance all night in presenting eleven distinct acts between sunset and sunrise. As soon as the disc of the sun has disappeared the performers dance wildly into the clearing almost naked, bedaubed with paint, and allowing their long hair to flow freely as they whirl about. They carry dancing staffs with tufts of feathers at the ends, and with wild bounds approach the high flames. These Indians dance with a clumsy constraint half crouching and creeping, in fact the fire is so hot that the performers have to wriggle on the ground in order to get near enough to set alight the feathers at the ends of their dancing sticks. A disc representing the sun is held aloft and around this the wild dancing continues ; each time the symbol is lowered and raised a new dance begins. Toward sunrise the sacred ceremonies draw to a close. Men daubed with white come forward and light pieces of bark at the dying embers, then they spring again into a wild chase round the fire, throwing sparks, smoke, and flames all over their bodies. They actually leap among the embers, trusting to the white clay to prevent serious burns.[304]

The Dakotas reverence fire and heat in a strange dance which takes place in a hut, around a cauldron of boiling water. The dancers wear no article of clothing except a conical cap of birch bark, but paint is liberally applied to their bodies. While hopping and singing round the cauldron shouting in honour of a giant called Ha-o-Kah, they dip their bare hands into the flesh pot, pull out and eat meat which is scalding hot. They splash the hot water over their bare bodies while dancing and singing ; one can readily believe that they dance quite vigorously. They pretend the hot water does not scald them and that the god of the clan will not allow them to be burnt. It is said that the performers cover themselves with an astringent which will not allow the heat to injure the skin. The dancers evidently believe in auto-suggestion, for they shout : " O how cold it is ! "[305]

THE MEDICINE MAN AND THE DEVIL DANCER

His name may be Shaman, wise man, or witch doctor, but we find him at work in all parts of the world. He may be of low status, a mere diviner or soothsayer, or a dancing man ; on the contrary, the medicine man may control the destiny of the tribe by going into ecstatic trance and learning the will of the spirits, which he communicates to his tribesfolk. The youth chosen for such an avocation is generally neurotic, even epileptic, with strange ideas about hearing the voices of spirits asking him to join them under threat of fearful penalties. A period of training begins with solitude, hunger, beating, living in a cave inhabited by spirits, or in some such way working on a sensitive nature until the novice is able to bring on fits of hysteria and trance by violent dancing. His craft may be exercised to cure sickness, which he generally does by sucking or blowing over the patient, then holding up for inspection some stone or other object which he claims to have removed. The clients believe in him, for during initiation he received from his tutor a mystic power perhaps by being rubbed with quartz crystals, or even by being stabbed with a knife on which there was the blood of his instructor.

The medicine man may be beating his drum in a snow hut, where he dances himself into a frenzy, or in the genial island of Ceylon he may be dancing in a hideous mask to drive away the demon of disease. On the shores of a beautiful coral island the wizard is at work in painted garb of red to make the sunshine, or in Central Australia he is driving away a comet, or pointing the bone at an enemy while singing : " May your heart be torn asunder." In a dark forest glade of Africa the witch doctor is dancing violently

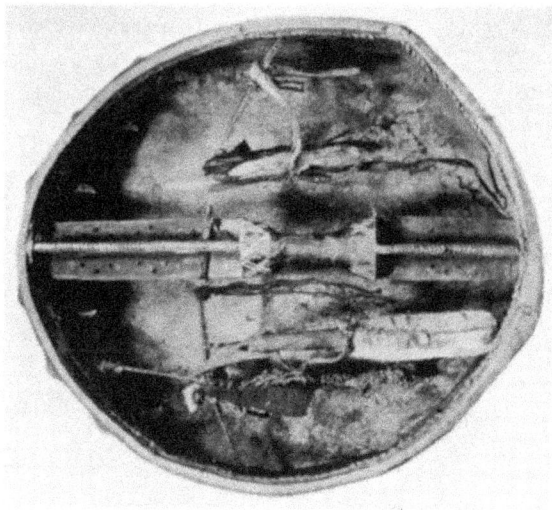

SACRED DRUM, USED AT SEANCES BY SHAMANS
OF LAPLAND.

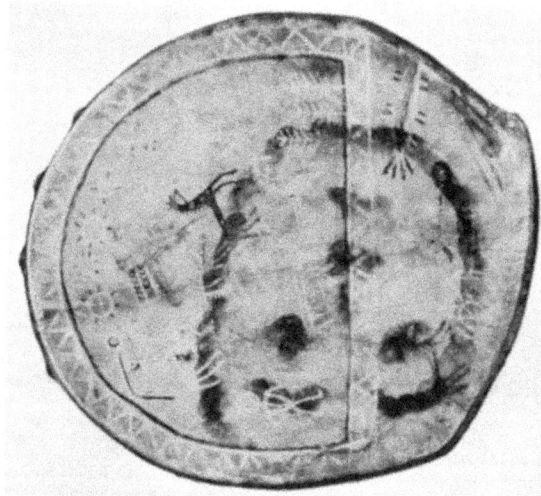

SHAMAN'S DRUM, SHOWING MYSTIC SYMBOLS
OF UPPER AND LOWER WORLDS.
(*By permission of Trustees, British Museum*)

amid a crowd of terrified natives from whom he is
" smelling out " the thief or adulterer.

So universal are the practices and dances of these
men that a few examples will have to suffice to show
the main objects of these wild performances.

The traveller Shklovsky reports that his servant
refused to carry a Shaman's drum on the sledge,
stating that the dogs would not pull, and the party
would surely be overtaken by a blizzard, or other
misfortune. The drum, which Shklovsky's[306] servant
described as a " devil's present," had been secured in
exchange for two bricks of tea, and after prolonged
argument the offending instrument was dragged
behind the sledge. Evening fell, and the party put
up for the night in a hut inhabited by Chukchee
people, who are not unlike the Eskimo in appearance.
These good folk regarded the introduction of the
Shaman's drum with great suspicion, and during the
evening showed much uneasiness when the warmed
drum skin began to crackle.

When about to begin a shamanistic performance
Ilighin, the medicine man, said : " Friends, there will
soon be a great change, whether for good or evil I do
not know. I shall call upon my guardian spirit and
ask him to take me on high in the western heavens,
and there I shall enquire of the gods."[307], [308] He then
went to rest on a bearskin in a corner of the hut,
while all sat still and downcast, save the old woman,
the special attendant of the Shaman, who made herself busy in preparing a robe covered with symbolic
signs, a breast ornament of mammoth ivory, and the
indispensable drum. The fire was allowed to burn
low and when the room was almost in darkness the
Shaman moved from his corner, took up the drumsticks, and made the noise of the instrument reverber-
ate through the dwelling until all shrank in terror.
Meanwhile he chanted: " Mighty master, fulfil all my

Q

desires, grant all my requests." All present fully believed that with the sound of the drum the spirit of the medicine man had gone forth to the mountain tops, there to converse with the terrible god Chapak. The music and chanting continued until Ilighin, the Shaman, crashed to the floor in a state of hypnotic trance. Bone castanets were rattled while the company chanted: " The heavy clouds roll, Chapak is coming, terrible as a homeless bear roaming in winter. Awake, Shaman ! " At this juncture fresh logs were thrown on the dying embers, and, as if in response to the crackling of the timber, Ilighin arose from his trance and immediately threw himself into a frenzied dance. Rapidly he twirled, now pirouetting, or leaping high into the air, while his eyes grew bloodshot, and the foam flew from his lips, as the hysteria grew more acute.

Presently the dancer paused, grew calm, and listening with one hand to his ear received the spirit message. " O friends," he said, " slavery and death await us in the future; " then followed a prophecy of the coming of hostile strangers whose advent should make the lives of the Chukchee people morose and bitter. Such then is the function of drum music, dancing, and chanting among the Chukchee, Yakuts, Ostiaks, Koryaks, and other aborigines of Siberia, who appear to regard the primitive music of the Shaman as an indispensable prelude to spirit possession and prophecy.

At a Chukchee funeral the rolling note of the drum is heard, and after the corpse has had an offering of refreshment, three drummers, usually old men, visit the four cardinal points of the camp, chanting in a slow drawling manner, and producing a continuous rolling vibration by means of whalebone drumsticks. The wailing chant is an appeal to the spirit of the deceased person, who is asked to intercede

with the great gods who have it within their power
to ward off smallpox, and cause the herds of reindeer
to multiply and flourish.   The ceremonies are concluded by stabbing a white deer to the heart, while
the old men, whose faces are smeared with the animal's
blood, perform a dance around the fire.

There appears to be a very sharp distinction
between sacred and profane uses of the drum among
Siberian tribes, though in some instances, notably
with the Koryaks, the Shamans have no drums of
their own to aid in spiritualistic performances.   The
instrument used for ordinary musical festivals is
requisitioned for magical ceremonies.   A common
belief is that spirits will not listen unless the drum
is beaten, and the use of these instruments may at
times be prohibited by the spirits.   Shamans of the
Buryat tribe state that their familiar spirits have
forbidden the manufacture of drums, and   as   a
substitute   two   long   sticks   are   beaten   together.
Amongst the Chukchee the Shaman's drum has a
wooden handle, and the membrane, some forty or
fifty centimetres in diameter, is lashed to a wooden
hoop by means of sinews.   The membrane, which is
generally made from the stomach of a walrus, is
tightly stretched when moist, and the drumsticks
used in Shamanistic performances are constructed
from pieces of whalebone thirty to forty centimetres
long.   Shamans of the Gilyak tribe manufacture drum
membranes from skins of the goat and reindeer, and
as an addition to the music of the drum there is
clanking of pieces of metal and tinkling of copper
bells which are attached to the robe donned by the
Shaman when about to begin his séance.

Among the Yakut tribe the craft of the blacksmith
is very closely allied with that of the Shaman, for
the former has an exclusive right of manufacturing
the jingling iron ornaments which decorate ceremonial

robes of the latter, and add their noise to the reverberation of the drum.   These iron accessories are not
merely scraps of metal, their function is primarily
musical, but in addition to this they are thought to
possess spirit counterparts, and to have the power
of remaining untarnished.   Shamans sometimes employ, in addition to the magical drum, a stringed
instrument resembling a banjo, also the " jews'
harp ", which consists of a frame having a wooden or
metal tongue.   The narrow end of the instrument is
held between the teeth, and an expiration of breath
produces a note by causing the tongue of the instrument to vibrate, while the mouth of the operator
acts as a sounding-board and amplifies the resonance.
In the Yakut tribe the jew's harp is used not only in
Shamanistic practices, but functions as a toy and
musical instrument in secular performances.   On the
contrary, among Buryats and Uriankhai, the instrument is used only by Shamans, who dispense with
the usual drum and gyrate to the notes of their jews'
harp.   The iron ornaments are regarded both as a
musical adjunct and as a defence against the blows
of hostile spirits.

The use of bells having a magical significance is
exemplified among the Altai, whose Shamans attach
these instruments to the collars of their ceremonial
robes.   The jingling serves as an accompaniment to
the dancing, and is regarded as the voice of seven
mythical maidens who have power to call spirits to
the aid of the Shaman.   Altai magicians combine the
drum with a series of rattles, which vary in number
with the ability of the performer, and are attached
to a rod inside the drum.   In North West Siberia
magical drums are usually provided with pictorial
representations of the lower world, inhabited by
human beings, also of a higher world regarded as the
dwelling place of spirits.

Buryats possess a strange belief in spirits who are symbolised by the presence of horns, usually an odd number, attached to the Shaman's drum.   In connection with these people it is interesting to note the use of " horse staves ", ornamented with bells and the carved head of a horse, on which the Shaman is supposed to ride when he visits the world of spirits. Drums, bells, rattles, jews' harps, have all an important place in the magician's outfit in various parts of Siberia, and, in addition to these musical instruments, there is a species of tuning fork, consisting of a wire tongue between two wooden sidepieces, which has a very wide distribution among Shamans from the Amur to the Urals, and from the Arctic Ocean to Tashkent.   Magicians among the Samoyedes have round drums ornamented with metal discs and plates, and, in the manufacture of these musical instruments, very elaborate precautions are taken.   The Shaman is required to kill a male reindeer calf, the skin of which he must prepare in such a way that no veins remain :   no woman is permitted to see or assist the manufacture, lest the sacredness of the instrument be lost.

Amongst the Lapps, too, no woman is allowed to touch the drums, which are extremely well preserved by being wrapped in furs, and like the drums of North West Siberia, these instruments of the Laplanders are pictorially divided into upper and nether worlds.   Family drums, on which all members of the household are obliged to perform at stipulated times, are found among the Koryak, Asiatic Eskimo, Chukchee, and Yukaghir, and during such recitals, which are probably given in honour of ancestral spirits, musical recitative melodies have to be rendered.

The musical performances of Shamans bear a striking resemblance to one another throughout the whole of Siberia, and their primary function is always to bring the magician into touch with the spirit world, usually with a view to obtaining information, which may be given to the Shaman's audience in the form of a prophecy respecting the welfare of the village community, the family, or possibly of some individual only.

Usually the drum is very softly beaten at the commencement of the performance, but gradually the volume of sound increases and is weirdly accompanied by singing noises representing sounds made by the guardian animals of the Shaman. Ventriloquism is frequently employed ; the falsetto voice being used to make replies from the spirit with whom the medicine man is supposed to be in communication. Gymnastic dancing of a violent kind works the magician into a state of frenzy from which he usually passes into a comatose condition. Probably there is considerable conscious deception, and the Shaman has to keep up his prestige by intentional imposture. Nevertheless he is a man of abnormal psychic power, a person who, from childhood, has felt that he must obey the call of the spirits and take up this strange avocation, from which he would gladly escape. As a medical practitioner the Shaman is in great demand, and in many instances his services obtain no pecuniary reward ; it may even transpire that traditional etiquette requires him to attend the poor before the rich. In the capacity of a trickster the Shaman horrifies his audience by swallowing burning oil and stabbing himself, while his supernatural powers are displayed in the readiness with which he frees himself from the strongest knotted ropes.

Chukchee inhabiting the shores of Behring Strait in the extreme North East of Siberia have a peculiar ceremony in honour of the sea god Keretkun, who is represented by a wooden image placed near a lamp in the hut specially prepared for this social and magico-religious function. During the first day the family unit only takes part in the celebration, which is marked by a sacrifice of food to Keretkun accompanied by a series of dances, songs and drum beatings. The second day of this honorific performance is heralded by the arrival of visitors, who exchange presents with the hosts, and at this juncture Shamanistic performances are introduced. The advent of the sea god is encouraged by the Shaman, who entices his spirit to the hut by keeping watch all night while he plays the magic drum in a subdued key, meanwhile accompanying the performance with weird chants and incantations. The music is regarded as an invitation to Keretkun to come and dwell with his people, who finally sacrifice a reindeer and conclude with a ceremonial feast.

A sacrificial feast held in honour of Bai-Yulgen, a god of the Altaians, illustrates the use of the tambourine for the purpose of encouraging spirit manifestations. The Shaman on this occasion erects a decorated tent in a thicket of birch trees, and to this he repairs, taking with him the mystic tambourine, which he flourishes in the air, going through the motions of ensnaring something which answers in a falsetto voice, " Behold I am here." When all the spirits are collected the Shaman flaps his arms in imitation of the wings of a goose, while he sings :—

" Beneath the white sky,
Above the white cloud,
Beneath the blue sky,
Skyward ascend O bird.

A subsequent part of the performance has for its object the freeing of the soul from the horse which is about to be sacrificed, after which the animal is killed and a ceremonial feast is made. Next day

after sunset the Shaman goes through the performance of feeding the spirits known as " Lords of the
Tambourine ", to whom he sings :—

> "Accept this, O Khairakhan !
> Master of the tambourine with six horns.
> Draw near with the sound of the bell !
> When I cry ' Chokk ', make obeisance !
> When I cry ' Me ' accept this ! "[309]

The magician next takes a cup and, holding it
high, imitates the noise made by spirits who are
supposed to be refreshing themselves. Once again
the tambourine, specially fumigated, is requisitioned
in order to attract spirits, who utter an exclamation
on arrival ; probably at this juncture the Shaman
makes use of his ventriloquial powers in order to
deceive his credulous audience. Louder and louder
he sounds the tambourine, until at last he pretends
to stagger under the weight of the numerous spirits
which he has enticed into it.

Now walking slowly round an upright birch
sapling the Shaman vigorously beats his tambourine,
mutters incantations, and keeps time to the music
by making convulsive movements with the upper part
of his body. This ceremony being concluded, there
follows the purification of the onlookers, who are
embraced by the Shaman in such a way that the
drumstick touches the back and the tambourine
the breast of each person in turn, in order to free
them from malign influences, by contact with sacred
musical instruments which have power to attract
friendly spirits. The Shaman now undertakes a long
journey to various heavens, his progress being assisted
by vigorous dancing and beating of the tambourine,
until the operator is almost in a condition of frenzy.
In these heavens the magician learns the will of
the gods, foresees future calamities, and is instructed

how to avoid impending evil by sacrifices and observances, the details of which he communicates to the awestricken folk around him.

In all Shamanistic performances the crisis comes when the magician, thoroughly exhausted by physical exertions and mental excitement, falls to the ground in a trance, which may endure for hours. These phases of arctic hysteria, not yet scientifically studied, appear to be somewhat akin to epilepsy, but they have no exact parallel in any other part of the world.

Medicine men among the Winnebago Indians have a secret society to which novices are admitted after special initiation ceremonies. Men wishing to join will exercise the most rigid economy for years in order to pay the fees which are required before the candidate is allowed to perform the dances and partake of the feast. The novices have to fast for three days before the ceremony, and during this period they are taken to some secluded spot and instructed in the mysteries of their society. They undergo a sweating process, followed by dancing, singing, and praying before the actual day of reception arrives. At the final ceremony the novices remain on their knees while fully initiated medicine men with their medicine bags round their necks dance for hours to the accompaniment of drums and rattles.[310]

The Abipoines of Paraguay, says Dobrizhoffer, have a prophetess, and when some circumstance is to be feared or anything done they consult an evil spirit. About the beginning of night a company of old women assemble in a huge tent. The mistress of the band is an old woman remarkable for her wrinkles and grey hair. She strikes every now and then two discordant drums,and whilst these instruments return a horrid bellowing, she, with a harsh voice, mutters songs like a person mourning. The surrounding women, with their hair dishevelled and breasts bare, rattle gourds while loudly chanting funeral verses, which are accompanied by a continual motion of the feet and tossing about of arms ; but this infernal music is rendered still more insupportable by other performers, who keep constantly beating pans, which are covered with deer's skin, so that they sound very loudly when beaten with a stick. In this manner the night is passed. At daybreak all flock towards the woman's tent as to a Delphic oracle. The singers receive presents and are asked what their grandfather has said. The replies of the old women are of such doubtful import that whatever happens they may seem to have predicted the truth. Sometimes the devil is consulted by different women in different tents on the same night.[311]

This phenomenon of ecstasy and trance after violent dancing is curious, for it is reported from civilised societies of modern times, for example in so-called evangelical revivals, when, under the stimulus of singing and violent oratory, people become greatly agitated and pray with vehemence as if under spirit possession. The Ghost Dance Religion reported from many parts of North America by James Mooney[312] in 1890 expresses the belief that after death all Indians will be reunited in one community. There are no musical accompaniments, but dancing ends in hypnosis, and supposed visits to heaven. Photographs taken in 1890 show participants " Inspired ", " Rigid ", and " Unconscious."[313]

The " Molonga,"[314] or devil dance, is widely known and practised among Australian aborigines, always with infallible accuracy, for there prevails a belief that " Molonga " will resent an inaccurate performance by inflicting death on men of the tribe, and carrying off women and children. In this case, as

was observed with regard to the dancing ground of
the Arunta of Central Australia, the clearing to be
used by performers is regarded as sacred, consequently
it may not be approached by women or children,
and to render demarcation quite clear a fence of
saplings is erected between sacred and profane areas.
About sunset a few males take their places in a row
on the edge of a clearing, and at once clash boomerangs
and shout a few syllables as a signal for the assembly
of an audience of women and children, who always
approach with trepidation which continues throughout the performance, manifesting itself at intervals
by a desire to rush headlong from the spot. Two
masters of the ceremonies are distinguished by red
streaks of paint across the face, broad armlets, tufts
of feathers, down stuck to the body with human
blood, and finally by a kind of anklet manufactured
from dried leaves which give out a crackling noise
during the dance, so serving as castanets.

There is a preliminary introduction of performers
who emerge in turn from the canopy of saplings,
each man being heralded by much shouting and
clashing of boomerangs until all performers have
made their début before the company. The actual
dance closely resembles that described for the Arunta
of Central Australia, for the performers advance
and retire in lines which at times pass through one
another, or, turning into file, follow a leader with
prancing high knee-action. Orchestral music consisting of hand clapping and improvised drum
beating by women, who work in relays, so enabling
the performance to be continued without interruption
from sunset to sunrise.

On the second night of corroboree additional
streaks of paint are given to the performers, and as
a rule four nightly performances may be regarded
as a " curtain raiser " for the grand finale of the

fifth night, when " Molonga ", the devil himself, is the " star turn." His appearance is made in dramatic manner, for without warning, and rendered hideous by a liberal application of grease and red ochre, he charges at the dancers, who retreat before him in confusion, while women and children give shrieks of alarm while retiring hastily from the scene. The ceremony terminates with a grand conflagration, during which all who have taken part dance round the fire, on which are thrown the time sticks used for controlling rhythmical movements during the performance.

One specialised form of singing is important because of its connection with magical practices to which the Australian native is much addicted. A man wishing to harm an enemy will retire to the bush carrying a long sharp bone or pointing stick, which is jabbed in the direction of his enemy, while the magician sings in a low voice : " May your life fail and your heart be torn asunder." Again in the "Kurdaitcha," or secret tracking of an enemy, magical shoes are worn in order to make the pursuer swift, accurate of aim and invisible to the foe. On this occasion,when the death of an opponent is compassed, the magical bull roarer, the simplest of musical instruments, is carried in the mouth, and to complete the preparations the " Kurdaitcha " shoes are " sung " in order to endow them with magical properties. In solemn accents the medicine man, who is to accompany the assassin, sings

> " Interlinia turla attipa
> Interlinia attipa."[315]

a murmured song which sets the magic in motion, and causes the shoes to stick fast to the man who is stalking his victim.

The Australian native adopts the policy of private retributive justice, consequently blood feuds between hostile tribes are carried on for long periods. Perhaps the medicine man has decided that the death of a tribesman was due to magical practices operated by some member of a hostile tribe. If this be so, nothing but the life of a man from the tribe which shelters the worker of black magic will satisfy popular demand. An avenging party armed with spears, boomerangs and shields, is gathered, and the success of the venture is assured by the performance of a magical ceremony in which stereotyped dances play an important part. These dances are interspersed with stealthy movements ; there is launching of spears at an imaginary foe.[316] shouting of " wah-wah," and at intervals the party executes a dance with prancing action, and high lifting of the knees. Veins of the arms are opened, there is drinking of blood, and sprinkling of the members of the avenging party in order to show unity of purpose, and as a magical charm for making the body lithe and active. Men who are to do the spearing dance with hands clasped behind their heads, and in regarding the performance as a whole we cannot escape from the significance of dancing as an adjunct to magical ceremony, while its social significance is evident in the employment of bodily movements in connection with a ritual which seeks to unify the members who participate.

Among the Ewe speaking peoples of the Slave Coast, boys who are dedicated to the gods serve three years in a seminary where they learn chants, dancing, and the general ceremonial of religious festivals. After three years of specialised education, the candidate has to show that his service as a priest would be acceptable to the gods. A sacrifice is offered, the boy is shaved, lubricated with oil, and girded with palm-leaves. He is then led in procession

round the shrine, while priests chant an invocation to
the gods, and relatives and friends prostrate themselves. The novice, robed in white, is seated on a
stool reserved for use during dedications ; then in
the form of a wild chant, repeated three times, a
priest asks the god whether the youth is acceptable.
Should the deity accept the novice, the latter trembles,
dances wildly, simulates convulsions, then suddenly
becomes quiet and normal.[317]

Niam Niam minstrels hardly have the status of
medicine men, but they are magicians of a low order
who make their appearance decked out in a most
fantastic way with feathers, and covered with a
promiscuous array of bits of wood, roots and all
pretentious emblems of the magic art, such as feet
of earth pigs, shells of tortoises, beaks of eagles,
claws of birds, and teeth in every variety. Whenever
one of this fraternity presents himself he at once
begins to recite all the details of his travels and
experiences in an emphatic recitative, and never
forgets to conclude by an appeal to the liberality of
the audience, and to remind them that he looks for
a reward either of rings of copper or of beads. Under
minor differences of aspect these men may be found
nearly everywhere in Africa. They are called by
some travellers " minne singers ; " but " hashash,"
or " buffoon," bestowed on them by Arabs of the
Sudan, would more fairly describe their character.[318]

There is, however, in Northern Nigeria a species
of " Bori Dancing " which indicates an abnormal
mental condition, some details of which have been
furnished by the late Major Tremearne.[319]

The word " bori " is of somewhat indefinite
meaning, but may be said to connotate an evil spirit,
a demon, or a delirious person. The dances indulged
in by people of hysterical and abnormal tendencies
are not so much the expression of an abnormal mental

state as an attempt to exorcise the demon of disease by violent muscular exertions. Such exorcism of demons is very common among primitive people, whose leader, the medicine man, is, as a rule, the principal performer. He is assisted in his task by special masks, dresses, and musical instruments. The case of the " bori " dancer is unique in this respect, that the patient himself has to undergo a long period of training and initiation, before undertaking his own curative treatment by means of gymnastic dances. Both Muhammedan and British rulers have attempted to suppress this hysterical dancing, which serves to aggravate rather than mollify a nervous malady. Nevertheless there are still many criminally or morbidly inclined young people among the Hausa of Northern Nigeria, who pay a fee of fowls, goats, or cloth, before retiring to a secluded spot in the bush for a period varying from six to forty days. The tutor, specially skilled in knowledge of curative dances, receives the fee, but of his *modus operandi* very little is known, save that the initiate has to drink special concoctions of herbs.

The concluding rites consist of a dance, the sacrifice of a black goat, and the formation of a procession in which the patient is carried on a litter to his home. Dancers circle round and round a sacred tree from right to left, possibly in order to propitiate spirits which are supposed to dwell in tamarind and baobab trees. Near at hand is an upright wand, inserted in the ground by the person who has collected herbs for the potions given to novices. This wand is held in reverence because of its protective value against evil spirits, and around this sacred emblem the dancers work themselves into a state of hypnotic frenzy comparable to that exhibited by the Siberian Shamans. The results of

this mad " Bori " dancing are similar to those which
accrue from Shamanistic performances, for presently
the participants fall to the ground in a semi-conscious
condition with fixed and staring eyes, after which
a normal condition is regained. Musical accompaniments are of the most primitive description, and, as
a rule, the services of two instrumentalists are found
to suffice. One of these, known in Hausa as " the
doer of the calabash ", uses two sticks for beating
an inverted calabash placed on the ground. His
partner, " the doer of the rubbing " exerts himself
with a primitive stringed instrument.

Another form of hysterical dancing, indulged in
chiefly by Hausa women, begins by the performers
arranging themselves in circular formation in groups
of four, while the instrumentalists, drummers only
on this occasion, sit in groups outside the dancing
circle. A woman from each group dances twice round
the ring, and on returning to her companions feigns
a state of hysteria and abandon. With all appearance
of complete collapse she pretends to fall backward,
but is saved from falling by the intervention of her
three companions. The hysterical dancer next
assumes a rigid attitude, is lowered to the ground,
and another woman takes her place. Some women,
on completing the gyration, attempt to throw
themselves violently to the ground ; seldom does
this actually occur, but there is manifest delight in
falling backward as far as possible before being
caught.

Among the Ba Thonga[320] tribe of Portuguese
East Africa, there prevails a very peculiar dancing
ceremony which has as its object the location of an
evil spirit or influence. For purposes of divination
people are gathered in the principal village, and when
all are assembled the diviner enters, carrying in his
hand the magical whip and assagai. He commences

AZANDE (NIAM-NIAM) MEDICINE MEN, NILE—WELLE REGION.

(Photo, Sudan Government Railways)

a circling dance which is accompanied by hand-clapping and the rendering of a special chorus by the spectators, who chant :—

> " Beautiful dancer of slender figure,
>   Seek for it ! seek for it ! diviner.

Wilder, and more vigorous becomes the dancing until the diviner, in a state of ecstasy, flourishes his whip, rushes hither and thither, pauses, sniffs the air as if trying to locate the evil spirit, and finally rushes toward a hut, in the floor of which he plants the assegai. The dwelling is carefully searched for evidence of black magic, and on some occasions the digging of a hole results in the discovery of a gourd of blood, or objects of enchantment, which have, in all probability, been deposited there by the diviner himself.

The owner of the hut is disgraced and, in order to prevent recurrence of sickness and death within the community, the charms are publicly burned. In this instance again, primitive music and dancing are employed in order to stimulate the emotions until a state of frenzy is reached. The function is beneficent in character, for it has in view the protection of the community against insidious workings of black magic.

Among the Ba Thonga, disease and abnormal mental condition are deemed to result from spirit possession, which can be rendered innocuous by singing, drum beating, and playing of tambourines if by such methods the spirit can be persuaded to reveal his name. The patient, in melancholy mood, is seated in his hut, waiting for the exorcism to begin on the first evening of new moon. All who have previously suffered from spirit possession are requisitioned, and when the director of ceremonies strikes his tambourine

R

there is a mad rush in the direction of the call. The crowd repairs to the dwelling of the sick man, each doing his utmost to extract the maximum volume of sound from a drum, tambourine, or rattle. More important than the use of musical instruments is an incantation in the form of a song inviting the evil spirit to reveal his name, after which revelation conquest is supposed to be easy.

In flattering verse the spirit is asked to favour the crowd by surrendering, and should several hours of persistent effort be unavailing, the tone of flattery is replaced by a menacing attitude, and instead of chanting, " We salute thee, spirit, come out by the straight way," the angry performers threaten to abandon the demon. Presently the patient rises, and with the wildest dancing works himself into a frenzy, during which the name of the spirit is revealed. The possessed person throws himself at the onlookers, flings himself into the fire, and finally becomes calm to indicate that the evil spirit no longer enthralls him.

Such instances of music and dancing as remedial measures might be amplified indefinitely, for primitive man of all countries has placed great reliance on the efficacy of music and dancing, as a means of working upon the emotions, in order to defeat demons of disease.

Devil dancing, or exorcism, is well known in the Far East, and I think a continuity could be traced from China through Tibet and India to Ceylon, over which vast region the use of hideous masks is part of the ceremony. Chinese devils are disembodied spirits of dead people who often mingle with the living in order to work some mischief. They may however always be detected by their want of appetite, an aversion to the smell of sulphur, and the fact that their bodies throw no shadow. Sometimes these

(*Upper*) TIBETAN DEVIL DANCERS IN ANCIENT WOODEN MASKS.
(*Lower*) TIBETAN DEVIL DANCERS PERFORMING.

(*By permission of Dr. W. M. McGovern*)

devils are of a milder character, a case being on record of one who gained a literary degree for his friend.

In Tibet about one man in four becomes a Lama or priest who is willing to bless crops and say an unlimited number of prayers by mechanical means, such as a little wheel turned by water, or a hand rattle. These Lamas give entertainments in which they wear most hideous masks, saying that these represent the demons the people will have to see in the underworld, so they might as well be accustomed to them. These Tibetan demons have the forms of men and the heads of ogres and beasts so hideous that they appear to be the monstrosities of a night-mare. These demons date back to pre-Buddhist times when they were worshipped by sacrifice of blood and food. In some of the acting there is a black-hatted priest called " Chief of the Wizards." He dances frantically to quick music in clouds of incense burned from large swinging censers, and an offering of pastry cakes concludes the ceremony.[321]

Exorcism of demons by devil dancing is reported from Nayars of the Malabar Coast. " If a woman is possessed of a devil, and it is women who generally suffer from these things, an expensive and elaborate devil dance called Kolam Thullal has to be performed. The village is informed, and each family is supposed to contribute to the expenses while preparations are made a good many days beforehand. The Kaniyan, or the magico medicine man, though considered an inferior, has with twelve of his people to come to the house where the ceremony is to be performed, and each of them puts on a mask made for the occasion, then paints himself in such a way as to look really terrible. The mask of each has a different expression. At eight o'clock at night the girl possessed of a devil is brought in front of the house where are gathered

people of the village. The whole place is illuminated
with big lamps, and the girl sits alone or is sometimes
supported by her mother.   Then one by one the
masked magicians come before her and execute most
frightening dances to the accompaniment of terrifying
music."

Under this treatment the girl becomes hysterical,
and while she is in this condition the devil within her
confesses where he came from and who prompted
him.   Revelation of identity is supposed to render
the devil incapable of further harm, and this confession
during the hysterical state is a sign that the dance
has been successful.[322]

The Todas of the Nilgiri Hills, Southern India,
have certain men who are reputed to have special
power as diviners, and they are designated by a
native word meaning " God—gesticulating—men."
Such men (Teuols) are said to have inherited their
powers from a father or grandfather, in fact the
office of medicine man is usually hereditary in all
parts of the world, and, what is more important, these
Teuols are believed to be possessed of a special
frenzy, in which they speak with the voice of a god
in language differing from their usual tongue. They
exercise their reputed powers during human sickness,
or if the supply of milk given by buffalo fails, or the
calves are troublesome.

If a buffalo refuses to go to the place of sacrifice,
for example at a funeral, the Teuol is called, and
though the animal may be lying down obstinately
it will rise and proceed to the desired place, when
these medicine men have danced their wild measures
around it. The dancing is of a violent kind, in which
the hair of the performer flies out straight from his
head, while his eyes grow bright and there is every
appearance of great mental excitement. One of the
dancers chanted in a loud voice giving reasons for the

animal's obstinacy and prescribing what was to be done. He waved a red cloth before the buffalo, which rose quietly and walked to the place where it was to be slaughtered.[323]

In South Canara there are three devil dancing castes, who allow their hair to grow long so that it flows out during their wild gyrations, during which a beautiful curved sword of the finest steel is flourished. Their eyes are wild and excited, possibly on account of drug taking, and though the exorcism begins with low mutterings, these soon rise to a wild chant, which accompanies the violent trembling of the limbs and marks time for the backward and forward movement of the body. The dance always begins about nine o'clock at night with a performance by the assistant of the chief exorcist. This attendant, named *Pujari*, whirls about in imitation of the mien and gestures of demons, but he does not aspire to full possession, which is reserved for a *Pombada*, a man of lowest class who comes forward when the *pujari* has exhibited himself for about half an hour. He is naked save for a waistband; his face is painted with ochre, and he wears a sort of arch made of coco-nut leaves and a metal mask. He paces up and down and so gradually works himself to a pitch of hysterical frenzy while tom-toms are beaten furiously and spectators join in raising a long monotonous howling cry with a peculiar vibration. At length he stops, and everyone is addressed according to rank. If the *Pombada* offends a rich Bant by omitting any of his numerous titles he is made to suffer for it. A night's reward is eight rupees for these frantic labours. Performers of very low castes and even a Koraga, who himself is low, expects a Parava devil dancer to raise his hand in salute, but the custom is not now observed.[324]

The Andamanese have a medicine man, " *Kobo*,"

who is said to have died and come to life again. Among
other things he learnt from the spirits a dance which
he remembered and is now willing to perform.
Women and children are allowed to witness the ceremony, which is performed on the village ground, where
many spectators are squatting on their haunches.[325]
In the Nicobar Islands, not far away from the
Andamans, medicine men are recruited from sickly
boys who undergo a special initiation by witch
doctors, who thump the ground under the hut of the
novice to call him to the ceremony. He is decorated,
placed on a throne, and given a sacred spear with
which to slay spirits. After a few days the novice
is plunged into the land of spirits, a marsh in the
jungle, where he remains for several days alone, for
all have left him at a pre-arranged spot where they
perform the dances connected with initiation. There
is continued dancing for several nights, whether there
is a moon or no moon, until the novice is danced into
fellowship of the first stage.[326]

The Kayan medicine man of Sarawak, Borneo,
dances in dramatic representation of his struggle
with the soul of a sick man which may actually have
left the body. He becomes wildly excited while
dancing, and chants a song the refrain of which is
taken up by all present. The chant runs :—

> O Holy Dayong (Medicine Man) Thou who lovest mankind
> Bring back thy servant from Leman,
> The region between the lands of life and death.
> O Holy Dayong.[327]

Women are by no means excluded from the witch
doctor's profession, and in Borneo, among the
Malanaus, it not infrequently happens that when a
woman, or more rarely a man, is ill or insane, she is
urged to admit that a devil has possessed her, and
to become well she graduates as a medicine woman

and so acquires power to help others. She repeatedly
goes through   a ceremony called *bayoh* (artificial
hysteria),and is then considered to have been accepted
by both men and spirits in her new rôle of exorcisor.
If it is supposed that some illness is due to possession
by an evil spirit it is decided to call the medicine
woman and get the unwelcome visitor to depart.
Offerings of eggs and fowls to good spirits having
proved fruitless, a day is fixed for the *bayoh*, preferably
shortly after a good harvest. The room is decked to
welcome good spirits, and rice and tobacco are displayed in a tempting manner to appease the various
appetites of the spirits invoked.   Just after sundown
the neighbours troop in and settle themselves round
the room, the ill-mannered pushing themselves in
front.   Certain of the villagers agree to form the
band. Soon the house is full of people,including boys,
and old men who are contentedly chewing and
smoking, while women rctire to the darker parts of
the room to gossip. Incense dispenses a not unpleasant
smell. Then the fun begins, gongs and drums are
struck, and the strains of music sound through the
village with intervals of a quarter of an hour every
two hours. The monotonous melody proceeds in this
way until seven the next morning.

At first the people collect round the earthenware
censers to warm their hands. They then begin to
step with the music, and wave their arms, hissing
loudly through their teeth the while, and occasionally
breaking into a whistle. After a time they sit down
and nod this way and that to music as though engaged
in training the muscles of the neck. But the drums
and gongs go faster till the long hair of the woman
flies round extended from her head. The whistling
is varied by an ancient chant *Sadong*, in an archaic
language now barely understood. There is question
and answer from the medicine woman to the spirits.

One of the women goes to the patient who, clad in black, sits alone on a mat, and brings her a pinang blossom to hold, covering her hand with a cloth. The unfortunate patient is spun round in a cone of shavings. Gradually the sick person is worked up to a frenzy, and keeping time with the music the medicine women sway about and wag their heads. So the proceedings go on with weird fantastic dancing, nodding, howling, whistling, chanting, for all the hours of a tropical night. Then the medicine women are whirled in the cone, and one by one they fall into a faint, stagger round the room, brush the onlookers in a giddiness of hysteria comparable with drunkenness. The explanation is that little demons come first. These are sent for their masters, but when a big spirit comes into the medicine woman she feels its presence, but does not see its form.[328], [329]

From Arctic snows to Indian jungles, and through the coral islands of the Pacific to the sandy wastes of Central Australia, we have seen the medicine man dancing his way into communication with the spirit world; controlling demons, and always vigorously exercising his craft. Frequently his wild incantations and dramatic dances are intended to serve the community well; or in darker mood he may be acting against the best interests of society as a worker of evil spells, or the bribed perpetrator of some black magic directed against one of his own tribesmen.

Whether we like the man or not he has to be regarded as an intermediary between visible and unseen worlds, he is a priest in embryo; one who learns the will of the gods and communicates it to mortal man. He knows how to enter the holy of holies; and with confidence he may advance into the world of spirits while a trembling audience awaits his return and prophecy.

CHAPTER VII

THE LAST DANCE

THE DEATH DANCE

In a great variety of scenes changing from arctic snows, through jungle swamps and coral islands, to sandy wastes, we have seen men still unchanged by civilisation dancing from cradle to grave. Even then the ghost has to be satisfied by many rites, most of which include ceremonial dancing ; for tying the toes of the corpse, prohibiting the name to be spoken, and making food offerings and a fire on the grave, will not suffice to check the wandering tendencies of spirits that are almost universally regarded as malevolent.

Methods of recognising death vary with racial history and development, for while a wretched Melanesian widow may have to live for a long period with the corpse of her late husband suspended from the roof until the death feast and dance have been celebrated, the poetical Maori may content herself with the lines :—

Brightly flashed the lightning's spear
On Turamoe's peak.
Portent of warrior's death and woman's woe,
O Tiopira, why did'st thou fall ?
Thou who stood'st so boldly forth in the bows of the canoe,
And thou, Hapeta, cold thou liest.
Death spread his lure for thee,
The dragon of the cave was loosed on thee.

Such is the lament for Maori Hauhau warriors who fell on Sentry Hill in 1864 under a shower of British lead. Yes ; the Maori is poetical and intellectual, but he favoured a cannibal feast in order to acquire the excellent qualities of the dead. Sometimes there is not merely fear of spirits, but worship of the dead who may be reincarnated as famous medicine men, or helpful animals. Sir William Ridgeway develops the hypothesis that tragedy originated in the worship of the dead.[330] Our immediate interest, however, is to glance at primitive methods of dealing with the last calamity, and there is no doubt that dancing may be classed with laceration to give mourning scars, and many other acts which assure the spirit that due respect has been paid.

Shokas of Tibet ascribe death to the departure of the soul from the body, and the ceremonies described by Henry Savage Landor[331] show that the community is concerned, not merely with the disposal of the body, but likewise with the complete removal of the sins of the deceased. Friends of the deceased smeared the corpse with butter, bent it double, and mounted it on a rough wooden hearse which at sunset left for the cremation ground, on which there was a circle of stones with logs around them. On this pyre the corpse was placed, a bowl of wine was poured over the head, and the pile was fired, after all valuable ornaments had been removed from the body.

Then followed the more congenial task of providing amusement for the dead man's soul, and to aid the process an effigy of straw was made, inside which were placed bones from the funeral pyre. A sheep was killed, and the women-folk mourned round the effigy, resting their hands upon it, and asking their relative to return to earth. Other women turned their hoods inside out as a sign of mourning, then danced a graceful measure round the dummy, while men capered in

(*Upper*) GOAT WITH SOUL AND CLOTHES OF DECEASED.
(*Lower*) DANCE IN FRONT OF DECEASED MAN'S HOUSE.
(*Photos, Messrs. Heinemann, Ltd*)

doleful manner to drum music that continued all day.

There were solos, trios, and duets accompanied by drummers,who beat their instruments on one end with a stick, on the other with their hands. In certain solo dances the drummer played with frequent changes of time, but the dancer cleverly varied from frenzy to slow shuffle in quick response to the music.

A goat laden with the clothes of the deceased was led into the throng, and following a martial dance by three hundred men, sandal wood was burnt beneath the nostrils of the goat in order to tempt the soul of the deceased man to enter the animal. All the clothes and ornaments were torn from the effigy and piled on the goat which impersonated the dead man. The creature was fed to repletion, even wine and other liquors were poured down its throat, and large dishes containing delicacies were placed before it. Women wept over the goat, then it was chased out of the village to be sacrificed, and the heart was cut out. At times a yak is substituted for the goat, and at the end of the ceremony described the people say: "Go ! Go! we have fêted and fed you. We have done all in our power, and cannot do more. Go now ! " and the animal is pushed over a precipice.[332]

Probably Marco Polo saw a ceremony of this kind in the thirteenth century when travelling in Shensi. He refers to placing meats and liquors before the body prior to cremation. The account mentions the burning of paper pieces painted with figures of women servants, and animals, which are supposed to accompany the deceased to the next world. " During the whole of these proceedings all the musical instruments belonging to the place are sounded with an incessant din."[333]

The Shans of Upper Burma arrange for a band to play outside the house of a deceased person of importance. There is beating of drums, gongs, and cymbals to scare the evil spirits which might attack the recently liberated soul. Inside the house women are chanting sentences in praise of the dead, and in a minor key reciting aphorisms on the uncertainty of life.[334]

The Tibetan custom of allowing a goat or yak to bear away the soul and sins of the deceased is called to mind by a practice of the Badagas of the Nilgiri hills in Southern India. These people send away a calf bearing the sins of the dead person from the funeral ceremony.[335]

Among the Todas dancing takes place at the funeral of a male within the circular walls of the funeral hut. A buffalo is slaughtered, and on the day after this sacrifice there is more dancing by males only, and a recitative chorus in praise of the dead.[336]

The Veddas of Ceylon invoke the *yaka*, or spirits, to receive a newly-liberated spirit by performing a dance several days after life has left the body. The *yaka* of the dead is asked to help those left behind, and in order to approach the spirit world the Shaman dances himself into a frenzy. He recites his charm over and over again until his voice is hoarse and he becomes possessed by the *yaka*.[337]

The Nicobarese hold a series of dances at intervals of three or four years, when a council decides to dig up the bones of people who died a few years ago. After all night dancing the ghoulish work begins, while women wail, and the witch doctor fans away evil spirits with a bunch of leaves. A lamp is left burning, for spirits dislike a light, and, as is the case in the Andaman islands, the disinterred bones are treated with great respect. A final dancing ceremony removes the uncleanliness of those who have taken part in this procedure.[337]

At Pulu in Torres Strait a death dance custom of a peculiar kind is observed, one likely to disturb the

gravity of the reporter. The ceremony is performed
once a year by men who dress in masks and ornaments
of leaves. These mummers mimic the gait of persons
who have passed away recently, and their impersona-
tion is realistic, for women in the audience cry out,
amid tears and lamentations, " That's my husband,"
" O my son ", according to their relationship with the
deceased whose gait is mimicked. The melancholy
of the performance is relieved by a dancing buffoon
who prances about behind the principal actors.[339]

A somewhat similar pantomimic display, including
mimicry of people and a travesty of recent events, is
given at funeral ceremonies in the island of Mer, New
Guinea. The dance is of a spectacular kind, at which
rattles are employed to suggest the rattling of the
bones of a skeleton, and the shaking is so vigorous
that the noise can be heard for miles through the
jungle.[340]

Along the Congo, funeral songs of the Boloki
usually recount the exploits of the deceased and
extol his good qualities, and directly the death of a
man of position is announced, preparations are made
for celebrating the burial rites. When large quantities
of sugar-cane wine have been prepared the ceremonies
are commenced by beating a hardwood drum as a
summons for men and women to assemble, in order
to celebrate the occasion by dances which may be
continued for three days and nights. Long lines of
male dancers form up opposite to females, and at a
signal from the drum men, evidently selected according to their position in the line, advance and meet
the women from the opposite rank. These couples
perform a wriggling shuffling dance, and on their
return to former positions other couples advance
toward one another after the manner of opposed
couples in a figure of the lancers. Another form of
funeral dance performed only by women is executed

in honour of a deceased female of social standing who is honoured on account of her exceptional success as a cultivator of the soil. The mourners decorate themselves with leaves, twigs, and creepers, then form a procession which passes through the village, singing praises of the deceased. This musical rite has a very practical conclusion, for all who have taken part in the ceremony proceed to the ground of the deceased, and there plant a large patch of cassava for the use of her family.[341]

An ethnologist acquainted with the Bushongo, in speaking of a man recently deceased, says : " During his lifetime the now defunct Bambi had been, I have no doubt, a very pleasant fellow, but dead he was objectionable." The exposed coffin, which had been watched for several days by the wife and other female relatives, was at last buried and a dance was given.[342]

The importance of dancing among primitive people is much greater than among civilised nations; and among the former, emotional life,whether sombre or gay, is capable of expression in bodily movement. With the Salish,who dwell on the West Coast of North America,tribal and family bereavement are recognised by a " death dance," which follows a mortuary feast, and distribution of small gifts provided by the nearest of kin to the deceased. Feasting is the order of the day, and, during the banquet, songs composed by the chief mourner are sung in commemoration of the deceased as a hunter, fighter, and wrestler. After the meal all guests dance to music composed by the nearest relatives of the dead, the time being kept by women, who beat rhythmically on a piece of painted wood. Soon music gives place to games, which are in progress for several days, at the end of which period wrestling, racing, and gymnastics bring the ceremonies to a close.[343]

After watching the dances of undeveloped people

from birth to death there remains the task of dis-
covering some general truths, which seem to group
themselves naturally under : (1) Historical problems
relating to origins and migration of rhythm, song,
and instrumental music. (2) Social and psychological
explanations. (3) Physiological aspects of the dance.
(4) Practical applications of our knowledge.

HISTORICAL ASPECT

So far as dancing is concerned we cannot get
to any fact more fundamental than that relating
to sense of rhythm. Recent research in factories
has shown conclusively that a task performed
with regular muscular movements is one accomplished
with great economy of energy and consequent
reduction of fatigue. Nature, by long and painful
experiments, often resulting in the elimination of
species and creation of new orders, established the
physiological basis of dancing by founding a sense of
rhythm in all animals. The elementary principle of
the dance is that of the co-ordinated muscular movements of flight, swimming, walking and running.
At what very early stage in the childhood of man
there came a consciousness of rhythm and a pleasure
resulting from its use and artificial development will
never be known. Archaeological evidence shows us
human figures of the Old Stone Age in what are
probably dancing attitudes, and these paintings are
associated in time and place with pictorial representations of animal life, for man in this remote period was
a hunter, and one of consummate skill. There was
perhaps in the first place a deliberate invention in
order to bring rhythmical motion into the daily life
of the clan, and it is not improbable that these early
experiments in giving rhythm a place in social and

religious development emerged from imitation of animal movements. No doubt there were *individual* efforts in mimicry of animals before some genius applied the practice and skill to the formation of a united social effort. This was intended to increase the supply of game by giving mimetic dances which still survive among most primitive people. As the psychologist would say, " It is necessary to bring the motions of music into some sort of correspondence with the character of the acts and energies of man in order to be able to express his soul's life." That is to say, expression of emotion is a natural law, repression is a product of education. Whether the rhythm is fast or slow, vigorous or reposeful, sombre or gay, loquacious or reflective, clear or suspended in doubt, no mood can occur that cannot be depicted in its general character and course.[344]

In one sense Professor A. R. Brown[345] is correct in saying that the psychology of dancing offers a wide field for study which has been barely touched. The dances of primitive man have not been comparatively studied, though psychologists have speculated considerably in an abstract philosophical way with regard to origins and development.[346]

I do not think it is true that song and music, with dancing must necessarily develop side by side, though it is natural for them to do so. The Tasmanians of Stone Age culture, long isolated, had a well developed sense of rhythm, vocal music, and dancing, but they had no musical instruments ; and the same may be said of Australian aborigines and Veddas of Ceylon.

Most animals, and especially the primates, have powers of imitation which they exercise, and this fact, combined with nature's early establishment of economy of effort by muscular rhythm, accounts perhaps for the origin of the dance, in imitation of the movements of animals. Karl Groos has some such idea in mind throughout his book " The Play of Man " ;[347] mimicry of animals was probably play before the capers were organised into a system of magical acts. Rhythm is certainly more elemental and earlier to appear in child development than is a sense of pitch. Dudley Kidd remarks that rhythm appeals to Kafir children more than singing,[348] and most people will agree that children of the Kindergarten class are easily taught rhythmical displays long before they could give an exhibition of vocal or instrumental music. There is great interest in the fact that many primitive people trace their knowledge of animal dances to information received from animal ancestors, and I have no doubt that the development of mimetic dances and totemism were mutually dependent.

When dancing as a definitely organised procedure was established, one can realise the power it must have had over a community by its intoxicating effect [349] and practical utility in expressing hopes, fears and anticipations with regard to the success of hunting.

From very early times in the Old Stone Age, archaeological evidence suggests that man had probably an idea of survival after death, and in the intoxication of the dance he fell into a hypnotic state resembling death. How did the office of sorcerer and magician arise ? Some people, more than others, would succumb to this hysteria and collapse, for there are always different degrees of any natural phenomenon. Did these dancers of peculiar temperament become the magicians and sorcerers, the wizards, and medicine men ? Were they quick to see the social advantage gained by dancing themselves into an ecstasy, stiffening out, and prophecying with regard to the location of honey and game ? Mimetic dances, ecstatic dances, and agricultural dances are I think the oldest and most fundamental instances of

s

rhythmical movements being employed to aid communal life. This intoxicating effect of the dance
accounts for the wide use of rhythmical action in
expressing every form of social emotion and herd instinct,whether of anger, fear, or joy. In the war dance,
the movements of which are based on the actual
motions of warfare, the intoxicating effect of combined
rhythms arouses the collective anger and sense of
unity which are necessary for success. In funeral
dances the fear of ghosts is expressed and a painful
emotion relieved by united rhythmical effort.

We have perhaps been guilty of a " just so "
imaginative speculation of the early development of
dancing, but the suggestions are made in relation to
a substantial background of classified facts, and such
guesswork is justifiable because in the earliest
historical times the various types of dancing were
well established, and without doubt dancing had a
long period of prehistoric evolution which must
necessarily be a matter for surmise. Vocal effort may
have originated in imitation of the cries of animals
which were mimicked, but of the origin of musical
instruments it is difficult to speak with any certainty.
The most elementary instrument of percussion is the
beating of a skin stretched across the knees, or even
the clapping of hands, snapping fingers, and slapping
the body. Thus instrumental accompaniment, like
dancing, is posture and gesture language, a form of
self-expression through the performer's own body.[350]

" Evolution " has been the keynote of scientific
thought for half a century, an " open sesame " to
many a problem of biological inquiry, a word of vital
importance to the scientist, the man of art, and in
no small measure to the musician. These enquirers
seek to interpret present complexity by reference to
the past, in the hope that they may strike the trail
followed by early progenitors in their crude endeavours

to express adequately the simple primary emotions and accompanying instincts. These emotions are ever and ever urging toward a refined and more elaborate fulfilment in religious processions, also in complex orchestral and vocal renderings of great musical compositions. Comparative study of musical instruments with a view to their classification and arrangement in evolutionary series is a highly technical task which at the best leaves a broad margin of doubt respecting relationship of types.

Certain musical instruments and dances are too peculiar and infrequent in occurrence to support a theory of migration from a centre. Thus the aeolian harp, consisting of bamboo rods pierced with holes, is exposed in treetops in Aurora Island, Melanesia, also in British Guiana, but a chain of connection is not, I think, established. In West Africa there are " hammock " and " rowing " dances which appear to have no parallels in other parts of the world.

On the contrary, the slat of wood known as a " bull roarer " gives out a whining note when whirled at the end of a string. Such a contrivance is of almost world-wide distribution in connection with magical ceremonies.

Mr. Henry Balfour has worked out the origin, development, and distribution of the musical bow[351], and has prepared maps showing the distribution of nose flutes ; but I am unable to say to what extent he supports a theory of migration against one of possible independent origins. The Pygmies in many parts of the world, chiefly Central Africa, Andaman Islands, Malay Peninsula, and New Guinea have been comparatively studied,[352] so providing an example of the kind of detailed and intensive investigation which is so essential to clearing up sociological problems.

Detailed study of songs and dances, especially those relating to animal mimicry, moon worship, sun cults, agriculture, ghosts, test of endurance, initiation into tribes and secret societies, and satirical drama, could be competently carried out only by detailed analysis of records taken on the rhythmograph, and phonograph. There are probably not in existence sufficient of these records to ensure reliable comparisons and groupings. But if such comparative study could be made, there is a probability that identity of terpsichorean technique would, if accompanied by notes on the meaning and legendary origin, provide the clue to migratory lines of such practices as initiation, human sacrifice, animal cults, and other complex social events which have, undoubtedly, had a long history. This mapping and comparative study, though essential from the historical standpoint, is a detailed and technical procedure unsuitable for a small popular publication.

THE DANCE AND SOCIETY

To provide reading of general interest it is but necessary to turn to social and psychological aspects of musical expression. The foregoing pages have been an elaboration of the schematic table given in the introduction, reference to which will show the many ramifications of the dance. A useful classification groups dances around the facts of (1) Food supply, animal and vegetable. (2) Sexual impulse. (3) Approach to a spirit world. Here we have the great basic factors of human existence ever since it has been such, and it is no exaggeration to say that dancing is a complete expression of social and communal life. Society dancing, as we know it in England to-day, also exhibition dancing as we find it in Asiatic countries, and as a popular entertainment at home, are offshoots and denegerate forms of the great communal system of dancing which has been the essence of human progress.

The remarks of Cureau[353] succinctly express what dancing still is to primitive societies in which combined rhythmical action gives mental fusion and convergence of purpose. Primitive men in particular are very fond of hypnotic sensations, and it needs only the monotonous throb of the tom-tom, combined with a regular repetition of movements and words, to bring about a communicable ecstasy, in which dancing is not so much a pleasure as an expression of love, war, and religion.

PHYSIOLOGY AND THE DANCE

The physiological aspect of the dance has been very fully dealt with by a recent writer,[354] who points out that in primitive women the muscles of the abdominal, pelvic, and gluteal regions are much more highly developed than they are in civilised women. Dancing improves the general health by relieving constipation and making parturition easy. " Too much ridicule and obloquy have been thrown on such valuable exercises as the *danse du ventre*, and the *danse du derrière*, which are capable of imparting a very great amount of movement to the viscera." Value in promoting healthy and vigorous life is rightly regarded as of great value to the individual and his social group. Sexual selection with the choice of enduring and well developed mates are again to be valued as an outcome of primitive dancing. I am inclined to think, however, that these benefits are to a great extent a fortuitous unstudied outcome of the dance, and not the deliberately chosen reasons for inventing the exercise.

DANCING AND ADMINISTRATION

Thus far we have been concerned with problems of history and pre-history which arise when a large body of facts is collated with regard to specific dances ; vocal music ; recitative songs, especially those in an archaic language ; and the origin and distribution of musical instruments. Discussion of the question of innate musical abilities as racial characteristics, and the extent to which these may be developed or repressed by racial history, geographical environment, and social and religious forces, leaves the impression that musical ability is a variable racial quality, but subject to the influence of the factors mentioned.

On the practical side there is for the missionary and administrator material worthy of careful study in ethnological reports on the dancing and music of backward peoples. If dancing and music are, as we have endeavoured to show, the essence of communal life ; and if it be granted that primitive peoples are worthy of preservation, and incorporation in the march of human progress ; then there follows the deduction that racial decline in numbers and vigour will result from an unnecessary interference with the social and psychological environment which has grown with the race. This question is forcibly expressed in a Colonial Office Report for 1921 in which Captain Rattnay states that in Ashanti (and the same applies to many parts of the world) the people are at the parting of the ways :—

" One path leads, I believe, to the unrest and ferment we see on every hand among the peoples whose institutions we have either deliberately broken down or as deliberately allowed to decay. The other path at least leads to some surer hope, because it has landmarks which the genius of the people will recognise, and which will keep them upon the road when in difficulties. . . . Among the younger generation there is a tendency to ridicule the past. A youth who has passed the 5th, 6th or 7th standard, and who by clerical work earns a few pounds a month, and is dressed in European garb, in his heart despises his own institutions, and his own illiterate elders. But he takes his cue from the European, whom his end-all and be-all is to copy. I firmly believe that once the Government and Political Officers are seen to take more interest in his ancient customs, and are seen to encourage such customs and institutions as are good, the younger generation will themselves follow suit, and come to realise that they should not throw away their priceless heritage."

BIBLIOGRAPHY

1 A. R. Brown. "The Andaman Islanders," 1922, pp. 249, 252, etc.
2 Dr. C. S. Myers. *British Journal Psychology*, 1905, pp. 252, 237, and
   "Ethnological Study of Music " in "Anthropological Essays
   to Sir E. B. Tylor," 1907.
3 C. G. Claridge. "Wild Bush Tribes of Tropical Africa, '' p. 224.
4 Krasheninnikoff. "History of Kamtschatka and the Kurile
   Islands." St. Petersburg 1764. Translation in English
   by Grieve. Pp. 176-7.
5 Turner, G. "Nineteen Years in Polynesia," London 1860, p. 210.
6 "Journal of The Resolution's Voyage of Discovery to the Southern
   Hemisphere," London 1775, p. 206.
7 Dieffenbach's "Travels in New Zealand," London 1843. Vol. II.,
   p. 19.
8 H. Ling Roth. "The Aborigines of Tasmania," Halifax, England,
   1899, pp. 138-9.
9 Williamson's "Ways of The South Sea Savage," London 1912,
   p. 139.
10 Polack, J. S. "Manners and Customs of the New Zealanders,"
   London 1838, Vol. I., p. 79-82.
11 A. R. Radcliffe Brown. "The Andaman Islanders," Cambridge
   1922, p. 132.
12 Dobrizoffer Martin. "The Abipoines of Paraguay," London
   1822, Vol. II., p. 431.
13 William Marsden's Translation of "Travels of Marco Polo,"
   revised by T. Wright, New York 1904, p. 171.
14 Poole, Stanley Lane. "Mediaeval India," Bombay, 1916,
   p. 10.
15 Hose, C., and McDougal, W. "Pagan Tribes of Borneo," London
   1912, Vol. II, p. 156-7.
16 Roscoe, Canon J. "The Bagesu," Cambridge 1924, p. 152.
17 Driberg, J. H. "The Lango—A Nilotic Tribe of Uganda," London
   1923, p. 142.
18 Rice, C. Colliver. "Persian Women and Their Ways," London
   1923, p. 124.
19 Seligman, C. G. "Melanesians of British New Guinea," Cambridge 1910, p.25, and Brown G. ''Melanesians and Polynesians,"
   London 1910, p. 59.
20 Routledge, W. S. and K. "With a Prehistoric People—The
   Akikuyu," London 1910, p. 154.
21 Werner, Alice, "Native Tribes of British Central Africa," London
   1906, p. 125.
22 Hardy, N., and Elkington, E. H. "Savage South Seas," London
   1907, p. 50.
23 Spencer, B., and Gillen, F. J. "Across Australia," Lond on
   1912, Vol. I., p. 247 *et seq.*
24 Melville Herman. "Typhee," London 1924, p. 156.

[25] ELLIS, W. "Polynesian Researches," London 1832, Vol. I., p 217.

[26] SHKLOVSKY, I. W. "In Far North East Siberia," London 1916. pp. 55-6.

[27] BOGORAS, V. "The Chukchee," *Journal* N. Pacific Expedition; Vol. VII, 1904-9., pp. 268-9.

[28] CATLIN. G. "Manners and Customs of North American Indians," London, 1841, Vol. I., pp. 127-8.

[29] SELIGMAN, C. S. "Veddas of Ceylon," Cambridge 1906, pp. 336-8.

[30] GRUBB, W. B. "In The Paraguayan Chaco," London 1904, p. 72.

[31] LANE, E. "An Account of Manners and Customs of The Modern Egyptians," London 1871, Vol. II., p. 272; and LANDOR HENRY SAVAGE, "In the Forbidden Land", London 1898, Vol. I., p. 124.

[32] HOSE and McDOUGALL's "Pagan Tribes of Borneo," Vol. I., p. 115.

[33] BREUIL, H.; GOMEZ, P. S., and CABRE, J. "Les Abris del Basque a Alpera;" L'Anthropologie 1912, Vol. XXIII., pp. 529-562.

[34] SOLLAS. W. J. "Ancient Hunters," London 1924, p. 483. Fig. 261 ; and PROZESKY in *Zeitschrift für Ethnologie* 1896, Vol. XXXVIII., p. 909.

[35] SOLLAS. "Ancient Hunters," p. 481.

[36] *Ibid.*, p. 485, Fig. 263. See M. H. Tongue, "Bushman Paintings," Oxford 1909.

[37] "First Three Years of Childhood," London 1885, p. 267.

[38] BRITISH MUSEUM "Guide to Stone Age Antiquities," Second Ed., Fig. 46, No. 5.

[39] MUNRO, R. "Palaeolithic Man and the Terramara Settlements," Edinburgh 1912. Plate XX., p. 450, Fig 4.

[40] BRITISH MUSEUM. "Bronze Age Guide," 2nd Ed., Plate VIII.

[41] BALFOUR H. "The Natural History of the Musical Bow," Oxford 1899.

[42] McCLINTOCK. W. "The Old North Trail," London 1910, p. 457.

[43] BONWICK, JAMES. "Life and Origins of The Tasmanians," 1870, p. 38.

[44] LING ROTH, H. "Aborigines of Tasmania," Halifax, England 1899, p. 134, notes, Peron, Francois, and Freycinet, Louis. "Voyage de Decouvertes aux Ternes Australie," 2 vols., Paris 1807, 1816, 1824.

[45] "Account of a Voyage in Search of La Perouse," 2 vols., London 1800, Bk. II., Ch. 10, p. 45.

[46] "Narrative of a Visit to the Australian Colonies," London 1843, Vol. I., p. 93.

[47] BROWN, A. R. "The Andaman Islanders," Cambridge 1922, pp. 32., 132-3.

[48] SELIGMAN, C. G. "The Veddas of Ceylon," Cambridge 1906, pp. 135, etc.

[49] *Ibid.*, pp. 341-65.

[50] "Life in Ancient Egypt," London and New York 1894, pp. 248-9.

[51] PETRIE, Sir W. M. F. "Social Life in Ancient Egypt," London 1923, p. 105.

[52] SACHS CURT. "Altagyptische Musikinstrumente," Leipzig 1920, pp. 17-23, many illustrations.
do. "Handbuch der Muisikinstrumentenkunde," Leipzig 1920.
NEWBERY,P. C. "Beni Hassan." Part I. Archaeological Survey of Egypt, London 1893. Plate XII.

[53] STANFORD, Sir C. V. " A History of Music," 1916, pp. 1-10.
[54] BUDGE, W. " Osiris and The Egyptian Resurrection," Vol. I., p. 232, and OESTERLEY, W. O. E. " The Sacred Dance," Camb. 1922.
[55] " Heart of Africa," Vol. II., p. 129.
[56] " Osiris and The Egyptian Resurrection," London 1911. Vol. I., p. 233.
[57] SAYCE, A. H. " Babylonians and Assyrians—Their Life and Customs," London 1900.
[58] Personal Communication. Mr. C. J. GADD. British Museum.
[59] A large drum beaten by two performers is shewn on a fragment of a Sumerian bowl (Revue d'Assyriologie, Paris 1910, Tome IX., Planche III. Horizontal Assyrian harps can be seen in the relief of Assurbanipal pouring a libation over dead lions. Assyrian Saloon, British Museum, Slab 118). An earlier kind of harp is shown on a relief from Lagash in Sarzec's " Decouvertes en Chaldee," Planche 23. The double flute and a kind of vertical harp are shown on the lowest register of the Assyrian reliefs in the Nineveh Gallery, British Museum. Slabs 49, 50. See also Kurt Jacks, " Die Musik des Altertums," Munich, 1925.
[60] JOYCE, T. A. " Mexican Archaeology," London 1912, p. 168.
[61] Ibid.; Fig. 63.
[62] Ibid.; p. 300.
[63] JOYCE, T. A. " South American Archaeology," London 1912, Plate IV, Fig 6, op. p. 42.
[64] Ibid.; p. 32.
[65] PETRIE, W. M. F., Sir. " Social Life in Ancient Egypt," p. 105.
[66] Journal Royal Anthropological Institute of Great Britain 1917. Vol. 47, p. 413.
[67] CROOKE, W. " Things Indian," London 1906, p. 119.
[68] do. " Northern India," London 1906, p. 187.
[69] Ibid., p. 121.
[70] Ibid., p. 122.
[71] See description of the " Rasa Dance " in Chapter XIII., Bk. V.
[72] DALTON, E. T. " Descriptive Ethnology of Bengal," p. 215.
[73] RAHAMIN FYZEE. " Indian Music," London 1914, p. 67.
[74] Ibid., Plate IV., p. 59.
[75] Ibid., Plate VI., p. 61.
[76] SCOTT, Sir J. G. " The Burman, His Life and Notions," London 1910.
[77] GILES, H. A. " Glossary of Reference on Subjects connected with the Far East," London 1884, p. 157.
[78] COULING, S. Encyclopaedia Sinica, 1917, p. 386, et seq—Couling give a long list of references useful to specialists.
[79] SAUNDERS, J. R. " The Chinese as They Are," London 1919, Chapter VI.
[80] British Museum, Asiatic Saloon, Table Case F., presentation by J. EDGE, Partington.
[81] PARKER, E. H. " John Chinaman and a Few Others," London 1909, p. 266, Ibid., p. 282, and " Ancient China Simplified," London 1908, pp. 30, 62.
[82] F. W. CAREY, Esq., Chinese Customs Service, personal communication.
[83] DOUGLAS, R. K. " Society in China," London 1894, p. 376.
[84] GRAY, J. H. " China—A History of the Laws, Manners and Customs," London 1878, Vol. I., p. 383.

284 BIBLIOGRAPHY

[85] WIT, AUGUSTA DE, "Java, Facts and Fancies," London 1905.
[86] PIGGOTT, Sir FRANCIS. "Music and Musical Instruments of Japan," London 1909, pp. 133-145.
[87] Ibid., p. 40.
[88] CHAMBERLAIN, B. H. "Things Japanese," London 1898, p. 307. INOUYE, JUKICHI. "Sketches of Tokyo Life," Yokohama 1895., Ch. IV., pp. 48-50, "The Geisha's Calling."
[89] GILES, H. A. "Glossary of Reference on Subjects connected with the Far East," London 1884.
[90] JOHNSTON SAINT, T. R. "Islanders of the Pacific," London 1921, p. 117.
[91] "Pagan Tribes of Borneo," Vol. I., p. 188.
[92] HOSE and McDOUGALL. "Pagan Tribes of Borneo," Vol. I., pp. 174-7.
[93] Ibid., Vol. II., pp. 20, 167-8.
[94] Ibid., Vol. II., pp. 168.
[95] HADDON, A. C. "Head Hunters, Black, White, Brown," London, 1901, p. 358.
[96] McGOVERN, J. B. "Among the Head Hunters of Formosa," London 1922, p. 112.
[97] DALTON, E. T. "Descriptive Ethnology of Bengal," London 1872, p. 41.
[98] HUTTON, J. H., "The Angami Nagas," London 1921, p. 104.
[99] CROOKE, W. "Things Indian," London 1906, p. 124.
[100] BIRT, B. "The Story of an Indian Upland," London 1905, pp. 142, 258-60.
[101] SPENCER, B., and GILLEN, F. J. "Across Australia," Vol. II., pp. 294-7.
[102] "Journal of a Journey of Discovery into Central Australia," London 1844, Vol. II., p. 236.
[103] WILLIAMSON, R. W. "Ways of the South Sea Savage," London 1914, p. 147.
[104] "Head Hunters—Black, White and Brown," London 1901, p. 187.
[105] "The Fijians—A study in Decay of Custom," London 1908, pp. 484-6.
[106] JOHNSON MARTIN, "Cannibal Land—Adventures with a Camera in the New Hebrides," London 1922, p. 154.
[107] DIEFFENBACH, E. "Travels in New Zealand," London 1843, Vol. II., p. 63.
[108] POLACK, J. S. "Manners and Customs of New Zealanders," London 1838, p. 79.
[109] EARLE AUGUSTUS, "Narrative of Nine Months Residence in New Zealand in 1827," London 1832, p. 159.
[110] ROBLEY, H. G. "Moko," London 1896, p. 32 et seq.
[111] POLACK, J. S. "Manners and Customs of New Zealand," London 1838, Vol. II., pp. 166-7.
[112] COOMBE, FLORENCE, "Islands of Enchantment," London 1911, pp. 299-300.
[113] DECLE, L. "Three Years in Savage Africa," London 1898, p. 156.
[114] DRIBERG, J. H. "The Lango, A Nilotic Tribe of Uganda," London 1923, p. 110.
[115] WERNER, A. "British Central Africa," London 1906, p. 228.
[116] WEEKS, Rev. J. H. "Among Congo Cannibals," London 1913, p. 227.
[117] NEWLAND, H. O. "Sierra Leone—Its People, Products, and Secret Societies," London 1916, p. 106.

[118] FIFE, C. W. DOMVILLE. "Among Wild Tribes of the Amazon," London 1924, p. 153.

[119] *Ibid.*, pp. 140, 152.

[120] *Ibid.*, p. 176.

[121] FARABEE, W. C. "Indian Tribes of Eastern Peru," Cambridge, Mass, 1922, p. 123.

[122] WHIFFEN, T. "The North West Amazons," London 1915, p. 204.

[123] McCLINTOCK, W. "The Old North Trail," London 1910, pp. 277-8, 421.

[124] CATLIN, G. "North American Indians," Vol. I., pp. 131, 245, Plate 104.

[125] McCLINTOCK's "The Old North Trail," pp. 277-8, 421.

[126] BOLLER, H. A. "Among the Indians—Eight Years in The Far West," Pa. 1867, p. 84.

[127] "The Abipoines of Paraguay," London 1822, Vol. II., p. 428.

[128] MALINOWSKI, "Mate Selection in Primitive Society," a Lecture given before the Eugenics Education Society and reported in the London *Times*, February 28th, 1925.

[129] PLOSS, H. "Das Weib in der Natur und Volkerkunde," Leipzig, 1905.

[130] HARDY, N. and ELKINGTON, E. H. "The Savage South Seas," London 1907, pp. 31, 50.

[131] ROUT, ETTIE. "Sex and Exercise," London 1920, p. 12.

[132] HADDON, A. C. "Reports of Cambridge Anthropological Expedition to Torres Strait," 1898, Vol. IV., p. 312, Vol. V., pp. 222-3.

[133] SELIGMAN, C. G. "Melanesians of British New Guinea," Cambridge 1910, p. 145.

[134] WILLIAMSON, R. W. "Ways of the South Sea Savage," London 1914, p. 145.

[135] MILNE, Mrs. LESLIE. "The Shans at Home," London 1910, p. 71.

[136] COWAN, J. "Maoris of New Zealand," London and Auckland, 1910, p. 218.

[137] KRASHINNIKOFF, S. P. "The History of Kamschatka and the Kurile Islands," St. Petersburg 1764. English Translation by James Grieve, p. 209.

[138] "Abipiones of Paraguay," London 1822, Vol. II., p. 208.

[139] FARABEE, W. C. "Indian Tribes of Eastern Peru," Pa. 1922, p. 123.

[140] FIFE, C. W. DOMVILLE. "Among Wild Tribes of the Amazon," London 1924, p. 225.

[141] RICE, C. COLLIVER, "Persian Women and their Ways," London 1923, p. 33.

[142] "Among Congo Cannibals," London 1913, pp. 119-20.

[143] SPENCER, B., and GILLEN, F. J. "Across Australia," London 1912, p. 237 ; and MATHEW, J., "Eagle Hawk and Crow," London 1899, p. 140.

[144] "Ethnological Studies Among North West Central Queensland Aborigines," Brisbane 1897, pp. 121, 151. Plates XV., XVI.

[145] WORSNOP, THOMAS, "The Aborigines of Australia," Adelaide 1897, p. 151.

[146] WORSNOP's "Aborigines of Australia," pp. 148.

[147] CODRINGTON, R. H. "The Melanesians," Oxford 1891, p. 33 ; and WILLIAMSON, R. W., "Ways of the South Sea Savage," London 1914, p. 141.

286 BIBLIOGRAPHY

[148] "Pearls and Savages," London 1924, pp. 240.
[149] DAUNCEY, H. M. "Papuan Pictures," London 1913, p. 75.
[150] WILLIAMSON, R. W. "Ways of a South Sea Savage," London 1914, p. 137.
[151] MARINER, W. "Tonga Islands," London 1817, Vol. II., p. 329.
[152] RUTTER, OWEN. "British North Borneo," London 1922, pp. 69, 328-31.
[153] FARABEE, W. C. "The Central Arawaks," Pa. 1918, p. 85.
[154] HILL-TOUT, T. "British North America," London 1907, p. 251.
[155] CATLIN, G. "North American Indians," London 1841, Vol. I., p. 245, Plate 103.
[156] WILLIAMSON, R. W. "Ways of the South Sea Savage," pp. 158, 222. Plates 71, 72.
[157] HADDON, A. C. "Cambridge Expedition to Torres Strait," Vol. V., p. 201.
[158] Ibid., Vol. V., p. 202.
[159] WEULE, K. "Native Life in East Africa," Leipzig 1909, p. 220. Translation by A. Werner.
[160] WERNER's "Native Tribes of British Central Africa," pp. 126-7.
[161] Ibid., p. 127.
[162] HOLLIS, A. C. "The Nandi," Oxford 1909, pp. 57.
[163] RUST, HORATIO N. "American Anthropologist," Vol. VIII 1906, p. 28, "A Puberty Ceremony of the Mission Indians."
[164] WHIFFEN. "The North West Amazons," pp. 157-8.
[165] THURSTON, E. "Ethnographical Notes in Southern India,' Madras, 1906, pp. 29, 383, 400.
[166] BROWN, A. R. "The Andaman Islands," Cambridge 1922, 128. Plate XI.
[167] HORNE, G. and AISTON, G. "Savage Life in Central Australia," London 1924, p. 172.
CURR, E. M. "The Australian Race," London 1886, Vol. II., p. 58.
SCHURMAN, C. W. "Aboriginal Tribes of Port Lincoln," London 1879, pp. 228-31.
SPENCER, B. and GILLEN, F. J. "Across Australia," London 1912, Vol. I., p. 24.
[168] HADDON, A. C. "Head Hunters Black, White, Brown," London 1901, p. 51, and "Customs of the World," London 1912, Vol. I., p. 3.
[169] Cambridge Expedition to Torres Strait, Vol. VI., pp. 283, 308, Plate XXVI., Fig. 1.
[170] HILL-TOUT, C. "British North America," pp. 53, 163-4, 252.
[171] ROSCOE, Canon J. S. "The Bagesu," Cambridge 1924, p. 28.
[172] FROBENIUS, L. "The Childhood of Man," London 1909, pp. 338, Fig. 273.
[173] NEWLAND, H. O. "Sierra Leone," London 1916, p. 125.
[174] DRIBERG, J. H. "The Lango—A Nilotic Tribe of Uganda," 1923, p. 127.
[175] IM THURN, Sir E. F. "Among The Indians of Guiana," London 1883, p. 326, Fig. 33, picture of the whip.
[176] TREMEARNE, Major A. J. N. "Tailed Head Hunters of Nigeria," London 1912, p. 104.
[177] NEWLAND, H. OSMAN. "Sierra Leone," London 1916, pp. 83.
[178] BASDEN, G. T. "Among the Ibos of Nigeria," London 1921, p. 132.

BIBLIOGRAPHY 287

[179] WERNER, A. " British Central Africa," p. 226.
[180] SCOTT, Sir J. (Shway-Yoe). " The Burman, His Life and Notions," London 1910, p. 312.
[181] Ibid., p. 305.
[182] MEAKIN, ANNETTE B. "Customs of the World," Ed. A. C. Haddon, 1912, Vol. II., pp. 585, 589. See also illustrations, Meakin's " In Russian Turkestan," London 1903.
[183] WILLS, C. J. " In the Land of the Lion and the Sun," London 1883, p. 114.
[184] LANDOR, HENRY SAVAGE. " In the Forbidden Land," London 1898, Vol. II., p. 182.
[185] WADDELL, L. A. " Lhasa and Its Mysteries," London 1905, p. 422.
[186] ROCKHILL, W. W. " Diary of a Journey through Mongolia and Tibet," Washington 1894, p. 91.
[187] DAUNCEY, H. M. " Papuan Pictures," London 1913, pp. 36, 73.
[188] HAMBLY, W. D. " History and Significance of Tattooing," London 1925.
[189] This work, Ch. IV.
[190] " Tätowiren," Berlin 1887.
[191] HOSE, C., and MCDOUGALL,W. " Pagan Tribes of Borneo," Vol. I., pp. 265, London 1912.
[192] ELLIS, W. " Polynesian Researches," Vol. I., p. 262.
[193] BREWSTER, A. B. 1922. " The Hill Tribes of Fiji," p. 185.
[194] CHRISTIAN, F. W. " Eastern Pacific Islands," 1910, p. 93.
[195] McGOVERN, J. B. M. " Among Head Hunters of Formosa," 1922, p. 189.
[196] " Die Tatowirung bider Geschlecter in Samoa," 1899, p. 17.
[197] JOEST WILHELM, " Tätowirung," 1887, pp. 60-65.
[198] TURNER's " Samoa " and " Nineteen Years in Polynesia," 1861, p. 192.
[199] BROWN, G. " Melanesians and Polynesians," London 1910, pp. 96, 101, 108.
[200] MARQUARDT, CARL, " Die Tätowirung in Samoa," 1899, p. 15, etc.
[201] Ibid., p. 15, etc.
[202] WHIFFEN. " The North West Amazons," p. 190.
[203] FARABEE, WILLIAM CURTIS. " Indian Tribes of Eastern Peru," p. 123.
[204] MILNE's " Shans at Home," p. 105.
[205] SKEAT and BLAGDEN. " Pagan Races of The Malay Peninsula," Vol. II., pp. 117, Vol. I., p. 364.
[206] MacGOVERN, J. B. " Among the Head Hunters of Formosa," London 1922, p. 184.
[207] SELIGMAN, C. G. " The Veddas of Ceylon," Cambridge 1906, pp. 341-65.
[208] CODRINGTON's " Melanesians," p. 334.
HUTTON's " Angami Nagas," p. 195.
[209] " The Making of Hawaii," London 1899, p. 19.
[210] " The Old North Trail," London 1910, p. 282.
[211] WILLIAMSON's " Ways of the South Sea Savage," p. 234.
[212] Ibid., p. 141.
[213] Ibid., p. 26.
[214] HADDON, A. C. " Races of Man," Halifax, England 1911.
[215] " North West Central Queensland Aborigines," London 1897, p. 117.

288 BIBLIOGRAPHY

216 DAVIES, R. H. "The Aborigines of Van Diemen's Land," *Tasmanian Journal of Science*," Launceston and London 1846, Vol. II., p. 416.

217 LLOYD, G. T. "Thirty-Three Years in Tasmania and Victoria," London 1862, pp. 49-50.

218 ROTH, HENRY LING. "Aborigines of Tasmania," Halifax, England 1899, p. 134 *et seq*.

219 ELLIS, W. "Polynesian Researches," Four Vols. London 1832. Vol. I., p. 195.

220 BROWN, J. M. "Maori and Polynesian," London 1907, p. 203.

221 THOMSON, BASIL. "Savage Island," London 1902, p. 218.

222 *Ibid.*, p. 22.

223 *Ibid.*, p. 226.

224 CODRINGTON, R. H. "The Melanesians," Oxford 1891, p. 337.

225 WILLIAMSON, R. W. "The Ways of The South Sea Savage," London 1914, p. 258.

226 HADFIELD, EMMA. "Loyalty Islands," London 1920, p. 133.

227 BROWN, J. M. "The Riddle of the Pacific," London 1924, p. 242 *etc*. See also for general archaeology.
ROUTLEDGE, E. K. "The Mystery of Easter Island," London 1919.

228 TORDAY, E. "On The Trail of The Bushongo," London 1925, p. 202,

229 KIDD, DUDLEY, "Savage Childhood," London 1906, pp. 88, 124.

230 J. DOWD, "The Negro Races," London 1907, p. 42.

231 WERNER, A. "The Natives of British Central Africa," London 1906, p. 216.

232 WEEKS, J. H. "Among Congo Cannibals," London 1913, p. 91.

233 "The Tailed Head Hunters of Nigeria," London 1912, p. 269.

234 TALBOT, P. A. "In The Shadow of The Bush," London 1912, p. 297.

235 "On The Trail of The Bushongo," p. 272.

236 "Native Life in East Africa," London 1909, p. 290.

237 JUNOD, HENRI A. "Life of a South African Tribe," Neuchatel 1912, Vol. II., p. 291.

238 "The Life of a South African Tribe," Vol. I., p. 404 ; Vol. II., pp. 249, 265, 442

239 "Ethnology of the A-Kamba and other East African Tribes," Cambridge, 1910, p. 32.

240 CHRISTIE, CUTHBERT. "Big Game and Pygmies," London 1924 pp. 20, 39.

241 *Ibid.*, pp. 44-5.

242 BARNES ALEXANDER. "Wonderland of The Eastern Congo," London 1924, p. 152.

243 SCHWEINFURTH. G. "The Heart of Africa," London 1878, Vol. I., p. 130.

244 BALFOUR. H. "The Natural History of the Musical Bow," Oxford 1899, p. 5, 124, *etc*.

245 "Notes on North American Indians," London 1841. Vol. I., p. 241. Plate 10.

246 CATLIN'S "North American Indians," Vol. I., pp. 245. Plate 104.
ROBERTS. HELEN H. "New Phases in the Study of Primitive Music," American Anthropologist, No. 24, 1922, pp. 144-59.

247 JENNESS. D. "Report of Canadian Arctic Expedition, 1913-18," Vol. XII., Part A.
"Life of The Copper Eskimos," Ottawa 1922, p. 222.

[248] *Journal* Jesup North Pacific Expedition, New York, Vol. 7, 1904-9 p. 402.

[249] "Among the Indians of Guiana," London 1883, pp. 310, 319,323, etc.

[250] IM THURN'S " Among the Indians of Guiana," p. 310.

[251] WHIFFEN, T. " The North West Amazons," London, 1915, pp. 190, 194-6.

[252] SCHOMBURGK, RICHARD. " Travels in British Guiana " (Translation by W. E. ROTH, London, 1922), Vol. II., p. 152.

[253] GRUBB, W. B. " Among Indians of The Paraguayan Chaco," London, 1904, p. 95.

[254] LANDOR. HENRY SAVAGE. " Across Unknown South America," London, 1913. Vol. I. p. 237.

[255] Spalding Club Miscellanies, 1. pp. 97-8.

[256] MURRAY, M. A. " Witch Cult in Western Europe," Oxford 1921, p. 135, gives a large bibliography dealing with initiation of witches, their cults, rites, and reports of law court trials.

[257] REINACH, S. " Cultes, Mythes et Religions," London 1906, Vol I., p. 173-83.

[258] HADDON, A. C. " Customs of the World " London 1912. Vol. II., p. 625. BROWNE, G. E. " A Year Among the Persians," London 1893. WEIR, T. H. " Sheikhs of Morocco," London, 1904. MEAKIN, A. B. " The Moors," London 1902.

[259] MEAKIN. " In Russian Turkestan," London, 1903, p. 66-7.

[260] McCLINTOCK, WALTER. " The Old North Trail," London, 1910.

[261] CATLIN, GEORGE. " Manners, Customs and Ceremonies of The North American Indians—" London 1886, pp. 127-8.

[262] McCLINTOCK, WALTER. " The Old North Trail," London, 1910, pp. 78-85, 92 *et seq.*

[263] HILL-TOUT, T. " British North America," London 1907, p. 163.

[264] IM THURN, Sir E. F. " Among The Indians of Guiana," London 1883, p. 324.

[265] BATCHELOR, Rev. J. " The Ainu and Their Folk Lore," London 1901, p. 273.

[266] HOSE, C. and McDOUGALL, W. "Pagan Tribes of Borneo," London 1912. Vol. I., pp. 111-13.

[267] SCHOMBURGK, R. " Travels in British Guiana," Translation by W. E. ROTH. London, 1922. Vol. II. p. 151.

[268] BOGORAS, V. *Journal* North Pacific Expedition. New York, 1904-9. Vol. VII. pp. 389, 403.

[269] BILBY, J. W. " Among Unknown Eskimo," London 1923. p. 211.

[270] *Ibid.*, p. 217.

[271] STOW, G. W. " The Native Races of South Africa," 1905, p. 113.

[272] SKEAT, W. W., and BLAGDEN, O. " Pagan Races of The Malay Peninsula," London 1906. Vol. II., p. 119.

[273] SELIGMAN, C. G. "Veddas of Ceylon," Cambridge 1906, p. 214 ; and SARASINS, P. and F. " Ergebnisse Naturvissenschaftlich Forschungen auf Ceylon in den Jahren, 1884-6," Wiesbaden 1887, pp. 512-13.

[274] BONWICK, JAMES. "Daily Life and Origin of Tasmanians," London 1870, p. 186.

[275] SPENCER, B., and GILLEN, F. J. " Across Australia," London 1912, Vol. II., p. 268. Fig. 117. Ceremony of the Emu Totem. The head-dress represents the head and neck of an emu.

[276] WILLIAMSON, R.W. " Ways of the Soutn Sea Savage, " p. 236.

[277] *Ibid.*, p. 145.

[278] BROWN, J. M. "The Riddle of the Pacific." London 1924, p. 157.

[279] HADDON, A. C. "Head Hunters, Black, White and Brown," London, 1901, p. 184.

[280] *Ibid.*, p. 114.

[281] THURSTON, E. 'Ethnographical Notes on Southern India," Madras, 1906, p. 511.

[282] "A Personal narrative of Thirteen Years' Experience among the Wild Tribes of Khondistan, for suppression of Human Sacrifice." London, 1864. Ch. II., p. 43.

[283] DALTON, E. T. "Descriptive Ethnology of Bengal." London, 1872.

[284] HADDON, A. C. "Customs of The World." London 1912, p. 196. Article by BRADLEY BIRT. Vol. I., p. 541.

[285] SKEAT and BLAGDEN. "Pagan Races of The Malay Peninsula." Vol. I., p. 362.

[286] "Pagan Tribes of Borneo." Vol. I., pp. 111-13.

[287] BEAVER, W. N. "Unexplored New Guinea." London, 1920, p. 180.

[288] BROWN, J. M. "Maori and Polynesian." London 1907, p. 203.

[289] "Head Hunters, Black, White, Brown," p. 217.

[290] WHIFFEN, T. "North West Amazons." London, 1915, p. 195.

[291] ROSCOE, Rev. Canon J. "The Bagesu." Cambridge 1924, pp. 16, 70.

[292] DRIBERG, J. H. "The Lango, A Nilotic Tribe of Uganda," p. 249.

[293] HOBLEY, C. W. "Ethnology of the A-Kamba and other East African Tribes." Cambridge 1910, pp. 32, 53.

[294] "The Old North Trail," p. 320.

[295] *Ibid.*, p. 410.

[296] HILL-TOUT, C. "British North America," London 1907, p. 170.

[297] DRAKE, FRANCIS. "Indian Tribes of United States of America," London 1891. Vol. I., p. 147. Plate 53. In editing this work Drake drew much information from H. R. Schoolcraft's "Indian Tribes of U.S.A." Philadelphia, 1851-60.

[298] JOYCE, T. A. "Mexican Archaeology." London 1912, p. 73.

[299] LUMHOLTZ, CARL. "Unknown Mexico," London 1903. Vol. II., p. 32.

[300] *Ibid.*, Vol. I., p. 331.

[301] DORSEY, G. A. "The Sun Dance of the Arapaho," Field Columbian Museum Publication. No. 75. Vol. IV., pp. 183, 191. Chicago, 1903. See Plates CX., VIII., and CXXXVII. for ceremonial painting.

[302] McGEE, W. J. Bureau American Ethnology. 17th Report, Washington, 1896. Pt. I., p. 242.

[303] BOURKE, J. G. "Snake Dance of The Moquis of Arizona," New York, 1884, p. 246 (musical instruments), pp. 158, 167. The Snake dance.

[304] FROBENIUS, L. "The Childhood of Man," London, 1909, p. 402.

[305] DRAKE, FRANCIS. "Indian Tribes of U.S.A.," London 1891. 2 Vols., p. 146. Plate 32.

[306] SHKLOVSKY, I. W. "In Far North East Siberia." London 1916, pp. 30, 155.

[307] HAMBLY, W. D. "Origins of Education Among Primitive People," London, 1926. Ch. III. deals with morbid psychology, training, and methods of work among medicine men.

BIBLIOGRAPHY 291

[308] SHKLOVSKY, I. W. "In Far North East Siberia," London 1916, pp. 30, 155

[309] CZAPLICKA, M. A. "Aboriginal Siberia," London, 1914, p. 298. For Sacred drums and other instruments see :—Zeitschrift fur Ethnologie, 1910, p. 6. "Die Lappische ZauberTrommel in Meiningen," and Koltmann "Bastian Festschrift," p. 559. "Floten und Pfeifen aus Aet Mexico." Also "Finnisch Ugrische Forschungen," by E. N. Sctälä (Helsingfors), Vol. VI. 1906.

[310] DRAKE, FRANCIS. "Indian Tribes of U.S.A.", Vol., I., Plate 54.

[311] DOBRIZHOFFER, MARTIN. "Abipoines of Paraguay," London, 1822. Vol. II. p. 72.

[312] Bureau American Ethnology. No. 14. 1892, Part II. "Doctrine of the Ghost Dance Religion," p. 921, etc.

[313] Ibid., Plate CXVI., p. 929 ; CXVII., p. 9315; and CXVIII., p. 933.

[314] THOMAS, N. W. "Natives of Australia," London, 1906, p. 121 ; and ROTH, W. E. "North West Central Queensland Aborigines," London, 1897, p. 120.

[315] SPENCER, B., and GILLEN, F. J. "Across Australia", Vol. II., p. 354.

[316] See This Work, Chapter III, "The War Dance."

[317] ELLIS, A. B. "Ewe Speaking Peoples of The Slave Coast of West Africa." London, 1890, pp. 142-3.

[318] SCHWEINFURTH, G. "Heart of Africa," 1878. Vol. I., p. 295.

[319] TREMEARNE, Major A. J. N. "The Tailed Head Hunters of Nigeria," London, 1912.

[320] JUNOD, HENRI, A. "Life of a South African Tribe," London, 1912. Vol. II., pp. 439-447.

[321] LANDOR, HENRY SAVAGE. "In the Forbidden Land," London 1898, Vol. I., p. 229 ; also McGOVERN, W. MONTGOMERY, "To Lhasa in Disguise," London 1924, p. 196 ; ROCKHILL, W. W., "Diary of a Journey through Mongolia and Tibet," in 1891-2, Washington 1894, p. 344.

[322] PANIKKAR, K. M. Journal of Royal Anthropological Institute, London, Vol. XLVIII., 1918, pp. 280-1.

[323] RIVERS, W. H. R. "The Todas," London 1906, p. 248.

[324] THURSTON, E. "Castes and Tribes of Southern India," Madras 1909, Vol. VI., p. 141 ; Vol. V., pp. 143-5.

[325] BROWN, A. R. "The Andaman Islands," Cambridge 1922, p. 163.

[326] WHITEHEAD, G. "In the Nicobar Islands," London 1924, p. 60.

[327] HOSE, C., and McDOUGALL, W. "Pagan Tribes of Borneo," Vol. II. p. 120.

[328] Ibid., Vol. II. pp. 130-3.

[329] LUMHOLTZ, CARL. "Through Central Borneo," New York 1920, Vol. I., p. 121.

[330] "Origin of Tragedy," Cambridge 1910.

[331] "In the Forbidden Land," London 1898, Vol. I., p. 117 et seq.

[332] Ibid., pp. 124, 128.

[333] WRIGHT, THOMAS—revision of Marsden's translation of "Travels of Marco Polo," New York 1904.

[334] MILNE, Mrs. LESLIE. "The Shans at Home," London 1910, p. 91.

[335] RIVERS, W. H. R. "The Todas," London 1906, p. 377.

[336] Ibid., p. 377 et seq.

[337] SELIGMAN, C. G. "The Veddas of Ceylon," Cambridge 1906, p. 132.

[338] WHITEHEAD, G. "In the Nicobar Islands," London 1924, p. 197.

292 BIBLIOGRAPHY

[339] HADDON, A. C. "Head Hunters, Black White and Brown," p. 139, Plate XII.

[340] HURLEY, FRANK. "Pearls and Savages," London 1924, p. 38.

[341] WEEKS, Rev. J. H. "Among Congo Cannibals," London 1913, p. 91.

[342] TORDAY, E. "On the Trail of the Bushongo," London 1925, p. 157.

[343] HILL-TOUT, C. "British North America," London 1907, p. 194.

[344] WATT, HENRY J. "The Foundations of Music," Cambridge 1911, pp. 91, 137, 178, 230.

[345] "The Andaman Islands," Cambridge 1922, p. 249.

[346] VOSS, R. "Der Tanz und seine Geschichte," Berlin 1869, pp. 3-15. are devoted to various definitions of origin of dancing.

[347] London, 1901, p. 368, etc.

[348] "Savage Childhood," London 1906, p. 88.

[349] GROSSE, E. "Die Anfange der Kunst," Leipzig, 1894.

[350] TALBOT, P. AMAURY. "In the Shadow of The Bush," London 1912, pp. 293-5.

[351] "The Natural History of the Musical Bow," Oxford 1899.

[352] SCHMIDT, W. "Die Stellung der Pygmaenvolker in der Entwicklungs Geschichte des Menschen." Stuttgart 1910.

[353] CUREAU, A. L. "Savage Man in Central Africa," London 1915.

[354] ROUT, ETTIE A. (Mrs. Hornibrook). "Sex and Exercise," London 1925.

INDEX

www.ingramcontent.com/pod-product-compliance
Lightning Source LLC
Chambersburg PA
CBHW021849020426
42334CB00013B/244